[illegible] born in 1931 in Halifax, West Yorkshire, into an Irish-Catholic family. Due to ill-health, her grammar-school education was cut short at the age of fourteen. After a series of unskilled jobs, she married and had four children. Always conscious of her unfinished education, in her thirties she began a programme of self-education via the local College of Further Education, which qualified her to enter the Civil Service. In 1975 she enrolled in the Open University and in 1976 went to Bradford University to study full-time. After gaining a Joint Honours degree in Politics, Literature and the History of Ideas, she went on to study for a Postgraduate Certificate of Education. Once qualified, she was employed as a teacher by Calderdale Education Department and also began to work on the Anne Lister journals. The two books of edited extracts which resulted from her work are published in Britain and America. Now retired, Helena is working on a biography of Anne Lister.

By Helena Whitbread

The Secret Diaries of Miss Anne Lister 1816–1824:
I Know My Own Heart

The Secret Diaries of Miss Anne Lister 1824–1826:
No Priest But Love

THE SECRET DIARIES OF
MISS ANNE LISTER
1824–1826

No Priest But Love

Edited by

Helena Whitbread

VIRAGO

This edition published in Great Britain in 2020 by Virago Press
First published in Great Britain in 1992 by Smith Settle Ltd, as *No Priest But Love*

1 3 5 7 9 10 8 6 4 2

This selection from Anne Lister's journals held by
Calderdale District Archives, refs SH:7/ML/E/I-26

A CIP catalogue record for this book
is available from the British Library.

ISBN 978-0-349-01333-6

Typeset in Goudy by M Rules
Printed and bound in Great Britain by
Clays Ltd, Elcograf S.p.A.

Papers used by Virago are from well-managed forests
and other responsible sources.

Virago Press
An imprint of
Little, Brown Book Group
Carmelite House
50 Victoria Embankment
London EC4Y 0DZ

An Hachette UK Company
www.hachette.co.uk

www.virago.co.uk

Love shook my heart
like the wind on the mountain
rushing over the oak trees
Beautiful women,
my feelings for you
will never falter
I tell you:
in time to come,
someone will remember us.

SAPPHO, c600 BC

Taken from *Sappho's Poems and Fragments*
(translated by Josephine Balmer,
London, Bloodaxe Books, 1992)

1823
Aug[ust] [illegible]

[illegible]

[illegible] Thurs. 21 Aug[ust] 3 55/60 p.m. [illegible]

[illegible] – How w[oul]d a cou[l]d [illegible] dar[e]d th[e] [illegible] storm, & in desper[a]te desp[air], my mind indig[nan]t th[a]t watch'd it skulk away – How few & high[t]e[r] feel[ings] [illegible] c[oul]d ha[ve] [illegible] chival[ry] of heart w[as] gone – Hope's brightest hues were brush'd away – yet still one melanch[oly] point of union rem[aine]d – the w[orl]d unhap[py] [illegible] to leave & ruin devot[ion]; a time [illegible] my heart still lingers in its old ab[ode] [illegible] [illegible] – [illegible] & heart [illegible] it is [illegible] – Je sens mon cœur, et je connois les hommes. Je ne suis fait comme aucun de ceux que j'ai vus; j'ose croire n'être fait comme aucun de ceux qui existent" [illegible]

[illegible] – [illegible] of romant[ic] youth [illegible] je sens mon cœur – B[u]t no mo[re] – no more –!
[illegible] dry detail of a [illegible] — [illegible]

A page from Anne Lister's journal

To the memory of my late husband Robert (1929–1996).

Contents

Preface

My involvement with the life of Anne Lister began with a visit to the Calderdale Archives one late autumn afternoon in 1984. Due to work and family commitments I had decided that any writing or research I wished to do must be centred upon a subject close to home. My mind immediately focused upon Anne Lister of Shibden Hall, Halifax. I knew that her letters were deposited in the archives and, on further enquiry, I found that her voluminous journals, extending from 1817 to 1840, were also held there. An added bonus was that they had recently been put on to microfilm and could be photocopied page by page, enlarged and taken home for in-depth study. This was essential, for Anne's journals are a mixture of passages written in small, cramped handwriting – her 'plainhand', as she called it – alternating with passages written in a secret code of her own devising – her 'crypthand'. The plainhand was far from 'plain' and needed deciphering as it was full of abbreviations and semi-archaic or near-obsolete English terms interspersed with French words and phrases, along with a smattering of Greek and Latin. But even more challenging was her elaborate crypthand – a mixture of Greek letters and symbols of her own devising. Luckily, I found that the code had been cracked by her descendent John Lister (1847–1933), the last Lister of Shibden Hall.

The key to the code, then, was available and I took a copy of it home with me, along with the first fifty pages of the journal. The next day I set myself the task of reading and decoding it. From that day to this I have found myself engaged in a literary, historical and cultural adventure, the interest of which never ceases. Halifax, for me, became two different places: physically, I moved around in my modern hometown; mentally, I lived in Anne Lister's small nineteenth-century market town. Similarly, I travelled to twentieth-century Paris for research – but it was Anne's nineteenth-century Paris that I uncovered, emotionally and psychologically, the spirit of which I have attempted to portray in this book through the excerpts I have chosen.

The process of selection from 7,722 pages of Anne's journals, containing an estimated 4,633,200 words, was not easy. The writing of a diary isn't comparable to the writing of a novel as the diarist, obviously, does not know in advance what is going to happen and what will be significant. Anne scrupulously recorded every day's events as fully as possible but, although fascinating for a historian, the minutiae of each day is less engrossing for the general reader. It is therefore the task of the editor to sift through the mass of material, teasing out key themes and highlighting the most pertinent experiences that will allow the diarist to tell her own story in her own authentic voice.

Selecting and editing excerpts from the private diary of an unknown person was a complex process as I had no preformed idea of what sort of person was likely to emerge, or what her story might be. My knowledge of Anne Lister was confined to the bare fact that she had once lived at Shibden Hall, a place to which I was taken as a child many times by my parents and to which I took my own children in turn. Short extracts of her diaries had been published from time to time in the local press to illustrate historical events in Halifax, but Anne's lifestyle and personality – and, indeed, her sexual orientation – were unknown to me until I studied her journals.

After a period of two years' reading and decoding, I knew that the uniqueness of the material lay in the depiction of how a woman in the first half of the nineteenth century could live her life and satisfy her emotional and sexual needs when she could 'love, and only love, the fairer sex'. How did a lesbian conduct her life during an era so radically different from our own, managing to balance sexual fulfilment with social acceptability? Anne's secret journal tells us. My decision to share Anne Lister's story with the world was not taken lightly; having spent so long decoding her intimate diary, I felt an affinity with her – I was her confidante across the centuries – and she would have hated her private life being made public. Yet I remain convinced of the importance of gaining a new insight into the mores of women's lives and sexuality. I know now that enabling readers to discover this piece of lesbian history had a positive impact on many: as Jeanette Winterson commented, 'The diaries gave me courage.'

I made the decision to create two volumes of the diaries for publication: the first, *I Know My Own Heart*, covers the years 1817–1824 and tells the story of the clandestine, long-running love-affair between Anne and her married lover, Mariana Lawton (with the ineffectual figure of Charles Lawton hovering in the background); the second, *No Priest But Love*, follows straight on chronologically, detailing Anne's sojourn in Paris and her infatuation there with a young widow, Maria Barlow.

I Know My Own Heart was published in 1988, the year that Section 28 was enacted, the controversial law that forbade local councils and schools to promote or teach the acceptability of homosexuality. As I was then employed as a teacher in a Catholic school, I was worried about whether my employment would be terminated when the contents of my book became known. Fortunately, the headmaster, an Oxbridge classicist who was very aware of the importance of the Anne Lister journals, reassured me on that point. His comment, 'You have lit a slow fuse,' has stayed with me to this day.

This second volume followed in 1992 under the title *No Priest but Love* and takes place mainly in Paris during the Restoration of the Bourbon monarchy period. In an attempt to recover from her heartbreak over Mariana's marriage, Anne stayed in Paris from the beginning of September 1824 until the end of the following March and revisited the city in autumn 1826. Set against a backdrop of political intrigue and cultural revival, Anne's love affair with Maria Barlow provides an absorbing social and sexual drama, which not only brings Paris vividly to life but provides an astonishingly intimate insight into the explicit love life of two women who became entangled in a compelling and complex relationship.

I made the decision to exclude some material which, although interesting and of historical importance, has been well documented elsewhere. For instance, Anne's descriptions of the tourist sights in and around Paris cover the same ground as many other English diarists of the period who visited the city. It is only where I felt that Anne witnessed an event, rather than a place, of historical importance that I have relaxed my rule: for example, the entry of Charles X into Paris to be proclaimed the new king of France. I have also included instances where Anne's observations were of particular interest or sharpness during her sightseeing expeditions, revealing certain aspects of her character.

Other deletions concern long and detailed accounts of work done on the Shibden estate when Anne returned from Paris as their inclusion isn't relevant to the main theme of this book. I have, however, included sufficient material to indicate Anne's altered lifestyle and degree of responsibility for managing the estate after her uncle died and she became the mistress of

Shibden Hall. The placing of the three-point ellipsis (...) in any part of an extract from the journal signals the deletion of the type of material outlined above and has also been used to delete repetitive material. I have used italics to distinguish the 'crypthand' passages from the ones written in 'plainhand'.

Thirty-five years have elapsed since I began transcribing these diaries. Released from the obscurity of the archives, Anne Lister emerged as one of the most charismatic characters any historian could hope to find. Her life has been celebrated on stage and screen and she is now recognised as 'the first modern lesbian'. Thousands of people from all over the world visit Shibden Hall and make a pilgrimage to Holy Trinity Church in York where Anne and her lover Ann Walker took the sacrament together to seal their union. In 2011 her monumental diaries were recognised by Unesco as a 'pivotal document' in British history and added to the register of the UNESCO Memory of the World Programme. The register citation notes that, while a valuable account of the times, it was the 'comprehensive and painfully honest account of lesbian life and reflections on her nature, however, which have made these diaries unique. They have shaped and continue to shape the direction of UK Gender Studies and Women's History.' The diaries are now internationally known – their profound impact on many lives has made Anne Lister a global icon whose place in history is secured for posterity.

Helena Whitbread

Dramatis Personae

I have included the main characters who were alive and involved in Anne's life during the period covered by this book. I have not included people who were peripheral to the main drama.

Halifax

Anne Lister (junior)	1791–1840	
Anne Lister (senior)	1765–1836	Anne's aunt
James Lister	1748–1826	Anne's uncle
Captain Jeremy Lister	1752–1836	Anne's father
Marian Lister	1797–1882	Anne's sister
Elizabeth Wilkes Cordingley		Maidservant at Shibden Hall
George Playforth		Manservant at Shibden Hall
MacDonald		Maidservant at Shibden Hall
James Briggs		Steward for the Shibden estate

York

Dr William Belcombe	1757–1828	Mariana Lawton's father
Mrs Marianne Belcombe	1760–1842	Mariana Lawton's mother
Sarah Anne Sherson Belcombe (Nantz)	1785–1847	Sisters to Mariana Lawton
Henrietta Willan Belcombe (Harriet Milne)	1787–1860	
Eliza Stibert Belcombe (Eli)	nd	
Louisa Meynell Travis Belcombe (Lou)	nd–1871	
Dr Henry Stephen Belcombe (Steph)		Brother to Mariana Lawton

Paris

Madame de Boyve		Proprietess of 24 Place Vendôme
Mrs Maria Barlow	1786–nd	Anne Lister's lover in Paris
Jane Barlow	1811–nd	Daughter of Maria Barlow
Mrs Page		Maidservant to Mrs Barlow
Madame Galvani		French tutor and friend to Anne

Lawton Hall, Cheshire

Charles Bourne Lawton	1771–1860	Husband to Mariana Percy Lawton (*née* Belcombe)
Mariana Percy Lawton (*née* Belcombe)	1790–1868	Anne Lister's lover – married Charles B Lawton, 9th March 1816
Watson		Housekeeper at Lawton Hall
Christopher		Manservant at Lawton Hall
Grantham		Lodgekeeper at Lawton Hall
Mrs Grantham		Wife of the above and alleged mistress of Charles B Lawton

Langton Hall, near Malton, Yorkshire

Mrs Anne Norcliffe	1762–1835	Widow of Thomas Norcliffe and mother to the Norcliffe family listed below
Isabella Norcliffe (Tib)	1785–1846	One-time lover of Anne Lister
Charlotte Norcliffe	1788–1844	Sister to Isabella Norcliffe
Mary Best (*née* Norcliffe)	1790–1837	Sister to Isabella Norcliffe and widow of Dr Charles Best, who was Dr Belcombe's medical partner prior to Dr Best's early death
Major Norcliffe Norcliffe	1791–1862	Brother to Isabella Norcliffe

Prologue

On a late August evening in the year 1824, in an upstairs room of an old fifteenth-century manor house, a woman called Anne Lister spent some time dawdling over arranging the contents of her writing desk to her satisfaction. She was about to leave her native Yorkshire and settle in Paris for an extended period of time. However much the adventure appealed to her, she could not avoid the 'sickly feeling of going'.

Shibden Hall, tucked away in a fold of the Pennine hills, had been in the Lister family's possession since the early seventeenth century. The Listers were of good social standing in the town of Halifax in the West Riding. The family had been one of the major landowners in the area, at one time owning much of the property in and around Halifax. By 1800, however, their estate had dwindled and by 1815, the time when Anne had come to live permanently at Shibden Hall, her bachelor uncle, James Lister, was content to live in quiet seclusion with his unmarried sister, Anne's aunt Anne. Their main income came from the rents of the small tenanted farms on their land. There was also some investment income from shares in canals and turnpike trusts. In addition, James Lister farmed some of the land and leased off other parts for stone-quarrying and coalmining. Lack of ambition on James Lister's part precluded any full-scale exploitation of his estate, but the family lived comfortably enough in their Pennine manor house with a few devoted servants to attend to their domestic comfort. James Lister was a quiet recluse, needing only his books and his farming activities. His sister, Anne, was an uneducated woman of simple, homely tastes, who spent her life organising the household around her brother's needs and battling with a crippling form of rheumatism which had afflicted her in her middle age. They did not attend the social gatherings in the town of Halifax and James firmly discouraged any attempts on his sister's part to entertain visitors at Shibden Hall.

Into this quiet, orderly, reclusive life burst the exuberant figure of their niece, Anne Lister.

Born in Halifax on the 3rd April 1791, Anne had been brought up in Market Weighton, a town in the then East Riding of Yorkshire. Her father, Captain Jeremy Lister, brother to James and Anne Lister of Shibden Hall, had married Rebecca Battle, from North Cave, East Yorkshire. She had brought to the marriage a small estate at Market Weighton, known as Skelfler. Captain Jeremy Lister, a veteran of the American War of Independence, eventually resigned his commission in the army and settled down with his wife to farm, very improvidently, the estate at Market Weighton. Of their original family of four boys and two girls, only the girls Anne and Marian (the latter born in 1797 and six years younger than Anne) survived. Three of the boys died during childhood and the fourth, Samuel, drowned in a boating accident in 1813 whilst serving in the army. He had been heir-presumptive to the Shibden estates in Halifax. Anne was twenty-two when he died. It was decided by the elder Listers that she should inherit Shibden on her Uncle James' death whilst her sister Marian should inherit the Skelfler property at Market Weighton. Accordingly, in May 1815, Anne, at the age of twenty-four, arrived in Halifax to live permanently at Shibden Hall in order to acquaint herself with the running of the estate and prepare herself for the role of eventual mistress there.

Anne's lifestyle was unusual for a woman of that time. Disdainful of anything resembling feminine pursuits, Anne's interests and hobbies were such as to cause a great deal of comment from people around her. Strenuous walking, horse riding, shooting and flute playing were hardly compatible with the air of delicacy required of the fashionable lady of leisure in the early years of the nineteenth century. In the year 1824, when this book begins, she was thirty-three. Her character was already formed and her determination to live her life according to the dictates of that character never wavered. At quite an early age she was a source of trouble to her mother. In later years, she describes herself, when a child, thus:

> '*... I was a great pickle. 'scaped my maid & got away among the workpeople. When my mother thought I was safe, I was running out in an evening. Saw curious scenes, bad women, etc. ...*'
>
> (Saturday 13 November 1824. Paris)

Her mother, in despair, sent her as a boarder at the age of seven to a dame school in Ripon, run by a Mrs Haigue and a Mrs Chettle. Anne remembers 'being whipped every day at Ripon', probably in an attempt to curb her madcap ways. However, the punishment seems to have been administered more in sorrow than in anger, for a Mrs Taylor, who attended the school when Anne was there, remembers Anne as being:

> '... a singular child & singularly drest but genteel-looking, very quick & independent & quite above telling an untruth ... whistled very well. A great favourite with Mrs Chettle ...'
>
> (19 November 1822. Halifax)

Anne's scholarly development began early. At the age of twelve she wrote to her aunt at Shibden Hall:

'... My library is one of my greatest pleasures after a good ramble in the fields ... The Grecian History has pleased me much. You know Mr Trant made me a present of the Roman History ... Have the goodness to purchase for me a dictionary. I mean one of the very best publications ... I have five guineas to spare & I don't know how I can expend it better to my own satisfaction ... It will be a valuable addition to my collection of books ...'

(Thursday 3 February 1803. Skelfleur [*sic*] House)

In April 1805, at the age of fourteen, Anne was sent to the Manor School in York as a parlour-boarder. It was about this time that Anne's reputation as a 'tomboy' began to be viewed in a more serious light. The fact that her sexual orientation was towards members of her own sex was, perhaps, not unusual at the age of fourteen, when 'crushes' and romantic friendship between young people of the same sex are considered the norm. But Anne's flirtations with her female contemporaries quickly acquired sexual overtones which she rapidly converted into sexual activity whenever the opportunity presented itself.

Anne's first intense relationship was with a girl whom she met at the Manor School, York, and with whom she shared a bedroom – Eliza Raine. Eliza's early life is obscure. She appears to have been the daughter of William Raine, a surgeon in the service of the East India Company. She was brought over to England in the legal care of a Mr and Mrs Duffin. William Duffin, an Irishman and also a surgeon working in India at the same time as Eliza's father, came to live at York where he continued to practise his profession. Eliza was sent to the Manor School. There she became probably the first of Anne's lovers, in a physical sense. The relationship was a doomed one. Anne herself admitted in later years that she used to flirt with other girls, causing Eliza much distress. The pathological jealousy displayed by Eliza seemed to be an early indication of mental derangement, according to the medical reasoning of the era. In 1814, Eliza was pronounced incurably insane and spent the rest of her life under the care of medical attendants in York. Anne, filled with remorse for her bad behaviour towards Eliza, never failed to pay her a visit – which was not always kindly received – when she was in York.

From this first affair, despite its traumatic end, Anne's emotional development was set in a search for fulfilment which was only to be found in sexual love with other women.

Socially, the Manor School was the catalyst which served to release Anne from her rural, rather sequestered background in Market Weighton. The people with whom she mixed at the school came mainly from wealthy families. Anne became fired with the ambition to gain entry into their more sophisticated milieu and so leave her rustic origins behind. These ambitions, formulated in her early teens, never left her. They were to become the driving force behind her adventurous and problematical life.

York, at that time, was a thriving place of economic and social importance. Debarred from travelling abroad due to the turmoil of the Napoleonic Wars, the fashionable English spent their time and money in their own capital cities. Although London and Bath were the more fashionable places in which to spend their wealth, nevertheless York, the then capital city of the North, with its imposing cathedral, medieval streets and its rich mixture of legal, military, political and economic worlds meeting and mixing at the winter assemblies and balls, at the racecourse and the glittering musical festivals, exuded a lively social atmosphere which made it the focus of the wealthy and privileged people who lived in the North of England.

Anne was fascinated by the lifestyles of the people in the York circle into which she was eventually introduced. Through her friendship with Eliza Raine, she met Mr and Mrs Duffin, who lived at the Red House, York. Mrs Duffin was, in 1806, an ailing woman in her sixties. Hovering in the background of the

Duffins' lives was Mr Duffin's mistress, a York woman called Miss Marsh who lived in lodgings at 58 Micklegate, York. Miss Marsh was playing a patient waiting game. Her aim, which she eventually achieved in 1826, was to become the second Mrs Duffin. Meanwhile, she virtually ran the Duffin household in place of the invalid wife, kept an eagle eye on all their business affairs, ministered to Mr Duffin's every comfort and pried into, and gossiped about, the affairs of all her friends and acquaintances, particularly where Anne and her friendships were concerned.

Once befriended by the Duffins and Miss Marsh, Anne's circle of acquaintances widened. She became friendly with the Norcliffe family, wealthy landowners who lived at Langton Hall in the small village of Langton near Malton, a market town situated between York and the east coast town of Scarborough.

To Anne, in her younger days, the Norcliffes represented the acme of sophistication. Rich, well-travelled, self-assured and socially confident people, they opened Anne's eyes to the glamour of the cosmopolitan lifestyle to which their wealth gave them access. They inspired Anne with ambitions which were eventually to take her into European court circles, an elevation which would cause her to view the Norcliffes as, in their turn, rather provincial. Anne was a very able student of society!

Meanwhile, the main interest for Anne lay in her liaison with Isabella, the Norcliffe's eldest daughter. Isabella was six years older than Anne, but they quickly realised that their friendship was more than ordinarily intense soon after their first meeting around 1810, when Anne was nineteen and Isabella was twenty-five. They embarked upon a serious and fairly long-running physical love affair. Isabella (or Tib, as Anne called her) badly wanted to become Anne's life-partner. Anne was not so sure that Isabella suited her but, because of the social advantages which the relationship brought, she was happy to indulge Isabella in her fantasies of their eventually living together.

That the Norcliffes were a formative influence on the development of Anne's social aspirations, there can be no doubt. All the more surprising, then, that when Isabella introduced Anne to Mariana Belcombe, Anne's immediate sexual passion for this pretty young daughter of a relatively socially insignificant York doctor should cause her to jettison her relationship with Isabella in favour of a new one with Mariana.

Dr and Mrs Belcombe lived with their large and gregarious family of five daughters and one son in Petergate, York, in the shadow of York Minster. The connection between the Norcliffes and the Belcombes lay in the fact that Dr Belcombe's partner, Dr Charles Best, had married Isabella Norcliffe's sister, Mary. The daughters of the two families, the Norcliffes and the Belcombes, had become firm friends, particularly as the Norcliffe girls often stayed in York for the various social gatherings which were also attended by the Belcombes. By introducing Anne Lister to the Belcombe family, Isabella sealed her own fate. Anne became irresistibly attracted to Mariana and, by 1814, Anne, then twenty-three years old, and Mariana, a year older than Anne, had become lovers.

Despite their passionate attachment to each other, the hard reality of economic circumstances intruded upon their idyll. Anne was not the independent woman of means which she was to be in later life. Even had the lovers braved public opinion and attempted to live together, they had absolutely no means of support. Dr Belcombe, also, was not a rich man. He had four unmarried daughters on his hands. When a wealthy Cheshire landowner approached him with an offer of marriage for Mariana, the Belcombe family were delighted. His offer was accepted with alacrity.

The suitor, Charles Lawton, was a widower, some twenty years older than Mariana. He was the owner of Lawton Hall and its surrounding estates in the village of Lawton, Cheshire. Mariana was dazzled by the prospect of rising from her humble status of daughter to an impecunious York doctor to that of wealthy mistress of Lawton Hall. The marriage took place in March 1816. Anne was literally heartbroken:

> '*. . . The time, the manner, of her marriage . . . Oh, how it broke the magic of my faith forever. How, spite of love, it burst the spell that bound my very reason . . .*'
>
> (Wednesday 20 August 1823. Halifax)

She became very ill and only the care of her York friends, Mr and Mrs Duffin and Miss Marsh, brought her back to her original state of good health.

The sense of betrayal never left Anne. Yet, despite her emotional trauma, she was unable to give Mariana up. They continued their sexual relationship whenever they found it possible to meet. They visited each other's homes or stayed in York at Mariana's family home. For, when Anne found that the marriage was inevitable, she and Mariana agreed that perhaps it need only be a temporary disruption, for economic purposes, to their life. They formed a plan to live together in the future when, hopefully, Charles' early death (he was nearing fifty and, given the life expectancy in those days, it was not so unrealistic to assume early widowhood for Mariana) would leave the way clear for them. It would also render their relationship respectable in the eyes of the world. What was more natural than a grieving widow taking refuge in the home of her best friend, where together they would keep the memory of the dead husband sacred? Should there be any children of the marriage, the two women would bring them up together, combining their incomes from the two estates of Lawton and Shibden.

The plan served to sustain Anne through the lonely years which followed Mariana's defection. During this long waiting period, Anne occupied herself by drawing up an intensive course of self-education. She felt that intellectual discipline was the only way to keep her unhappiness from overwhelming her:

'... If I was once to give way to idleness, I would be wretched. Nothing but keeping my mind so intent upon study can divert the melancholy reflections which would constantly prey upon me on account of Mariana. Alas! They are even now a source of bitterness & disquiet that words can ill describe ...'
(Thursday 22 May 1817. Halifax)

She timetabled her day fully:

'I ... mean to turn my attention, eventually & principally, to natural philosophy. For the present I mean to devote my mornings before breakfast to Greek & afterwards, till dinner, to divide the time equally between Euclid & arithmetic ... I shall recommence my long-neglected Algebra. I must read a page or two of French now & then, when I can. The afternoons & evenings are set apart for general reading, for walking, [for] ½ an hour, or ¾, practice on the flute ...'
(Tuesday 13 May 1817. Halifax)

This programme of study, exercise and music was supplemented by helping her uncle on the estate, by occasional visits to the more important families in the town of Halifax and by long visits to her friends in York. Her main emotional outlet lay in the snatched meetings with Mariana and their exchange of letters.

Unfortunately, one of Anne's letters, in which she had referred to their hope of Charles' early death, was found by him. He wrote a furious letter to Anne, forbidding her to visit Lawton Hall. He became extremely jealous of the friendship between his wife and Anne, intercepting all the mail and making it extremely difficult for the two women to meet. Anne's response to this situation was to use an esoteric code, or cypher, to which only she and Mariana had the key. Anne also used the code in her journals when she wished to write about her emotions and her bouts of physical lovemaking with Mariana and also with other women. For, as the years went on and Charles continued in robust health, Anne began to realise the futility of the arrangement. She began to look at the possibility of finding someone else to fill the role of life-partner.

There was also an added complication to Anne's sexual life with Mariana. In July 1821, Anne began to detect certain symptoms which led her to believe that she was suffering from some venereal disorder. It seems that Mariana had contracted a complaint from her loose-living husband and had infected Anne with it. Anne, in turn, had passed it on to Isabella Norcliffe, with whom she had sporadic and unenthusiastic sexual relations. Anne now began to feel a great sense of responsibility about indulging in sexual activity with any other woman. She made every effort to cure herself of the complaint, and included in these efforts was that of abstaining from sexual contact with Mariana for fear of further outbreaks of infection. Although she was not always successful in this last aim, the sobering fact of a venereal complaint certainly changed Anne's attitude towards Mariana and towards future sexual conquests.

In addition to Anne's emotional weariness, Mariana had become concerned about the lesbian nature of her relationship with Anne becoming known publicly. In 1823, after seven years of marriage, Mariana was a respectable figure in Cheshire society. She had a materially comfortable home with plenty of money and servants. Charles was away from home for long periods and, when he was at home, did not make excessive demands either on her person or her time. She was left pretty much to run her own life as she wanted. She had good women friends; she took up charitable causes, including the setting up of a small school for girls to whom she taught sewing; she had many hobbies and interests; and she was allowed to visit her parents in York frequently. Also, her sisters paid lengthy visits to Lawton Hall to keep her company. In short, she had become content with her station in life. She was prepared, at this stage, to overlook the fact that, basically, her marriage was far from ideal. She began to show an indifference to Anne, which served to heighten Anne's already disillusioned feelings about Mariana.

The situation between them came to a head in the late summer of 1823. On a visit to York and Scarborough, Mariana made it clear that she felt ashamed to be seen in public with Anne because of the latter's masculine appearance and unfashionable dress-sense. That Mariana was also mortally afraid of the world's censure of their lesbian relationship now became apparent to Anne. She records in her journal that, on the subject of their love becoming publicly known:

> '. . . [Mariana] *had a feeling she could not describe.* [She] *would make any sacrifice rather than have our connection suspected . . . The fear of discovery is strong. It rather increases, I think, but her conscience seems seared* [closed] *so long as concealment is secure . . .* [I] *told her she need not fear my conduct letting out our secret. I could deceive anyone . . .*'

In the same entry Anne goes on to condemn Mariana:

> '. . . *Mary, you have passion like the rest but your caution cheats the world out of its scandal & your courage is weak rather than your principal* [sic] *strong . . . It was a coward love that dare not brave the storm . . .*'
>
> (Wednesday 20 August 1823. Halifax)

The emotional shocks suffered by Anne from Mariana's increasingly worldly attitude to their (for Anne) idealistic love did irreparable damage to the relationship. Anne felt that it was time to come to terms with the fact that Mariana was 'another man's wife'; that Charles seemed unlikely to suffer premature death; that life held other promises, other happinesses. Her ambitious nature prompted her to search for a wealthy, more socially elevated woman than either Isabella Norcliffe or Mariana. Perhaps even a titled woman? Disinterested love was no longer on the agenda. As idealism left by the back door, cynicism entered by the front. In terms of finding a life-partner, Anne became what could be termed a careerist.

Anne herself was to become a woman of property when her uncle died. She now wished her future companion to bring wealth and what she termed *éclat* to the partnership. Mariana, if she left her husband or became a childless widow, would bring neither. Isabella's deterioration into drink and snuff-taking certainly wouldn't ensure *éclat*. It was time for Anne to move away from old associations and broaden her experience of the world. She decided to put into operation her long-cherished plans to travel and was determined to begin by going to Paris for a lengthy visit. She would become proficient in the language, absorb the culture and acquire the polish of a cosmopolitan woman. These things could only be assets in her new phase of life. At the age of thirty-three, Anne was no longer the lonely, yearning lover waiting, in the fastness of her Pennine hillside home, for her loved one to be released from the bondage of marriage. Now she was about to step out into the wider world of travel and sophistication to try her luck with other women in different social milieux. It is from the revealing pages of her journal that we are allowed a fascinating insight into the successes and failures of Anne's new direction in life.

A Parisian Prelude

'Half Paris seemed sitting in groups under the trees listening, some to music, some to singing ... It was altogether rather a fairy scene ...'

(Friday 3 September 1824. Paris)

Anne Lister's description of an evening stroll in the Champs Élysées captures the surface gaiety of a city which was famous throughout Europe for its culture, luxury and taste. The dark under-belly of vice, corruption and counter-intrigue in one of the most sophisticated cities of the world surfaces but little in the pages of Anne's journals. Like most visitors there, she was only too pleased to have the opportunity of being in Paris at all, for, during the period of the French Revolution and the subsequent Napoleonic Wars, the continent of Europe was virtually closed to all but the most intrepid of English travellers. Napoleon's final defeat at Waterloo in 1815 opened the floodgates. The sea route between Dover and Calais became busy once more with peaceful, enthusiastic travellers, eager to take advantage of the diversion of foreign travel and to widen their cultural and linguistic horizons.

Anne Lister was amongst those able to afford the cost of living and travelling on the Continent for prolonged periods of time. Her first visit to Paris with her aunt in 1819 had given her a taste for the life and climate there, and she was determined to repeat the experience. This time, in 1824, she took only her maid, Elizabeth Wilkes Cordingley, to accompany her. The two women left their home in Halifax, a small Pennine town in the West Riding of Yorkshire, on the 24th August 1824, and were not to return to England until the spring of 1825.

The journey from Halifax to Paris had not been without some adventures. In London, Anne felt an elevation of spirits that led her to record:

> '. . . In walking about London this morning could not help feeling proud of the metropolis of my country. What magnificence, what comfort, what luxury. Like Tyre of old, her merchants are princes.'
>
> (Thursday 26 August 1824. London)

A rather bizarre event occupied much of her thoughts during her stay in London. Anne had gained permission from the magistrates at Hatton Garden[1] to see the treadmill at Cold Bath Fields prison.[2] She then found, to her horror, that her visit there had been written up in *The Times* of the day. Mr Webb, the proprietor of Webb's Hotel[3] at 220 Piccadilly, where Anne and Cordingley were staying, brought up to Anne's room:

> '. . . a roast of mutton & a newspaper, asking me if I would like to look at it. I casually answered "Yes". He said there was this business at Hatton Gardens in it. He had never thought of it getting into the papers & now it would be in them all. "Ah," said I, "the thought & fear of it struck me last night. I am very sorry for it." It was the "Times" newspaper of today. The whole thing very fairly put in. At the moment I felt mortified & annoyed at the idea of what a quiz it would be against me. Mr Webb saw this, which was probably more than

he expected. I soon, however, grew reconciled, as I always do & told Mr Webb when he came in again. I could not help laughing at the thing . . .'

(Saturday 28 August 1824. London)

Anne decided to draft a letter in defence of her action. She did not, in the end, send off the letter, which contained the following explanation of her motives for the visit:

'. . . since the matter has been made public. I feel desirous that my motive should be divested of the "*scientific*" nature to which it had been attributed, & reduced to the simple wish of examining for myself the merits or demerits of the tread-mill . . . I cannot help feeling persuaded, from the ease with which all the persons, male & female, seemed to perform the exercise of the tread-mill, as well as from the short trial I myself made of it, that the labour is not so excessive as it has been represented, nor by any means so great as that daily undergone by a large portion of the lower classes of society . . .'

(Saturday 28 August 1824. London)

After this mortifying experience, Anne and Cordingley travelled to Dover, crossed the Channel by steam packet and arrived at their lodgings at 11.35 pm on Wednesday 1st September 1824.

For the English resident in Paris, life in a modest pension in the mid-1820s was hardly a passport to the highest circles of fashionable French society. It was at just such a small guest-house, run by Madame de Boyve and her husband, at 24 Place Vendôme, that Anne and her maid eventually arrived. There they were provided with the rather unexceptional round of eating, drinking, socialising and entertainment expected by genteel, upper middle-class people and, on a lower level commensurate with their class, their servants. Anne Lister at this stage of her life was not ambitious enough, wealthy enough or socially confident enough to desire entry into the aristocratic strata of Parisian society. For now, fully aware of her unpreparedness for the *haut ton* lifestyle, she was content to use her time in Paris to look about her, learn the language, familiarise herself with the cultural aspects of Parisian life and attempt to obtain an improvement in her health by consulting medical specialists in Paris.

Her arrival at 24 Place Vendôme, late, travel-weary and hungry, had not proved an auspicious start to her new life there:

> '... Arrived, & myself & my luggage upstairs (187 steps from the ground), in my room at 11–35. The family had gone to bed. Only servants up. They had expected me earlier. Thought I should not arrive tonight. The room looked dirty & untidy & felt desperately hot, even to one who had been nearly boiled to death in the cabriolet of a diligence. What could be had to eat & drink? Not much & that not in a hurry. At last, I had a teapot of hot water brought (could not get a 2d, there was no fire to heat more water) & some vin de pays & a little bread & butter & Cordingley got some tea after waiting about an hour. It required some contrivance to arrange that "order" which is "space". Cordingley not fit for anything. Sent her off to bed. I up till 2–20. A few thoughts of home & my journey passed in my mind ...'
>
> (Wednesday 1 September 1824. Paris)

It was only the resilience of Anne's nature which allowed her to overcome this depressing start and summon up a positive attitude in order to gain the maximum benefit from her Parisian experience. The structure of her daily life there left her very little time for privacy or study, which was one of her main passions in life, but her attention to her journal was never relaxed.

The guests at Place Vendôme took breakfast in their own

rooms at an hour of their choice. What was then left of the morning was devoted to walking, reading in the Tuileries gardens or shopping. Luncheon was at one o'clock, after which, sightseeing or excursions filled the afternoon. Dinner was officially at five-thirty but more often than not at six, and then, on fine evenings, Anne sat under the trees in the Champs Élysées listening to music and watching the spectacle of the Parisian world stroll by. Other evenings were spent in social entertainments organised by Madame de Boyve at Place Vendôme, when card games, word games designed to extend the guests' knowledge of the French language, other paper and pencil games, and musical soirées would fill the time. Eventually, visits to the opera and the French theatre added diversity to the chillier autumn and winter evenings.

Anne found herself comfortable at Place Vendôme despite the fact that her room was situated many steps above ground level. In letters to her friends, her main complaint was the noise of the carriages and the cracking of the coachman's whip as the vehicles rumbled past the house:

> '... Ill-hung, rattling carriages perpetually rolling over a rough pavement, making a din more easily imagined than expressed – the whole house vibrates like the needle of a mariner's compass ... The cracking of whips ... is quite indescribable. We have no whips in England clumsy enough to make such an infernal-sounding din ...'[4]

Anne's letters home to her friends and family give a good general impression of her life in Paris, but it is to her journal that she confides the more intimate and detailed accounts of her day to day living. At first she attempted to stand aloof from the social interaction which took place at Place Vendôme, but her own strong, forceful nature, her desire to be liked and accepted by people of her own class and, above all, her penchant for pretty women and her propensity for flirtations – and more – with them, soon made her the centre of the small dramas enacted behind the respectable façade of 24 Place Vendôme.

Thursday 2 September

Had Cordingley & had a thorough dusting of all the drawers, cupboards, etc., not before they wanted it. Arranged all my things & not dressed till 11¾. Then had my bed made & room swept. Mme de Boyve came up to pay her respects at 12½ ... [She] is very handsome. Has a very good address & I admire her. Introduced to an elderly lady, a Mrs Richardson of Chichester; a Mrs Mackenzie & daughter; & a Mrs Barlow & daughter. Not much style about any of them. I must make out who they are. Mrs Barlow, the widow (her daughter aet. 13) of a Lieutenant-Colonel ... Mrs Barlow's maid is an Englishwoman but speaks French well, a great comfort to Cordingley, but makes sad complaints of the servants' living. They can get breakfast but seldom anything fit for dinner ... The servants dine after us (we are said to dine at 5½ but it is always near 6) but the housekeeper takes everything away as it comes out of the room & lets the servants have little they can eat. There are 3 of them [servants] & she gives them each 1 bottle of wine to last a week. Mrs Barlow's maid has complained till she is tired, & is very miserable here. Her mistress has spoken to Mme de Boyve, who says no servant shall alter the regulation of her house.

Friday 3 September

Breakfast at 10¼. Then went down to consult Mrs Barlow what things (clothes) I should get. Looked at some shawls Mme de Boyve had sent for but did not purchase ... *I have nothing proper to dress in & cannot speak the language at all & feel as if I could not get on* . . . In the evening, went with M. & Mme de Boyve & Mr Franks, an Irishman who is in the house, to the Champs Élysées. Half Paris seemed sitting in groups under the trees listening, some to music, some to singing. Really very good. We formed a little party, joined by a French captain of the Garde du Corps, a de St Aubun, who returned home with us after we had been at least a couple of hours walking about & sitting under the shade. I enjoyed the music & singing. It was altogether rather a fairy scene. A beautiful evening. I had not ½ the clothing on I should have had at home. The air was so delightful it seemed like the gentle freshness of a lady's fan. On our return & sitting round the drawing room table, found Capt. de St Aubun a striking example of forward foppery, of what they say are the manners of the French gents. I was talking to the Misses Mackenzie & Barlow (quite girls in their teens) & observed some forfeit should be paid for speaking English; they knew not what. Said Capt. de St Aubun, 'Baiser un François' [Kiss a Frenchman]. But his afterwards coming to claim the penalty made me at once think how careful I should be in trusting daughters of my own in French society. It was all a joke on his part – but it shewed [*sic*] that he might have been in earnest with giddy girls & that when Frenchmen marry Englishwomen they probably pay their addresses 'tout droit' [straight on], or, *as we should say in low Yorkshire, 'court by the breeches buttonhole'*. In my memorandum made at the moment, M. le Capitaine is unceremoniously styled 'an impudent fellow'. Probably he neither meant to be nor thought of being so. Said Miss Mackenzie, 'They are all alike, at least all I have seen. Always something about "baiser" [kissing].' Came to my room at 11½.

Saturday 4 September

Mrs Barlow came about 11½ [am] & sat with me till 1. She is quiet & tolerably ladylike but a very heavy companion. Her spirits seem weak. She appears to have delicate health & talks of thinking much, & looks a look of melancholy. *The most good she did me was looking at the gown Madame Romatier made for me two years ago* [when Anne was last in Paris], advising me to put it on at dinner with a handkerchief & saying it would do very well & so it did. Mrs Barlow is a connoisseur in spelling but, as she herself observed, not very profound & this was one of her chief subjects of conversation & that Mme de Boyve was selfish . . . A Monsieur Sorteval (with mustaches [*sic*]) came in the evening. Not speaking French so beautifully as Capt. de St Aubun but not using the word baiser & tolerably agreeable. Mme de Boyve has a multiplicity of little games, etc., with which & with conversation we amuse ourselves in an evening. Tonight we have had a little lottery & les questions, e.g. everyone writes a question, then they are all jumbled together or given out as Mme de Boyve chooses for each one to answer. Then, this done, they are all returned & read aloud by Madame. We had also, as we always have at dinner, those little bonbons wrapt up in mottos. Last night we had letters forming different words to make out. If I could speak the language well I could get on agreeably enough – & I think Cordingley seems more reconciled. Tea is always brought in about 9 and each person has one cup.

Sunday 5 September

A soirée in the evening. A lady & her daughter (Mrs Kidd & her daughter) & a young man, really gentlemanly tho' a little priggishly dandyish, & Messrs Sorteval, whom we had last night, Phillip & Bellevue, a diminutive, rather deformed man but gentlemanly. Speaks French beautifully & intelligibly & I liked him the best of the 4 gents. The elderly lady played écarte the whole evening with M. Sorteval or M. Bellevue. The rest of us sat round the drawing room table, had a little lottery or 2 & different sorts of games et les questions. Yet there was not much conversation or play made & such a party would have been called stupid in England. Thought I, if I could speak French as well as English, I could improve all this if I chose & make the thing pleasant. The English crept away early, soon after 10, & I came upstairs at 10–55 & left the French to talk us over. *Mme de Boyve evidently likes me. She praises the questions & answers I write & is very civil. I am certainly attentive to her with something of flattery of manner she is not used to from ladies.* I could make my way if I could speak better & am in better hope about it tonight. In mannerism I have certainly the advantage of all our English party. The ease I feel ½ surprises myself.

Monday 6 September

At 11 we were all off to the fête, or fair, or rather feast St Germain, held 2 miles from the town in the forest close to a nunnery or school ... Stopt to see Malmaison[5] – the prince, Eugene Beauharnais[6] died a year ago & the place is kept very neat by the guardians of his son, quite a boy. Shewn over the house – upstairs, too. The bedrooms (we saw 3) low. The state room & bed hung with crimson damask & gold fringe. Another room with satin which, I should think [was] originally very light blue or pink. Another with white calico, as was also the bath room where Napoleon used to sit for hours & drink his coffee ... Passed thro' St Germain & got 2 miles into the forest to the site of the fête ... It was 6 before we squatted down on our carriage-cushions to the cold dinner we had brought with us & spread out on the ground. After dinner we walked about among the booths. As it became dark, the lighted lamps among the trees had a pretty effect. Yesterday was the vulgar day (being Sunday) – all the common people there. Today many genteel people were said to be among the crowd, this being considered the best & genteelest fête in the neighbourhood of Paris. Mr Brande supposed about 20,000 people there. 2 good bands played quadrilles, one for the higher orders in an inclosure [*sic*] under the trees, for admittance & which we paid 5 sols each. The other for peasants. Among the former we noticed some genteel-looking persons, a few English among them. Among the higher orders it is now the fashion, since the English have been so much here, not to dance too well. Before each lady & gentleman danced as well as an op[a]. dancer & thought of & studied little else than this & dress … Mme de Boyve delights in these things and I, for her sake & novelty's, made no objection. There was a circus, horse-riding, balancing, etc., but this, we thought, would keep us too long. Saw the cheval savant, a wise horse, which told the oldest, youngest, la plus amoureuse [the most loving], etc., of the party. Then we had a little sleight of hand and electricity but the people let go before the shock came round. And all this for 2 sols each person. Then we saw, for 2 sols also each person, a sort of puppet-shew, marionettes, representation of the life of our Saviour, his birth, being found in the Temple with the Jewish doctors, his condemnation, death, resurrection & ascension. The man who shewed it drawled out the explanation as he would have done that of any other puppet-shew & the people looked & seemed as interested as they might have been at the life & adventures of Tom Thumb. To us protestants these things seem blasphemous; to French Roman Catholics they are bien bon. Then for 2 sols each, we saw the marionettes perform Les Brigands.[7] We then walked about among the people & tents & booths. Ate some grapes at one of the latter & sauntered about till 10. Then got into our carriage & set off home. 3 hours in coming & got back at 1.

Tuesday 7 September

Mrs Barlow called about 11 & sat with me above an hour. *Came about ordering my gown. Very civil & communicative. Says she has a very affectionate disposition, etc.* Lt. Col. Barlow (I suppose he was) commanded the 61st Regiment & was killed at Salamanca.[8]

Friday 10 September

[From 9½ pm] to near 11, Mrs Barlow & Miss Mackenzie & I sat up talking, apparently all well satisfied with each other's company. Miss Mackenzie is a nice girl. *Mrs Barlow quiet & ladylike & manages her small income well but is not profound nor, after all, without vanity, which I know how to manage. I think I am the favourite in the house.*

Saturday 11 September

At 12, Madame Galvani[9] came. A countess in her own right. Her estates confiscated by Napoleon because her husband, being entrusted by him with 3 millions of public money on some particular service, ran off with the money & has never since been heard of. Mme Galvani's manners are good & I like her manner of teaching French very much ... I am to have Molière. She will bring me a 8vo. edition. The smaller ones are very incorrect & it is necessary to me to have one correctly accented. Mme Galvani has a pretty, ladylike hand & *very* good & beautifully clean nails & looks like a foreign gentlewoman. I see I have much to learn, much difficulty of pronunciation to surmount but I shall not despair ... Dinner at 6 ... I talked almost entirely to Mrs Barlow & a little to Mrs Mackenzie. *Mrs Barlow tells me I am certainly not plain. They all think me a fine woman & I am very sensible & agreeable. I rather gently compliment Mrs Barlow ...* [She was] born in Guernsey, her father a colonel at least, perhaps a general, Mackray.

Sunday 12 September

In the evening, all sorts of droll games. Hunting a thimble or some small thing passed from one to another; blind man's buff; with a lighted match, 'Martin vit, vit il toujours, il vit toujours' [Martin lives; does he still live; he still lives], those in whose hands it went out paying a forfeit; 'Are you content with your neighbour?' – changing seats & the one stood out trying to get one of the seats left. Never laughed more. The tears ran down my cheeks. Could not speak for laughing. No strangers, only our own family party tonight . . . *Mr Frank told me seriously tonight I was very clever & not he only but they all thought so.*

Monday 13 September

On coming upstairs to Mrs Mackenzie to ask what they were going to do, found them going to the Louvre to try to see the exhibition there of the new (modern) pictures done by living &, I believe, all French artists, for the king's death[10] was hourly expected & all public places would be closed for 6 weeks. His majesty had taken extreme unction.[11] The garde du corps to be changed. Monsieur the next king[12] will go to St Cloud[13] & there will be no fête there. What a stupid place, says everyone with accord, will Paris be! Away we went to the Louvre. Shut already sans aucune exception [without exception] till further orders. Sauntered in the Tuileries gardens. Got back at 4.

Thursday 14 September

At 12–20, Mme Galvani étoit arrivée chez moi a restoit [arrived, she stayed with me] 1½ hour . . . read aloud & I read after her. Asked if she thought I could ever get the French accent perfectly. Yes! She thought I could as perfectly as any English person. Said I fear I should never learn to speak French here. We were all English & spoke English perpetually. Asked if there was any pension where the people were all French. It seemed not. The French people live at hotels . . . I would inquire for some little girl to have constantly to talk to. Mme Galvani says there is nothing for it but parler Français toujours [to speak French always]. The little girl might do me good. In fact, I had my head full of ambition to conquer difficulties & full of undigested ideas . . .

Latterly I had so bad a pain in my knees it was quite miserable. I had a little of [it] yesterday evening. Ever since I came here I have felt a sensation of great cold in my knees when sitting in my room (there are airs in all directions) & they are so stiff if I stoop I cannot get up again. I felt it, too, sitting in the Tuileries gardens. I know not what to make of it.

Wednesday 15 September

Walked to Montmartre. Fine view from the top of the hill. Strolled along it among the windmills. Paris stretched out before [us] on one side & St Denis on the other . . . The quarries looked exactly like our limestone quarries up & down the wolds. Brought home 2 specimens of the stone. Went to the cemetery of Montmartre. They were walling it round (enlarging it) & would not, therefore, let us go in.

Thursday 16 September

At 12–50, Mme Galvani came & staid 1¼ hour. So late because she waited, in vain, for a black gown, not wishing to come out in colours on account of the king having expired at 4 o'clock this morning . . . Then came the Irish girl from Mme Romatier's with my new black gros de Naples gown, which fits me very well. Dinner at 6. In the evening came upstairs for ½ hour to eat some of my Fontainebleau grapes. Very good. Then sat ¾ hour with Mrs Barlow, in bed all the day from great suffering in cutting one of her wisdom teeth.

Friday 17 September

I sauntered along the boulevards. Quite a busy scene even at this early hour. My left eye swelled up this morning by a bite – very likely that of a bug, but I suppose it must have been a gnat . . . *I cannot go to the boulevards at night without a gentleman. I hate confinement. When I come with Mariana* [Lawton] *I will be at an hotel, if possible, & be at liberty*. My eye very uncomfortable. We all agree it must have been bitten by a bug.

Saturday 18 September

Went out direct to the Tuileries gardens at 8–55. In going, bought at the 1st shop on the left, under the arcades, a pamphlet by M. de Chateaubriand.[14] 'Le roi est mort, vive le roi' [The king is dead, long live the king]. Read this as I walked along. Then paid a sol for the Journal Politique,[15] which I read over in ½ hour while walking in the gardens. The king lies in state (the embalming was to be finished last night) in the Salon du Trône at the Tuileries & may be seen by the public from 10 to 6 today & Monday. All the world paid their respects yesterday at St Cloud to Charles X,[16] the dauphin & dauphine (duc & duchesse d'Angoulême),[17] Madame la duchesse de Berri[18] & the duc de Bordeaux.[19] The audience lasted from 10½ to 6. There were all the royal family – ambassadors, authorities civil & military. All the nobility. From 1,500 to 2,000 private carriages. The public carriages could not get along the road but were obliged to go round by Sèvres.

Monday 20 September

In the evening I sat about an hour with Mrs Barlow. *Her eyes sparkled when she saw me & she was evidently afraid lest anyone else was coming. She surely wished to have me tête-à-tête. She rather flatters me on my talents & agreeableness & I gently flatter her on being ladylike & pretty. She asked me if I had any male correspondents. I said one, between seventy & eighty, mentioning Mr Duffin* [Anne's old friend in York], *& said I was no believer in platonic attachments. Preferred ladies' company to gentlemen's. Did many things ladies in general could not do, but did them quietly. My education had been different from the common rule. I was suited to my circumstances. On my uncle's death should come in for my uncle's* *estate, at my own disposal. He had no high opinion of ladies – was not fond of leaving estates to females. Were I other than I am, would not leave his to me . . . Mrs Barlow wanted some confidence from me but I said nothing she might not repeat. It seems her father has been imprudent & is not, perhaps, well off now. Brought her up in extravagance. Would not have liked her to put a pair of stockings on twice. Thought I to myself, 'This is no good sign.' She had always a horse to ride & plenty of beaux, thirty or forty about & in riding could tire them out. She talked about my being an observer of character. I might be deceived, for I always looked on the best side. I declared I had never been deceived. She thought I had not been much tried for she asked me if I had been much out of my own country &* [I] *said no. 'There,' said she, 'you know something of everybody.' It struck me she might be hinting at herself when, in reply to something rather complimentary, she* [said], *'Perhaps you will change.' I said I was the most constant of the constant. I was not fickle as the summer's wind. She asked my opinion of Mrs Pope, as I had owned I had staid downstairs on her account. I answered she was not pretty, 'Ah,' said Mrs Barlow, as I went away, 'you must not be led by smiling eyes.' She had told me I had an expressive countenance & evidently seemed to like my company, but she tells me too much of the great attention of Sir Gore & Lady Ouseley*[20] *& of how much she has been, & indeed is, admired. She is vain & swallows all the flattery I give her readily. I hardly know what to make of her – whether she is rather puff & cheat or simply a foolish, silly little woman. She wants very much to know what I have said of her in my journal, which I mentioned this morning. I tell her it is too flattering. She wishes me to write it out for her that she may send it to one of her friends. Her widow's pension, she told me yesterday, is eighty pounds a year & government pays her, besides this, two hundred & fifty pounds a year. I begin to rather flirt with her but I think she has no consciousness of it, or why she begins to like* [me]. *I spoke against a classical education for ladies in general. It did no good if not pursued & if* [it was], *undrew a curtain better for them not to peep behind. Have all along told her I should not marry. She advised me taking the name of mistress if I travelled alone. Said I intended, but should not travel alone. Should have a friend with me. She asked if she was married. I said yes, meaning Mariana.*

Thursday 23 September

At 10, went down into the drawing room to see the procession attending the late king's funeral. The 1st troops passed our window at 10½. The body of the king, on a superb gilded carriage, passed at 11½. The carriages of the mayor & the municipality of Paris began to pass at 6 minutes before 12. Had all passed in about 7 minutes & the small division of troops which followed them had passed (& thus concluded the splendid cortège) at 2 or 3 minutes past 12. The troops of the Garde Royal & of the line marched well. Those of the National Guard[21] very indifferently, not near so well as our militia during the war & perhaps almost all our volunteer regiments would have kept better in line ... Stood near ½ hour talking to Mme Galvani about her husband & family. She has no very near relations but 1 brother – a patrician of Venice. She a Venetian & her family Venetian. Next to her own private troubles she mourns those of her country, ill-used by France & Austria. All the patricians ruined by the Revolution. All the palaces in Venice falling into ruins. Italy abased & disgraced as a nation but not as individuals.[22] *The French not degraded as a nation but degraded individually. She holds them very cheap in every respect. Says they will do anything for money & a riband* ... The French not well-informed in general. The higher orders of Italians, ladies as well as gents (except in Lombardy), generally as well-informed as Mme Galvani herself. A woman lately held the chair of Greek professor at the University of Bologna & 2 Sicilians (sisters) are now professors of mathematics, I forget where.

Sunday 27 September

[Charles X], after receiving the keys of the city at the Barrière l'Étoile, was, with all his court, to hear mass for the prosperity of his reign ... Mrs Barlow came in & told me by all means to go out & see the king. I ought not to miss it. It was nearly fair [after a rainy start to the day]. Off, therefore – I was by myself – at about 1½. Hastened thro' the Tuileries gardens, over the Pont Royal, & took my station mounted on a chair, for which I paid 10 sols, at the Louvre end of the Pont des Arts. After waiting till about 3½ (at 1 time almost stunned with the noise of the cannon fired from the platform of the Pont Neuf), the king & all his suit [*sic*] passed by on their return from Notre Dame. They passed me quite close & I had an excellent view. His Majesty smiled & looked the picture of good humour & as if he was in excellent health. The dauphin looked remarkably well on horseback. Ditto the dukes of Bourbon[23] & Orléans.[24] Troops, the National Guard, lined the way on both sides as far as I could see &, of course, all the way from the cathedral to the Tuileries. It rained pretty smartly every now & then while I was on the Pont des Arts & all my way back from there to the Tuileries. Returned as I came, by the Pont Royal. Troops & people blocked the road along the Louvre & the other way. The crowd was considerable – a moving shoal of umbrellas. Pushed my way. Seeing a crowd waiting before the balcony of the Tuileries, expecting the king to shew himself, I pushed in among the people & stood there ¾ hour ... I could wait no longer & hurried home to dress for dinner.

Thursday 30 September

Hurried down to dinner at 5–35. Sat downstairs talking chiefly to Miss Pope. Mr Moore paying court determinedly [to Miss Pope] as usual ... I cannot make him out – but do not admire, or think him like a gentleman. This evening he got me into an argument. He would have it the flame of love was as properly flame as the flame of fire & the flame of love was called flame without any figure of speech. He could prove it from Blair (Blair's Rhetoric).[25] I pressed him a little harder than he seemed to like or to have expected, & the manner in which he attempted to shew I mis-stated or misunderstood his argument, & the little attention he once or twice affected to pay when he could not fairly parry the argument used against him, made me think him a noodle & put me a little out of patience, & perhaps I shewed it a *little* when he seemed to quiz the thing by his manner of asking to resume it for an hour in the morning. *This led me to reflect, on coming upstairs, I have talked too much to this man & perhaps, too, to Miss Pope, who is goose enough to encourage him, & perhaps I have been too soon acquainted with them all. For who & what are they? They have none of them any style about them. Mrs Middleton is vulgar. Mrs Barlow is sillily vain & Mrs Mackenzie not genteel. The three daughters are merely rather improved editions of their respective mothers & poor, would-be genteel Miss Richardson went away yesterday. Mr Frank is stupid, & gentlemanly enough, but not, I think, a thoroughbred.*

Friday 1 October

Went to a milliner's shop in the Rue de Castiglione. Black gros de Naples bonnets, 22 to 28 francs each ... Then downstairs a little in the dining room with M. & Mme de Boyve & a Mlle de Sans – French but born in England, who speaks both languages equally well. Out of health. Pale and rather interesting in appearance.

Saturday 2 October

At about 1¾, Mme de Boyve, Mlle de Sans, the Misses Mackenzie & Barlow, Messrs Frank & Bellevue & myself, set off ... to the Jardin des Plantes ... Loitered in the museum above 1½ hour. Then sauntered perhaps ½ hour in the garden & seeing the wild beasts, & got home at 5 ... Perfectly attentive to Mlle de Sans. *We get on very well together & she seems to like me. She is out of health & I take care of her. We already talk of visiting each other. She asked me to dinner. We sit next each other. She is a rather nice girl. I asked her age this morning. She said she was in her twenty-sixth year. Her complaint is 'parting with blood the wrong way'. The bloody piles, I suppose. She has had them years. I daresay I shall flirt a little with her* ... Oh! that I could remain here till I gained the language & could then stay time enough to attend lectures & profit by the superb museum of natural history.

Sunday 3 October

At 1–10, set off to call on Mme Galvani ... I was just thinking of leaving when who should come in to Mme Galvani but Mr & Mrs Park, Cecilia Barlow (that was) & Mrs Barlow (Miss Hamer, that was) ... [The latter] asked if I had been here long & how long I meant to stay. [I] answered 1 month & meant to stay 2 more. Came to learn to speak French & was here, 24, Place Vendôme. They are going away in a month. *I wonder what they would say of me, or if they will call. Somehow I felt rather annoyed. I always doubt my own importance & if people are not civil in calling, etc., fancy they mean to cut, or not to know, me. I shall never feel right on this point till I am evidently in good society & rank, with a good establishment. It immediately struck me they had read this treadmill business & I felt annoyed but said to myself, 'Well, all is for the best.'*

Monday 4 October

Major & Mrs Norcliffe [Anne's friends from Langton Hall, near York] had called. Received them in the drawing room but only for 2 or 3 minutes, for the woman wanted to measure my head [for a new bonnet], & the Norcliffes went away. *She (Mrs Norcliffe) held out her hand & we shook as if she was cordial. Not a word said about my breakfasting with them . . . They were going directly to the Tuileries gardens. Perhaps I might meet them there? I seemed as if I intended it but I would not go on any account. Would rather be out of the way. I cannot appear as I should wish. I want someone with me that I need not be ashamed of – I feel this every day – to choose my dress, etc. Passed Mlle de Sans on the boulevard. Was it intentional that she did not know me? Suspected it was & mused upon it accordingly.*

Thursday 7 October

Breakfast at 9 in Mrs Mackenzie's room. *I thought it best to volunteer, fancying her a little jealous of my attentions to Mlle de Sans. I think I was correct but I have perhaps set all right again now. Mrs Barlow, I expect, will not like to find herself not first with me. I will take care in future not to get into this sort of thing. I will keep myself more aloof unless I really think their company pleasant* . . . Mlle de Sans had not dined at table yesterday or today. Too unwell. *Rather flirted with her, which she seems to like & understand well enough.*

Friday 8 October

Sat 10 minutes just before dinner with Mlle de Sans. She was very poorly. Could not come into dinner but came soon afterwards. I went to her directly after dinner & sat about ½ hour with her . . . *Arrant flirting. She likes me certainly. Mrs Barlow said at dinner I was fond of new friendships; was not consistent.* In the evening, no company. Played & won a long game of chess with Mrs Mackenzie. Came up to bed at 10–25.

Saturday 9 October

Speaking of different books, asked Mme Galvani if she had ever read the 'Basia' of Johannes Secundus.[26] *Yes, she has the work & will lend it to me, merely observing, when I said was it not a curious sort of thing, that it was a little free but so were all the poets.* Mme Galvani had read the Latin historians & merely observed, when I asked what she thought of Suetonius,[27] that he was a little free but so were all the historians. Perhaps it was not fit for quite young girls to read but women come to years of discretion might read anything of the kind.

Sunday 10 October

Mlle de Sans & I get on very well together. We give each other our mottos at dinner. She very specially gave me today, & desired me to keep, the following, 'Tendre amitie, doux asile des coeurs, c'est à toi que je sacrifie, si l'amour nous donné la vie toi seule en donné les douceurs.' [Tender friendship, sweet haven of the hearts, it is to you that I sacrifice; if love has given us life, only you can give its pleasures.] I believe Mrs Barlow would better like to have all my attentions herself. She rallies me about being inconstant, yet pays me great compliments every now & then ... Played at 'Les Resultats', in England called 'Consequences'. Each one writing the name of 2 ladies & 2 gents, then 2 papers of ou ils sont [where they are], then 2 of ce qu'ils font [what they are doing], then 2 of what was the result (les resultats). After which, they were all read aloud in the order that they happened to be taken up by Mme de Boyve. Occasionally formed ridiculous combinations & we all laughed exceedingly.

Tuesday 12 October

Mrs & Miss Mackenzie came to ask me to look at their caps & bonnets, etc., before they were packed up ... *Talked bavardage (gossip) to some cap women that came & amused the Macks who, I believe, like me very much.* Mrs Barlow came in. *Talked flattering nonsense to her, as usual. Said Miss Mack, 'I have a question to ask you.' She wrote it. 'Êtes-vous Achilles?'*[28] *I laughed & said she made me blush. She said it was from my manner of talking to Mrs Barlow just as she had heard gentlemen talking to her. Mrs Barlow declared my eyes were as speaking as hers. I laughed & said I should write down the character they all gave me. Mrs Mack said my eye diminished. She has made the observation when I have been looking at things. Miss Mack says that it embellishes, for that all my friends are so perfect in my eyes, imagination must do a great deal. Mrs Barlow says that I am volage, that is, inconstant & she is jealous. Brought Miss Mack into my room. Joked her about her question. Said it was exceedingly well put. She said I was the only one in the house to whom she could have written it, because the only one who would have so soon understood it, that is, who would have understood the allusion to take it that way . . . Miss Mack certainly likes me. She said she had never seen anyone so agreeable . . . Mme de Boyve came & sat with me ¼ hour . . . Somehow* [I was] *led to tell the story of the two sweethearts in the house at North Bridge whom I threatened to pistol.*[29] *She said I had the qualities d'un dame & d'un homme* [of a woman & a man]. *Professed to like me very much & said I was liked by all the house. I really believe she does like me . . . In the evening rattled away so & flirted with Mrs Barlow & seemed in so much greater spirits than usual, Mrs Mackenzie said she could not understand me. She thought it unkind. I said I knew she was low & so were we all at her going. What was the use of giving way? I wished to keep up the spirits of the party but in such a case, when our own spirits were forced, we could seldom hit the happy medium but generally overdid. Then said how, at a ball after my brother's death, I seemed in the best spirits while I was really in the worst. It was my way. She appeared satisfied & I was grave & quiet afterwards. It would have been better judged to have been so all along but*

I was rattling to Mrs Barlow, who evidently enjoyed it better than she would have done the dolefuls with Mrs Mack. I was complimenting Mrs Barlow. Said Mlle de Sans, 'I see you talk to her as you do to me.' 'No,' said I, 'I am not the same to any two persons.' She seemed satisfied. Fancies me serious with herself & flirting, perhaps, with Mrs Barlow. They are all jealous of my attentions.

Wednesday 13 October

Saw [the Mackenzies & Mr Frank] off in the fiacre at 3¾. They seemed very sorry to go and we all looked grave to lose them. They are amiable people yet I am not sorry they are gone because I find they would have interrupted me too much & I was always speaking English to them . . . Went down to dinner at 5–40. M. de Boyve not dining with us (he has been unwell this fortnight or more), we were only 5 & the smallness of the party looked dull. [There would have been Mme de Boyve, Mlle de Sans, Mrs Barlow and her daughter, Jane, and Anne herself.] *But in the evening we were rather dull because we had nothing to do – not much, I think, on account of the Macks. Felt pulses, mistaking Mlle de Sans' several times. Said I could not feel hers correctly. Said she reminded me of the following, which I gave her in pencil: 'When in my hand thy pulse is prest, I feel it alter mine, & draw another from my breast, in unison with thine.' 'Indeed,' said she, 'if you were a man I know not what would be the end of all this. I think Mme de Boyve would be right. I should be married before the year's end.' She certainly likes me. Mrs Barlow, too, has made up to me, particularly today. Has said several times she was jealous. Sat with hold of my hand tonight & looked as if she could like me. Half said as much several times. This morning, in shewing the Macks my greatcoat & putting it on, & my hat Mrs Barlow joked & called me her beau. In fact, they all like me . . . At dinner, gave Mlle de Sans a motto signifying Heaven made her to charm & me to love her. On leaving her, before dinner, she somehow shook hands, then saluted me in the*

French manner [kissing her on each cheek], *& then in the English manner* [kissing her on one cheek or on the lips]. *I immediately kissed her again, with a little more pressure of the lips, saying 'That is Yorkshire.' She had before remarked on my inquisitive, curious look. I said it was like the look of other people, the Macks, etc. 'No,' said she, 'it is only like yourself, but I don't dislike it.' She slightly coloured tonight when I gave her the four lines about her pulse. She certainly likes me, & Mrs Barlow flirts with me.*

---

1. The magistrates at Hatton Garden – In Anne's day, 52 and 53 Hatton Garden formed the site of a notorious police court, a 'dispensary of summary justice', presided over by a Mr Laing who was the original of Mr Fang in Dickens' *Oliver Twist*.
2. Cold Bath Fields prison – Built in 1794 in a district of that name (so called because a well of cold water was found there in 1697), the prison was notorious for its harsh regime. In 1820, the Cato Street conspirators were lodged there for a while before being sent to the Tower. The prison was closed down in 1877 and finally demolished in 1899. The site is now occupied by the Mount Pleasant sorting office in Farringdon Road.
3. Webb's Hotel – This was the Black Bear, Piccadilly, to which Anne always went when staying in London.
4. '... Ill-hung, rattling carriages ... infernal-sounding din' – See Ref SH:7/ML/147, Calderdale Archives. A letter from Anne Lister to Sibbella MacLean, dated Shibden Hall, 18th August 1824 – but finished in Paris, 12th September 1824.
5. Malmaison – 'House of Misfortune', so called because it was built on the site of Reuil, which was burnt in 1346 by the Black Prince, son of Edward III of England. The house was bought in 1799 and enlarged by Josephine Bonaparte, first wife of Napoleon and, later, Empress of the French. Napoleon frequently stayed there between campaigns. It is now a museum.
6. Eugene Beauharnais – (1791–1824). Stepson of Napoleon after 1796, when his mother, Josephine Tascher de la Pagerie, married Napoleon. Adopted by Napoleon in 1806. When Napoleon proclaimed himself

King of Italy in 1805, Eugene became his viceroy. He retired to Munich when Napoleon fell from power and died there in 1824.

7. Les Brigands – An adaptation of the drama *Die Räuber* (*The Robbers*) which was written by Schiller (1759–1805), German dramatist and poet. His *Die Räuber* (1781) placed him in the forefront of the *Sturm und Drang* period of German literature.
8. Salamanca – The Battle of Salamanca (22nd July 1812) took place in Spain during the Peninsular War. Wellington reputedly defeated '40,000 Frenchmen in 40 minutes'.
9. Mme Galvani – (nd) It appears that Mme Galvani was married to the nephew of Luigi Galvani (1737–1798), the Italian physician and physicist, whose work on the nature of electricity provided the major stimulus for the work of Volta (1745–1827). Volta, whose own name gave rise to the volt, coined the term galvanism. The combined works of the two men led to the subsequent age of electric power.
10. The king's death – (1755–1824). The first of the Bourbon monarchs to be restored to the throne of France, Louis XVIII was fifty-nine when he became king. Apart from the One Hundred Days of Napoleon's return to Paris after his escape from Elba in 1815, Louis XVIII reigned from 1814 to 1824. Previously the Comte de Provence, he was the fourth son of Louis, Dauphin of France (who died in 1765 before he could attain the throne of France) and Marie-Josèphe of Saxony. During the Revolution, Louis fled France, eventually living at Hartwell, in England, from 1809 until he was able to return to Paris as the constitutional king of France. On his death, in 1824, he was succeeded by his brother, Charles X, previously Comte d'Artois.
11. Extreme unction – meaning 'last anointing', i.e. of the sick with sacred oil. This is a sacrament of the Roman Catholic Church which is conferred by anointing the sense organs (eyes, ears, nostrils, lips and, formerly, the feet and loins) with blessed oils, accompanied by the pronunciation of a formula. It is an ancient rite that was seen as a continuation of Jesus' ministry of healing. Although it is now seen as a sacrament of the dying, it was a sacrament of the sick and its effects were meant to strengthen the body and the soul.
12. Monsieur, the next king – the word 'Monsieur' was an honorific title in the French court. It was used to address the eldest living brother of the king. In this case, it was applied to Charles, Comte d'Artois, who was about to become Charles X when his brother Louis XVIII died.

13. St Cloud – The château at St Cloud, built in the seventeenth century a few miles outside Paris, was originally a country residence of the Ducs d'Orléans. Later, it became Napoleon's favourite residence. It was destroyed in 1870 during the Franco-Prussian War.
14. M. de Chateaubriand – (1768–1848). François-Auguste-René, Vicomte de: diplomat and author. One of the first writers of the Romantic movement in France, he greatly influenced the youth of his day. He became Minister for Foreign Affairs from 1823–24, under the ultra-Royalist government of Joseph, Comte de Villèle. Chateaubriand's *Mémoires d'Outre-Tombe* (*Memoirs from Beyond the Tomb*) were written for posthumous publication and have proved to be his most enduring work.
15. Journal Politique – Anne may have been referring here to the official government newspaper, the *Moniteur ou Journal Politique*.
16. Charles X – (1757–1836). Formerly the Comte d'Artois, grandson of Louis XV and brother to Louis XVI and Louis XVIII. Charles spent the Revolutionary years in exile and returned to France a convinced reactionary. He became king on the death of Louis XVIII in 1824, but his increasingly authoritarian and religious policies forced him off the throne during the July Revolution of 1830. His cousin, the Duc d'Orléans, Louis-Philippe, became the 'citizen-king' of France in his stead.
17. Duc & duchesse d'Angoulême – (a) Duc d'Angoulême (1775–1844). Son of the Comte d'Artois (Charles X) and Marie-Therese of Savoy, he was the last Dauphin (heir-apparent to the French throne) and a prominent figure in the restoration of the Bourbon monarchy after the defeat of Napoleon in 1814. In 1830, when his father, Charles X, was compelled to abdicate, Angoulême renounced his claim to the throne and went into exile. (b) Duchesse d'Angoulême (1778–1851). Daughter of Louis XVI and Marie Antoinette, she was thus first cousin to her husband.
18. Duchesse de Berri – (1798–1870). Marie-Caroline de Bourbon-Sicile. Daughter of Francis I of the Two Sicilies. Her husband, the Duc de Berri, son of Charles X, had been assassinated in 1820. When Charles X abdicated in 1830, she tried to secure the succession for her son, leading a revolt in 1832, but was forced into exile. She lived in Italy and Austria until her death.
19. Duc de Bordeaux – (1820–1883). Henri-Charles-Ferdinand-Marie,

Comte de Chambord. Last heir of the elder branch of the Bourbons and, as Henry V, Pretender to the French throne from 1830. He was the posthumous son of the assassinated Duc de Berri (see note 18) and grandson of Charles X. He was forced to flee France with his mother when his cousin, Louis-Philippe, was made king in 1830.

20. Sir Gore Ouseley – (1770–1844). Diplomatist – created baronet in 1808. Appointed ambassador-extraordinary and minister-plenipotentiary to the Parisian court in 1810. An Oriental scholar, he assisted in founding the Royal Asiatic Society of London in 1823. In 1842, he was appointed president of the Society for the Publication of Oriental Texts. He was also a Fellow of the Royal Society and of the Antiquarian Society. In 1806, he married Harriet Georgina, daughter of John Whitelocke.
21. The National Guard – (The Garde Nationale). The nucleus of the Garde Nationale was formed when the Gardes-Français, previously the model regiment of the army, deserted and joined the attack on the Bastille in July 1789. Their ranks became swelled by volunteers, who were drawn exclusively from the propertied classes of the city. In 1814 and 1815, despite their revolutionary origins, the Garde Nationale played an important role in the restoration of the Bourbon monarchy.
22 Italy abased and disgraced ... – Napoleon's conquests in Italy during the Napoleonic Wars and his subsequent rule from Paris meant that Italy was re-divided into small states after he left. Frequent military interventions from Austria into Italy's affairs added to the stresses caused by an economic and agricultural slump, which lasted until 1830.
23. Duke of Bourbon – (1756–1830). Louis-Henri-Joseph, 9th Prince de Condé. The last of the Princes of Condé, a younger branch of the House of Bourbon. His son and sole heir, the Duc d'Enghien, had been tried and shot for treason, on Napoleon's orders, in 1804.
24. Duke of Orléans – (1773–1850). Louis-Philippe, eldest son of Louis-Philippe-Joseph, Duc d'Orléans (a cousin and enemy of Louis XVI) and of Adelaide de Bourbon-Penthièvre. He became Duc d'Orléans on the execution of his father by the Jacobin government in November 1793. In 1809, he married Marie-Amélie, a daughter of King Ferdinand IV of Naples. He became king of the French (the 'Citizen-King') in 1830, after the abdication of Charles X. In 1848,

he too was forced off the throne. He went to live in England where he died two years later.

25. Blair's Rhetoric – Hugh Blair (1718–1800) was a Protestant cleric and Regius Professor of Rhetoric and Belles-Lettres at Edinburgh University. His *Lectures on Rhetoric and Belles-Lettres* was published in 1783, when he resigned the professorship. He acknowledged his debt to Adam Smith's lectures on rhetoric, delivered in Scotland in 1748–1751. Blair was granted a pension of £200 a year by George III in 1780.
26. Johannes Secundus – (1511–1536). A neo-Latin poet of the Netherlands whose work followed the models provided by such as Catullus (*c*84 BC – *c*54 BC) and Propertius (*c*50 BC – after 16 BC). The *Basia* is a small collection of love songs, written by Johannes Secundus and much admired in his day. It became a model for other, particularly French, poets. The work of Secundus was instrumental in helping to move poetry away from the medieval into the modern era.
27. Suetonius – Gaius Suetonius Tranquillus (CAD 69 – CAD 140). A Roman historian who was also chief secretary to the Emperor Hadrian (AD 117 – AD 138). Suetonius wrote a number of books but the only extant book is *The Twelve Caesars* which paints a colourful picture of the more scandalous side of the Caesars. Robert Graves was much influenced by Suetonius in the writing of *I, Claudius*.
28. '*Êtes-vous Achilles?*' – Miss Mackenzie shows that she understands the nature of Anne's sexuality by this remark. Achilles, in Greek mythology, was sent by his father to the court of Lycomedes on Syros, to escape the fate, predicted by the oracle, of dying in the battle of Troy. He was dressed as a girl during his banishment and kept among the king's daughters, one of whom bore him a child.
29. '*Somehow I was led . . . to pistol*' See p. 186 *The Secret Diaries of Miss Anne Lister* (Volume One) – '. . . *After dinner, Mary* [Best] *made a flourishing story of my going upstairs with loaded pistols and turning out a man . . .* [who] *had a jobation for ogling the girls at one of their parties. I alluded to it and did not much like his manner of acknowledging it . . .*' [Tuesday 16 October 1821. York.]

Breaking the Ice

The small, almost hermetic group of women living at 24 Place Vendôme were now by no means unaware of the nature of Anne's sexuality. The libertine atmosphere which prevailed in that era, particularly in Paris, towards Sapphic love[1] or love between women, inclined people to view with an affectionate and amused tolerance what later ages were to condemn as inverted and unnatural. It is true that a great deal of flirtatious touching, holding of hands and kissing had taken place between the women at the pension but for Anne, idealistic and merely 'romantic' friendship between woman and woman was not enough. Her need for a woman companion to share her life included a strong sexual component.

At the time of Anne's visit to Place Vendôme, she and Mariana Lawton had necessarily been separated, because of Mariana's married state, for some months. Anne was getting restless. She had been a guest at Place Vendôme for six or seven weeks. The main sightseeing round had become routine. The company in the pension had become familiar and the atmosphere there was beginning to revolve around the personal rather than the general. Mlle de Sans, Mme de Boyve and Mrs Barlow had all become objects of Anne's amorous regard. They were all aware that any relationship with her which went beyond the socially conventional would not be merely platonic.

Of the three women, Mrs Barlow's position in society was the most precarious, living as she did on a widow's pension of £80 a year and a government gratuity of £250 a year. Some portion of this income would be lost once Jane, her thirteen-year-old daughter, attained her majority. The encouraging response which Mrs Barlow showed to Anne's flirtations with her and also, perhaps, her vulnerability, offered an opening for Anne's more predatory advances.

Thursday 14 October

Went to Mrs Barlow & sat with her an hour. *Somehow she began talking of that one of the things of which Marie Antoinette was accused of was being too fond of women.*[2] *I, with perfect mastery of countenance, said I had never heard of it before and could not understand or believe it. Did not see how such a thing could be – what good it could do – but owned I had heard of the thing. Mrs Barlow asked if Mme Galvani had told me. I said no, & that nobody could be more correct than Mme Galvani. I said I would not believe such a thing existed. Mrs Barlow said it was mentioned in scripture, not in the New Testament not Deuteronomy, nor Leviticus. I said I believed that when reduced to the last extremity —— I was going to mention the use of phalli but luckily Mrs Barlow said, 'You mean two men being fond of each other?' & I said 'Yes,' turning off the sentence about being reduced to the last extremity by saying men were often afraid of women for fear of injuring their health. Here Mrs Barlow feigned an ignorance, which gave me the hint that she wanted to pump me but I declared I was the most innocent person in the world considering all I had seen & heard, for everybody told me things. She said she should not have mentioned it but she knew she was not telling me anything I did not know before. I said I read of women being too fond of each other in the Latin parts of the works of Sir William Jones.*[3] *She told me an old gentleman here, a savant I understand, had made proposals to her to visit her. The French women knew how to manage this without risk of children. All the French ladies, the wives, had two & no more. Mme de Boyve said if she, Mrs Barlow, married again she would tell her how, if she dared. Mme de Boyve had not told her but somebody else has & I understand that old General Vincennes*[4] *did or was once going to tell her all about it. By the way, it was this – my manner of giving her to understand I knew the secret – that she asked if Mme Galvani had told me. Mrs Barlow said she had learnt all this since she came to France & seemed to insinuate that she knew a great deal. In fact, she suspected me and she was fishing to find it out but I think I was too deep for her. I told her she had more sense than I had & could turn me round her finger & thumb if she liked. 'No,' she said, 'it is Mlle de Sans.' 'No, no,' said I, 'you understand this sort of thing better than she does.' But I had before said I could go as far in friendship, love as warmly, as most but could not go beyond a certain degree & did not believe anyone could do it. We agreed it was a scandal invented by the men, who were bad enough for anything. She is a deepish hand &, I think, would not be sorry to gain me over, but I shall be on my guard. She said, this evening, she never talked of these things except to persons she liked. She was hemming a pocket handkerchief narrow because she thought mine was so, & undoubled the whole to make it broad merely because I asked her. She certainly flirts with me . . . & said sometime afterwards, that she was not so calm and cold as I supposed. [I] made love to Mlle de Sans in the fiacre. Said I began to think I neither knew her nor myself. Knew not what was the matter with me, etc. She owned she had had many offers. Said she was just the sort of girl for it, she could attach anyone, etc. She was poorly & low but still coquetted very well. I cannot help fancying she, too, is a knowing one, considering she is a girl not quite six & twenty.*

Friday 15 October

Walked with Mrs Barlow ¾ hour along the boulevard . . . she did not seem ennuyée with my company & we sat quietly in her room till 1¾, when luncheon was announced . . . *I asked her for her bible.* [I] *said I knew what she alluded to as the French way of preventing children. Shewed her Genesis 36, the verse about Onan. I was right, so therefore the French husbands spill their seed just before going to their wives which, being done, they take the pleasure without danger. I wonder the women like it. It must spend the men before they begin. 'I must shew you the other passage,' said Mrs Barlow, 'because I know you wish to know.' I asked the chapter. She said Romans. 'Yes,' said I, 'the first chapter' & pointed to that verse about women forgetting the natural use, etc. 'But,' said I, 'I do not believe it.' 'Oh,' said she, 'it might be taken in another way, with men.' I agreed but without saying anything to betray how well I understood her. 'Yes,' she said, 'as men do with men.' Thought I to myself, she is a deep one. She knows, at all rates, that men can use women in two ways. I said I had often wondered what was the crime of Ham. Said she, 'Was it sodomy?' 'I don't know,' said I, then made her believe how innocent I was, all things considered.* [I] *said we were a cold-blooded family in this particular. Warm as I was in other things, this one passion was wanting. I went to the utmost extent of friendship but this was enough. I should like to be instructed in the other (between two women) & would learn when I could but it would be of no use to me. I had no inclination. Could not imagine what good it could do. Nor could she & thought, therefore, there could be no harm in it. 'Oh, no,' said I slightly, 'they can do no harm.' She then shewed me the little book the gentleman had left here for her, 'Voyage a Plombières',*[5] *p. 126, where is the story of one woman intriguing with another. She has lent me the book . . . She gives me to understand she would live with me & is sure I could love very deeply. She believes me tho' that I know nothing about it*

& is persuaded of what she might have suspected, that I have had no connection with women. But she is decidedly making love to me. I tell her I am more childish than she is – more fond of nonsense after reading, etc. Like to relax in an evening. Should like to have a person always at my elbow, to share my bedroom & even bed, & to go as far as friendship can go, but this is enough. [I] said I was half in love with Mlle de Sans but if I had appointed to go with her & was with Mrs Barlow, I could not keep the appointment. But if sitting with Mlle de Sans I could leave her to go to Mrs Barlow. Mrs Barlow has more tact, more power over me . . . She then told me of her confinement; of Mr Barlow. She did not like honeymoons. How many a man she might have had here. I joked & said if I was my father's son I should be sure I was in love with her – should know what was the matter with me. She said I was crazy, at the same time looking as if she wished to lead me on. [I] laughed & said I was not accustomed to this sort of thing – should take pills or salts, etc., & so we went on till Cordingley, wondering I had not rung, came in to dress me & Mrs Barlow left . . . She sat next me in the evening & every now & then I felt her near me, touching me. My knees, my toes or something . . . Payed [sic] what attention I could to Mlle de Sans but Mrs Barlow evidently wished to engross me. We came up to bed together. Asked her to come into my room & she would but for fear of increasing her cold. She certainly makes absolute love to me. Tells me I don't know her – she can love deeply, etc. All I know about things, I pretend, is a mass of undigested knowledge which I had but know not how to use, for I am a very innocent sort of person. I really must be on my guard. What can she mean? Is she really amoureuse? This from a widow & mother like her is more than I could have thought of. I am safer with Mlle de Sans. I told Mrs Barlow I would not visit her soon again till I felt myself better. I have said & done nothing I cannot & do not lay to simplicity & innocence as yet & I really must take care. I keep telling her she is too deep, too knowing, for me . . . She had said before, this house

was a little world & I should think so if I had seen all she had. I begin to think so already.

Sunday 17 October

Mrs Barlow & I sat up tête-à-tête till 1–25. *My manner towards her kind but proper. Talked rationally of my great want of a companion & how much stronger my friendships were than those of people in general. She could not feel as I did. 'Ah,' said she, 'it is not those that shew the least who feel the least.' She put her arm round me. I might have kissed her but contented myself with shaking hands.*

Tuesday 19 October

[Mrs Barlow] sat by while Cordingley curled my hair & afterwards we had a cozy chit-chat. 11–50 when she left me. *The thing is decided enough. I am paying regular court to her & she admits it. She said I should soon forget her. I answered, 'No, never,' & once I was away & recovered from my folly I should always be obliged to her for the kindness with which she treated me. I thought she behaved very well. There was nothing for which I could blame* [her]. *'Perhaps,' said she, 'you will not always think so.' She is evidently aware that I must think she encourages me. Lord bless me, 'tis plain enough she would not allow me to go on in this manner, nor would she put herself so in my way if she did not like it. Just before her going, I put my arm round her waist & tried to pull her on my knee, she resisted & I gave up & apologized. I asked if she was angry as she went out. She said, 'No,' & was giving me her lips to kiss when she recollected & suddenly turned her cheek, which I kissed, saying 'Why did you not do as you were going to do?' I had told her before I wished she could stay all night with me & if she were at Shibden she should, to which she made no objection . . . She is fond of me certainly but I do not pay her attention as if I respect her . . . I ought not to have dared talk to her as I do. What can I think of women in general?*

Wednesday 20 October

Began my accounts & had nearly settled them about 2–20 when Mrs Barlow came to me. *She asked me if I did not mean to go out & would not sit down but after a long while standing, took her seat close to me & made love in the pathetics. This morning she seems to think she is to blame & expressed her wonder she should allow me to talk so to her. I declared none could behave better. Thanked her again & again. Said how lucky for me that, if I must be foolish, it was with a person so calm, so safe, as herself. Said I should always be obliged to her for this. She would have the thing as not new to me & asked for my word of honour. I pretended I could only give it in part & not altogether & on this account would not give it at all, pretending others had been attached to me but I not to them. Refused to explain because she would even despise me if I did. She observed my wedding ring* [given to Anne by Mariana Lawton]. [I] *said this ought to bind me but this was pure friendship & I began to dread the influence that was greater. She then said, as if a momentary feeling, that the fault was hers.* [She] *stole over – 'But, oh, you are so candid, so open.' She knows me not. I am as deep as she . . . I perpetually plead my want of vanity to persuade myself it is possible for her to care for me. She little knows who she has to deal with. Before all this, I had laughed & joked & declared I would go to Italy and try the experiment, that is, get a woman there. She knew what I meant – tho' wrapt up it was plain enough & she only begged me to take care. Should be sorry to see my name in the papers in such a scrape as that would be. I assured her I would manage the thing well & tell her all about it. I would always tell her everything.*

Thursday 21 October

At 2½, went out with Mrs Barlow. Walked thro' the Tuileries gardens, along the Rue de Seine, direct to the Luxembourgh.

Went to see the Observatory. Staid some time on top of it, enjoying the fine air & the fine view of Paris. Then sauntered about the gardens, returned as we went & got home at 5¼. Dinner at 5¾ ... Sat with Mlle de Sans (Mrs Barlow had been there ever since dinner) by her bedside till 9–20, when Mrs Barlow & I came up to my room & she sat with me till 10½. *A little nonsense as usual. Held her hand & would not let her* [go]. *'If,' said she, 'you do in this way, you will prevent my coming again.' Of course, I desisted. While with Mlle de Sans, she (Mrs Barlow) let me have my hand up her petticoats almost to her knee. At last, she whispered, 'Do not yet.' She afterwards let me do it nearly as high. She had before taken away her legs once or twice but always put them back again. Joking about whether my character was respectable, she hoped it was & I joked as if she thought it was a good deal in her power. She has said once or twice if she was not so calm, what would become of me.*

Friday 22 October

At 10–40, set off with Mrs Barlow to the Louvre ... *No nonsense today. Said I felt quite ashamed of myself. Was determined to get the better of the thing & insinuated it would be Mrs Barlow's fault if I behaved foolishly again ... Was not accustomed to this sort of folly. Would not have my friends know of it for worlds. She said she was very glad of it. She had evidently suspected me of all this towards them but I fancy begins to think differently now. Said she was cross last night.* [I] *apologized for myself & said that I must not invite her any more. She said I was right, casually repeating that I should not marry. I said, nonsensical as I had been, I felt that to marry would be more wrong in me than all this nonsense.*

Monday 25 October

At 2½, Mme de Boyve & I set off to the Passage des Panoramas to Felix; the best pâtisserie in Paris. After agreeing he deserved his reputation we sauntered along the Passage, afterwards along the boulevards. Got as far as the grille of the Tuileries gardens but it began to rain a little & this sent us back & we got home at 4¼ ... Left the drawing room at 9–50. Just called & wished goodnight to Mlle de Sans & then went to Mrs Barlow & sat with her till 11¾. Then came to my room, sent Cordingley to bed and stood eating grapes & musing for some time. Then curled my hair. *Made closer love than ever to Mrs Barlow. She seemed as if she liked – as if she loved – yet she will not own this. Declares not. Only wishes to be friends. At last she said she was low. I asked why. She seemed ready to cry & said she thought she, too, was a little crazy. I did not notice this but only dwelt on the folly of encouraging what could not be returned & on the impossibility of her feeling for me as I did for her. At last she said, 'If I adored you I would not live with you in this way. I would rather marry you.' . . . She said she could not bear to lose her own esteem & I should not love long what I did not respect. I owned this. 'But,' said I, 'if I could propose your settling at Shibden &, of course, made you understand on what terms?' 'Oh,' said she, 'I must be respected by the world.' 'So you would,' said I. 'Well but,' said she, 'what would your friends* [think]*?' 'Oh,' said I, 'only that you were a new friend. I could easily manage this.' 'Ah,' said she, 'that I would not like. It would have been better had you been brought up as your father's son.' I said, 'No, you mistake me. It would not have done at all. I could not have married & should have been shut out from ladies' society. I could not have been with you as I am.' 'But,' said she, 'you would have taken your chance with the rest.' She meant of gentlemen. 'But,' said she, 'if you are contented it is enough.' She asked if my friends, meaning my three favourites,*[6] *knew my situation. I said no. I thanked her for what she had said to me.* [I] *said it was my great comfort I could do her no harm. I must always remain quite indifferent in her eyes & all the consolation I asked was if she would say she would have married me if I had been my father's son. She said she should not have been so fortunate. 'Ah,'* *said I, 'do not say this. Say simply yes.' This she would not do but repeated the former. 'I wish,' said I, 'you may be happier than you might be at Shibden.' 'Ah,' said she, 'I shall never be happy but it is not for the cause you think.' She again seemed ready to cry. Bade me go & I left her.*

Tuesday 26 October

From 3 to 5, walked [with Mrs Barlow] in the Tuileries gardens ... *Conversation in our usual style. She believes I have had a great deal of experience but acquits all my friends. Thinks I respect them too much. Why did I not so respect her? I pretended I respected her as much but liked or loved her better & thus explained all satisfactorily. But whatever experience I had had, she did not blame me more than other men but even thought more allowance was to be made for me than for them . . . She said I astonished Mme Galvani at first, who once or twice said to the Mackenzies she thought I was a man & the Macks too had wondered. Mrs Barlow herself had thought at first I wished to imitate the manners of a gentleman but now she knows me better, it was not put on . . . Asked Mrs Barlow if she thought I was capable of being in love. She thought yes. I said then I was so with her. She said it would soon go off. She thought her being so much with me was the best way of curing me. 'Ah,' said I, 'you know better than that.' But she trusted me. Thought me most honourable & that was the greatest obligation by which she could bind me to deserve her confidence. She wondered what Cordingley thought of me. 'Oh, merely,' said I, 'that I have my own particular ways.' I happened to say that my aunt often said I was the oddest person she ever knew. Mrs Barlow said, 'But she knows all about it, does she not?' 'Oh,' said I, 'she & my friends are all in a mist about it.'* ... Mrs Barlow came to me at 7–25. Sat with me here till 8½ & then in her own room till 9, when we went down to join the party ... *On leaving my room, I had before said I liked to see her dressed & put her shawl a little back. She always drew it forward again. Mere coquetry. She begins to blush a little now & then & looks rather pathetic. I asked why she had said last night she could not be happy. She said she was low. She longed to have a home.* [I] *reminded her she might marry when she likes. She said she might if she had not shut herself up so many years. She likes attention & had not much from the men tonight. After waiting a while she said nobody had given her a word. Of course I gave her one directly. She would not suit me. I would tire of her – but flirting with her amuses me now.*

Thursday 28 October

Hurried off at 6¼ to the Porte St Martin theatre. 3 pieces. In the 1st, a girl travelling in a diligence told where her money was & was robbed. A quiz, too, against the English. Then dancing & wonderful feats of balancing & strength, wrestling & fine play of the muscles by 4 men dressed in flesh-coloured web so as to look almost as if naked, having merely smart shining middle cloths round them. Bits, too, of the same tinsel on their breasts. Dressed to imitate American Indians ... The display of muscular action when 2 of the men wrestled was very fine. Then more good dancing & lastly, a piece of pantomime in which Mesurier[7] was excellent, representing a soldier about to be shot for desertion, reprieved by the king, to whom the young man's intended bride fell down on her knees & presented her petition for her lover's life. There was the king & his staff and about a hundred veritable soldiers & the band paraded on the stage for a considerable time. A mimic representation of what the real thing would have been ... It was surprising to see how well they marched & counter-marched in so small a space on the stage. Surely all this would have seemed ridiculous to most English people but appeared to highly delight the French.

The affair between Anne and Maria Barlow continued with a certain amount of prevarication on both sides. Anne oscillated between infatuation and a deep-seated disinclination to commit herself too seriously. Mrs Barlow sensed that Anne's real loyalties were elsewhere. The affair, however, had not gone unnoticed by the other guests, nor by Madame de Boyve. The latter took it upon herself to relate some stories of Mrs Barlow's alleged activities and intrigues with various men callers, prior to the arrival of Anne, at Place Vendôme. It seemed to Anne, from Madame de Boyve's gossipy account, that Mrs Barlow was what would have been termed an 'adventuress'. Anne began to feel that she had reason to worry about her deepening involvement with Mrs Barlow but found it impossible to draw back from the excitement of the liaison.

Friday 29 October

Mme de Boyve's cold bad – kept her in bed all day. Sent my compliments & to say I should be glad to pay my respects. Almost immediately after dinner she sent for me. [I] left the drawing room & went to her at 6–50. Staid by her bedside till 8–40. *Admired her, etc., . . . Then got on to the subject of Mrs Barlow. I always try to put them in love with each other but I merely said tonight, Mrs Barlow always spoke well of her but they were such different characters they could never quite suit each other. Mme de Boyve agreed. She always felt afraid of annoying her & perhaps Mrs Barlow might feel the same towards her & they might be mutually not at ease. But five or six people had said they did not like Mrs Barlow. She had always something satirical, en critique, to say of everyone . . . Mme de Boyve declared whenever Mrs Barlow thought of going she would instantly take her at her word. Among other things I gave her my word of honour not to mention, she said she* [Mrs Barlow] *always* [thinks] *everyone in love with her. True enough . . . Mrs Barlow had at one time received a Mr* [Hancock], *an Englishman, perpetually in her room. Sat with him & talked with him tête-à-tête for hours together till all the servants began to joke & M. de Boyve desired Madame to tell her of it, for if it was not given up she really must leave the house . . . There was another one, a gay Frenchman, I forget his name, & M. de Nappe declared to Mme de Boyve this man had slept one night with Mrs Barlow . . . tho' Mme de Boyve did not believe what M. de Nappe said, she left me to judge for myself . . . Thought to myself again, 'Her* [Mrs Barlow's] *conduct has not given the lie to all this.' M. de Bellevue whispered to her the other night, 'Saint Enis touch', according to the sound, meaning sly, a saint in public but not in private . . . She looks so calm & quiet in the drawing room one would think her the least in the world for this sort of thing. 'Well,' said I to myself, 'what hands have I got into? How to get out again? Let this be a lesson for the future.' But I have asked her into my room* tonight . . . Had tea. Came upstairs at 9–35. *Had a good fire, my hair curled and had just done when Mrs Barlow came at ten. Told her I had rattled away to Mme de Boyve. Admired her. Should have been in love with her if I had been a man, but would not have married her. Would only have married an Englishwoman. Would not mix the blood . . . I was proud of my country. Loved the little spot where my ancestors had lived for centuries. Should inherit from them with pure English blood for five or six centuries and my children should not say I had mixed it. I loved my king & country & compatriots & would not take my fortune away from them. I should be head of my family & it should remain English still. She (Mme de Boyve) admired the nobleness of my sentiments & said England was the first country in the world & when I said I should never marry at all, said she was glad of it for then I should never change to my friends, adding (but I did not tell Mrs Barlow this) she was not worthy of my friendship. I kissed her* [Mme de Boyve] *kindly on leaving her. Well, but, said Mrs Barlow, I was volage. I sat close to* [Mrs Barlow] *with hold of her hands as usual, looking but not saying much. She got up to go at five minutes before eleven. I kept her at the door quarter-hour. Kissed her throat rather warmly. 'What are you doing?' said she & pretended anger, being surely a little excited. I begged forgiveness. Said I could not bear she should think me volage. What had I to call for constancy? Could I love whom I did not respect? Or could I attach myself to good wishes (meaning hers)? She said I had told her I could have married Mme de Boyve. I said it was nonsense. 'If you had said it downstairs I should not have thought of it but you have said it to me.' I protested against it. 'Well,' said she, 'perhaps you have not been in love – perhaps not attached properly or at least not for many years. But you say I am romantic. You are volage. It is best you should be so. You cannot love as I can.' Thought I, I could have her if I seriously chose it but she would require too much attention & I could never forget this flirting with these men. She was a little excited, I think, & surely she is conscious of liking me. She knows well enough all about it. What would Mariana say to all this if she knew? I am indeed unable, it seems, to take care of myself with women. I am always getting into some scrape with them. If Mrs Barlow did not like me she would not let me talk & do as I do. But no more. I shall be in the mire if I don't take care.*

Wednesday 3 November

Mrs Barlow told me this morning she was 21 when she was married in 1808 to Lt. Col. Barlow of the 61st Foot, by special licence in Guernsey. Colonel Barlow was 38, about 18 years older than she. She will be 38 the 28th December next . . . *In wishing her goodnight she quietly let me put my arms around her waist & gently press her & very gently kiss her. She stood, too, with her right thigh a little within my left, in contact – which she has never permitted before. She likes me certainly.*

Thursday 4 November

Sat cozily till 9–50, then came up to bed. Mrs Barlow soon followed & came to me at 9–50 & sat with me till 11–55. *Behaved very properly all the day tho' evidently making distant love. Kissed her gently several times, particularly saying she now behaved kindly and well & I was satisfied & would never make bad use of it . . . She understands me well enough. She knows I am making love & does not look as if it was impossible she could return it. At last, I said she was right & not* [right] *in saying I should not love long whom I did not respect. Right in the first instance, but we were at issue on the point that, if my love was returned, I should not respect the person. Why should I not? If she deserved to be respected for every other thing surely loving me could not sink her in my esteem? Why should she not love me? Was I not one who might hope to gain attachment & retain it when gained? And in loving me, there must be a great deal of mind, hinting that I had not the power to inspire any love which did not chiefly depend on mind. She looked as if not dissenting nor displeased. 'But,' said I, 'there are those whom I know I could both respect & love. They are not at the world's end but it matters not to give them a local habitation & name. Yet to know only one mind where it is necessary to know two, is nothing.'* [Mrs Barlow] *often looks at my gold rings & just presses them on my finger. She had done so tonight. Said I, 'I know you often think of those rings. Perhaps you attach too much importance to them & I too little.' She asked if I had described the friend who gave them. I somehow said, 'No.' 'Ah,' said she, 'she is your dearest friend. You told me it was Mrs Lawton. You told me wrong then.' To this I made no answer but – returning to the position – there are those whom I know I could both respect & love yet to know only one mind where there are two is nothing, said she directly, 'You ought to know your own mind before you ask that of others. You do not understand these things.' I was silent a moment, then said it was possible to unsay in a moment what it had required hours to say, & was going to ask whether she meant that if I was in the same mind three years hence, or if my own mind was really made up now, could she change hers. But she jumped up, must go, & went away . . . Speaking of my picture of happiness,* [I] *said I would not let my friend get into bed much before or after me. I should* [not like] *to find or be found asleep. She smiled. I said happiness, like all other things, required some tact. I thought I knew it a little & that I could make the person I loved happy. She said she thought I could. Surely she likes me. What would Mariana say? She has not written to me of too long.*

Friday 5 November

Went to Mrs Barlow at 11¾. Took down my breakfast things & breakfasted in her room & sat with her till 1½ & then very sorry to be called off to the Louvre. *Behaved properly, as far as it could be so in making love all the time. Asked if she thought a person just like her could make me happy. She said she could not answer yet – seemed to think yes. Speaking of herself,* [she] *said there was much for & against. She had a child, which must divide her attention, etc., & was a great objection. I stopt her, saying, 'No, no, it is not that,' in French, for we spoke it all the while. 'But there are two, & only two, things. You have been married – you must make comparisons. It is impossible you should love me well enough. And there is the thought of those rings, which does come across my conscience. But you could not love me well enough. You must make comparisons.' She merely answered, 'You do not know me.' . . . I said the best thing for me would be her marrying. 'Then,' she answered, 'I will hasten it.' 'No, no,' said I, 'it would give me more pain than I like to think of.' But I would deserve her friendship. Had hold of her hands all the while. Said I minded not what she said. It was what she did. I knew I had her good wishes & that she did not dislike me. Leaned on her shoulder a few moments. Squeezed her hands gently & perhaps she was conscious of the feelings of excitement which thrilled thro' me. She just said, 'You will squeeze me to death.' I desisted. She said it was time to go. She did not look as if she disliked me, nor do I believe she felt so. I asked her to give me my own place. She said no & resisted. I had kissed the left side of her throat in the morning & asked to have that for my own place. She said it was odd; another liked it – and then said a moment afterwards, when she had seen the expression of wonder in my countenance, that it was her daughter. I said friendship might allow me that & I would not abuse it. She still refused, then said, 'I am not fit for this world', & hurried off. From her manner altogether I fancied she, at that moment, felt to like me more than she would have owned to me or liked to own even to herself. Is it possible she should see me as she does and be so much with me & not relax a little sometimes? . . .* [A letter from Mariana Lawton had come that day] . . . *Mariana writes affectionately enough. Asks if I ever wished for her. Read this to Mrs Barlow, who observed she seemed much attached to me. It was the habit of some people to write so but she thought Mariana was not in this way and she felt all she wrote.* [I] *said she was in the habit of calling me 'Fred' from a joke of a story. I had had many nicknames but was never called by my own name except by my family. Mrs Barlow seemed to notice in silence then added, of Fred, did she so call her husband. Poor Mrs Barlow. She likes me certainly. I had told her last night I could not have married Mariana. Mrs Barlow guessed her family was not good enough for I had named her father being a physician at York.*

Sunday 7 November

A little before 3, went (there & back in a fiacre) with Mrs & Miss Barlow, Mlle de Sans, M. Dacier & M. Eugene de Boyve, to M. le Baron Denon's,[8] Quai Voltaire, to see his collection of Egyptian antiquities,[9] paintings, Greek & Roman medals, etc. Staid there near 1½ hours. Several rooms thrown open to us. Mummies & parts of mummies . . . Came upstairs at 10–50 with Mrs Barlow.

Stopt a few minutes talking to her in her anteroom. *Kissed her in a little dark passage as we came out of the dining room. She lets me kiss her now very quietly & sits with her feet close to mine . . . If I had a penis, tho' of but small length, I should surely* <u>*break the ice*</u> *some of these times, before I go. We were very much by ourselves at* M. *Denon's. I pointed out two phalli. Said the beetle was an indecent emblem & pointed out an indecent print of a wake, or fête, where the people seemed to be dancing & the breeches of the men made to shew their erections.*

Monday 8 November

At 11–50, set off with Mme Carbonnier to Chaillon. no. 12, to see her daughter, en pension there (19 young ladies there) at 500 francs a month, to be set straight. She is very much deformed. The whole right side much enlarged. A nice looking house, situate in a nice garden in which young ladies were walking. They lie on inclined planes all the day, except from 12 to 2, when they walk & from 6 to 8 in the evening. They are not allowed to sit down – must either stand or walk or lie down. While lying on the inclined planes (at least, saw 1 for this purpose, furnished with an apparatus for conveying a stream of cold water), they have cold water poured on the weak parts.

Tuesday 9 November

About 7¼, Mrs Barlow, Mrs Heath, Mlle de Sans, M. Dacier & myself, set off (in a fiacre) to the Italian [Opera] to see Madame Pasta[10] in 'Nina Mad For Love'.[11] She was certainly very great. Her voice & singing very fine; she, very graceful. Mme Galvani some time ago said she was decidedly a very much better singer than Catalani.[12] M. *Dacier paying attention to Mlle de Sans, to which she shews no dislike, & I to* Mrs *Barlow. Under our shawls, had my arm round her waist great part of the time. Felt a little excited by the music, etc., & she surely knew it full well. I think she felt something herself. Had my arm round her waist, too, as we returned* ... Got home at 11–20. Went immediately into Mrs Barlow's & sat with her till 12¾. We had tea & I had some of my grapes. *Dead lovemaking & talked a little foolishly. Said if I could not make a good hit, I should make a bad one, hinting at having a mistress. Seeing her look as if angry,* [I] *turned it that I should shut myself up from the world ... I had before told her I had once had a person with me with whom I had gone to bed at ten & lain till one, two, three & later, the next day & my father would not have us disturbed. She looked & said she would not have had such a person in her house. Just before going to the Opera, had come up to put my things on & kissed her left cheek till it was quite sore & three places quite raised. When she shewed me, I laughed heartily, declaring I knew not what I was doing. She said she was ashamed to go downstairs. I believe she was but she was not at all angry.*

Wednesday 10 November

Mrs Barlow came & sat with me till 12, when she was sent for to [go to] Colonel and Mrs Birch, who had called on her. [I] *said how ill I had behaved last night. The opera had set me all wrong & I would go no more . . . She leaned on my shoulder and seemed hurt. 'Ah,' said she, 'I should not mind it so if I did not think you blamed me so much.' She certainly seems fond of me & said that I spoilt her. I told her I did not blame her ... I said how happy I was when with her. She said she was just as happy when with me.* [I] *told her tonight I would call her Maria – asked if I might. She said she was obliged to me for the wish to do so. I asked if she would burn my letters* [if they corresponded at a later date]. *She said she would do whatever I asked her. I thanked her, saying I would then write more at my ease, assured that she would destroy all that it might be imprudent to keep. This is sanction enough to my writing what I like . . . She said, in the morning just before we went out, I should suit her entirely but she would not suit me. It would be difficult, at first, to be attentive to me without appearing to neglect her child. Speaking of her good figure & pretty hand and of her foot, asked her to let me span her ancle* [sic]. *She refused. I said I was contented she should refuse me this now but could not bear it if we were always together. 'Oh,' said she, 'then it would be a different thing.' She now stands nearer to me when I kiss her, yet she always withdraws the moment it becomes* [obvious] *that I am excited. She certainly knows how to gain one's affections. She has a tact & delicacy by which she owned she had retained the love of her husband. I really do like her now & I think she is much attached to me. She was rather low this morning – said she must exert herself for her child's sake, otherwise would not care how soon she was removed from this world. I think she regrets what she knows of my engagement to Mariana, tho' the handsome proper manner in which she speaks of it pleases me much. She told me today my only plan, when I hinted at breaking the engagement, that is, changing my mind* [about Mariana] *was not to pother* [sic] *myself about it but let things go on quietly till I was left to myself & then determine. She has a nice little figure. She is ladylike & quiet yet very affectionate. She really does seem to know how to manage me & I might choose worse.*

---

1. Sapphic love – The name is derived from Sappho, a Greek poetess, born in the late seventh century BC on the island of Lesbos. Her poetry is most famous for its eulogisation of love between women, thus linking it to lesbianism. Critics differ in their views, however. Some do see her poetry as concentrating on erotic love between women; others as an expression of maternal love for girls young enough to be her daughter. She did marry and also gave birth to a daughter, but the poetry does depict a sensual appreciation of female beauty.
2. Marie Antoinette – (1755–1793). Wife of Louis XVI of France. One of the charges brought against Marie Antoinette was that she had 'debauched liaisons with women as well as with men'. Even as early

as 1775 her strong friendships with women were looked upon with suspicion. Many of these accusations against her, made by the French, were grounded in the fear of Austrian domination, via 'petticoat power' wielded by Marie Antoinette and her mother, Maria Theresa, Empress of Austria.

3. Sir William Jones – (1746–1794). Latinist. Born in London and died in Calcutta. He studied at Oxford from 1764–1768, learning Latin, Greek, Hebrew, Arabic and Persian. During his lifetime he mastered twenty-eight languages, many of them self-taught. His work encouraged interest in Oriental studies in the West. Knighted in 1783, he became Judge of the Supreme Court in Calcutta.
4. General Vincennes – Anne could here be referring to General Vincent (1757–1834), Austrian Ambassador to Paris from 1814 to 1825. He was born in Florence, into a noble family of Lorraine, many of which served the Habsburgs, emperors of Austria.
5. 'Voyage a Plombières' – Plombières is a spa town in eastern France. The book to which Anne refers has been difficult to locate. The only likely reference found was *Les Nymphes de Plombières, ou Relation Veridique des Fêtes Curieuses qui viennent de se donner dans ces Bains. Anecdote Historique Tirée du Journal de la Ville* ('*The Nymphs of Plombières, or True Relation of the Curious Feasts which have just happened in the Baths. Historical Anecdotes extracted from the Town's Newspaper*') pp4. Paris, 1789. This is listed in *The British Library General Catalogue of Printed Books to 1975* (vol 260), K G Saur. London/München/Paris. 1984.
6. . . . *my three favourites* . . . – Two of Anne's 'favourites' were definitely Mariana Lawton and Sibbella MacLean, a Scottish woman of noble descent whom she had met in York. The third is debatable. It could have been Isabella Norcliffe (but Anne had tired of her by now) or, alternatively, Mariana's sister, Anne (Nantz) Belcombe. All were, in fact, aware of the nature of Anne's sexuality – Sibbella MacLean less so, perhaps, than the others who had all had sexually active love affairs with Anne.
7. Mesurier – Anne here probably refers to Mazurier (c1799–1828), mime artist and acrobatic dancer. His fame, in fact, dated from his appearances at the Porte St Martin Theatre, Paris, in 1824. (See the entry in the *Dictionnaire des Comediens Français de Lyonnet*, p 413.) The sketch seen by Anne was probably 'The Deserter'. Mazurier was,

in his time, the most talented mime artist in Paris. His earnings of 1,000 francs a day exceeded those of the celebrated actor, Talma.

8. Baron Denon – Dominique Vivant Denon (1747–1825), a French artist, Egyptologist and museum official who played a crucial role in the development of the Louvre Museum. During the French Revolution he was protected by his friend, the painter David (1748–1825), who was a member of the extremist Jacobin group of revolutionaries. In 1798, Denon went with Napoleon on his Egyptian campaign, where he made many sketches of the ancient monuments, even whilst under enemy fire. His book, *Voyage dans la Basse et le Haute Egypt* (*'Travels in Lower and Upper Egypt'*) was published in 1802.
9. Egyptian antiquities – In the first half of the nineteenth century, vast numbers of antiquities were exported from Egypt. Napoleon's pillaging of many of these treasures included the Rosetta Stone which, in 1801, was, in turn, acquired by the British and is now in the British Museum.
10. Madame Pasta – Guiditta Maria Constanza *née* Negri (1797–1865), opera singer. She was the reigning Italian soprano of the time, acclaimed for her vocal range and expressiveness. In 1850 she retired to teach at her villa on Lake Como.
11. 'Nina Mad for Love' – This would be *Nina Ossia la Pozza per Amore* (1789), a one-act opera written by Giovanni Paisiello (or Paesiello), (1740–1816). He was a Neapolitan composer of operas, the best of which is thought to be *The Barber of Seville* (1782), based on a play of the same title by French author Beaumarchais (1732–1799), who also wrote *The Marriage of Figaro*. Paisiello was invited to Paris by Napoleon in 1802, where he conducted the music of the Court in the Tuileries. His fortunes fell when the Bonaparte family fell.
12. Catalani – Angelica (1780–1849), Italian operatic soprano. She made her debut as a singer at Venice in 1795, then at La Scala in 1801. In 1814 she took over the management of the Theatre des Italiens in Paris, a job she held until 1817. In 1819 she retired from the operatic stage and founded a school near Florence. Her talents commanded high fees. She was paid 200 guineas for singing 'Rule Brittannia' or 'God Save the King'.

No Priest But Love

Both Anne and Maria Barlow had become deeply involved with each other in the space of a few short weeks. Yet both had doubts about the other. Anne felt, in some way, that Maria Barlow was out to 'trap' her into a lifelong relationship for reasons which had more to do with providing security for herself and her daughter than with real, disinterested love for Anne. Mariana Lawton's hold on Anne's emotions had its roots in the fact that, despite her traitorous marriage, Mariana's love still endured. Anne could not feel the same security in this new, rootless relationship with an unknown woman which had developed so quickly in the artificial, hothouse atmosphere of a pension situated in the romantic city of Paris.

On Maria Barlow's part, there was no doubt that she wanted a serious relationship with Anne and that she knew that such a relationship would be of a strong sexual nature. That, for Maria Barlow, had to go hand in hand with the dignity and rights which marriage would confer upon a woman of her social status. Given the fact that Anne obviously could not marry her in the eyes of the law or of the church, Mrs Barlow was unsure how far she could go in resisting Anne sexually without jeopardising her chance of a life relationship between them. As it was, she had a decision to make, and the thought of Mariana Lawton hovering in the background of Anne's life made Mrs Barlow's position much less strong than it might otherwise have been. If she refused to consummate their relationship sexually, Anne could always return to the sanctuary of Mariana's love and the security of Shibden Hall. For Maria Barlow, alone in Paris and relatively poor, no such cosy option existed. On the other hand, if she yielded to Anne's sexual requests, the whole affair might founder upon Anne's capacity for indulging in casual sexual affairs (for which Maria Barlow had already excused Anne, holding her no more guilty than 'other men') whilst retaining her real love for Mariana Lawton.

However, whatever private doubts and insecurities the two women harboured, the affair continued to intensify.

Thursday 11 November

Breakfast at 9–35. Mrs Barlow came at 10–10, ready to go out shopping immediately. *Asked her to sit down for one minute & we sat lovemaking till ten minutes before twelve.* Went to a shop in the Rue Neuve St Roch (not far from here) & bought 4 ells each of cambric at 18 francs per ell, Mrs Barlow to hem me 6 handkerchiefs. Got back at 12¾. Found Mme Galvani waiting for me. Spent all the time in conversation. She left me at 2–10. *Then immediately came Mrs Barlow to go out again. She jumped on the window seat to see if it rained. I locked the door as usual, then lifted her down and placed her on my knee. By & by she said, 'Is the door fast?' I, forgetting, got up to see, then took her again on my knee & there she sat till four & threequarters, when Mlle de Sans sent to ask if I could receive.* [I] *told the maid I was sorry, I could not, I had got so bad a headache. The fact was I was heated & in a state not fit to see anyone. I had kissed & pressed Mrs Barlow on my knee till I had had a complete fit of passion. My knees & thighs shook, my breathing & everything told her what was the matter. She said she did me no good. I said it was a little headache & I should go to sleep. I then leaned on her bosom &, pretending to sleep, kept pottering about & rubbing the surface of her queer.*[1] *Then made several gentle efforts to put my hand up her petticoats which, however, she prevented. But she so crossed her legs & leaned against me that I put my hand over & grubbled her on the outside of her petticoats till she was evidently a little excited, & it was from this that Mlle de Sans' maid roused us. Mrs Barlow had once whispered, holding her head on my shoulder, a word or two which, I think, were, 'Do you love me?' But I took no notice, still pretending to be asleep. She afterwards said once or twice, 'It is good to pretend to be asleep,' & then once, while I was grubbling pretty strongly, 'You know you pinch me.' From this she never attempted to escape. Before, when rubbing her in front, she had every now & then held my hand but always let me have it back again. After Mlle de Sans' maid roused us, she* [drew] *her chair close to the bed. I sat on the bed & partly knelt on one knee so as to have her quite close & she began to reproach herself, saying she was a poor, weak creature & what should I think of her. I protested love & respect. Said it was all my fault & I would be miserable if she was too severe to herself. 'Can you not love me one little bit for all the great deal I love you? If you do not love me, I cannot forgive you. You are too cruel thus to sport with the feelings of another – but if you do love me, I am happy.' 'What do you think?' said she. 'Oh,' I replied, 'that you do.' She answered that if she did not love me she could not have done as she did. I kissed her mouth several times when it was a little open & rather warmly. Just before she left she said she was a little tired. I asked why. She answered because her feelings had been excited. She told me she had always kept all others at a great distance. I said I did not doubt it for if she could keep me at a distance under present circumstances, she certainly could others when not so tried. I said she frightened me. She had talked to me before we went out this morning about settling near Southampton with the widow of her husband's oldest brother, General Barlow, who was also her aunt, her mother's sister & about fifty. She had a son & daughter grown up.* Dinner at 5½. Saying I had a headache, came upstairs immediately after dinner ... Mrs Barlow came at 10¼ & ... staid with me till 11¾. *She looked a little grave, as if half-ashamed & wondering how I should treat her. I was very respectful tho' affectionate. Said I had fancied I had much to say to her but all seemed gone & I had not a word to say. I was happy, yet could cry like a child if I chose, little as this was ever my custom. She said this would better suit her. I denied this. Asked her to sit on my knee. She refused, saying she did me harm. I still entreated & she yielded on my promise to behave well. I wished she could remain with me. Instead of expressing any objection, she said, 'But as it is impossible, I had better go,' & then went. Now that the ice was a little broken, what will it end in? Has she any hope of attaching me really? She is sufficiently yielding.* [On my] *saying to Mme Galvani that she was pretty, 'No, not at all,' said she, 'beaucoup plus laide que moi'* ['uglier than me'], *& that she looked eight & thirty. Her skin & complexion were bad. I thought of all this when kissing her & thought it would not do for always . . . Said Mrs Barlow* [earlier], *'Go to bed early. Do not write tonight.' I answered, 'I have not much to write. No need of it. I can remember today without writing.'*

Friday 12 November

Dinner at 5–40. Mrs Barlow & I went up together immediately from table into her room where we sat very cozily till 8–35, when (Mrs Barlow not liking to go down) I went by myself & joined the party in the drawing room till 10 & then returned to Mrs Barlow & sat with her till 11–40, when I came up to bed. *Loverlike as usual. No recurrence to yesterday that she disliked. She sat cutting out my pocket handkerchief. I said how much happier I was within these few days. I was now assured I was not indifferent to her & that the distance at which she chose to keep me was less the result of inclination than of what she deemed propriety. She did not contradict this. Her manner acknowledged, I maintained, that my very folly was the effect of everything she wished, tho' not itself what she wished. It did not spring from regard so unworthy her acceptance as she imagined. She said she wondered how I could like an old woman as she was. I said if she really thought this, I only hoped it was an argument in favour of what I had just said about my regard. She was not passé, not old, to me – yet, still, it could not be the bloom of youth or beauty that I loved her for. In stooping over her, the waist of my new gown hung off a little. She put her hand down on the left side, almost touching the nipple of the breast, evidently wishing to feel it. She felt the stuffing but made no remark. I let her do it, observing I should hope to do the same. She did not much notice this but with a half no. She said it looked as if ready for anyone. I said for no one but herself, but she might do anything. She said others might who liked. 'No,' said I, 'I do what I like but never permit them to do so.' This seemed to please her. She still fancies Mariana likes me. Tonight* [she] *insinuated what might have passed* [between Anne & Mariana], *saying, 'But of course you would never tell me.' I turned this off dexterously as usual & I think, considering Mariana's marriage, she feels unwillingly constrained to believe me. I kissed her neck over her habit-shirt. She said she was all skin & bone now, her pillows were gone. I said she satisfied me. She afterwards drew her shawl close round her saying, as she found me a little empassioned, I did myself harm. She did not like to see me in that state. I kissed her lips & forehead several times & on coming away put my tongue a very little into her mouth. She said, tho' without the least appearance of anger, that I had forgotten myself. I said it was much more difficult to forget myself a little than to remember myself so well, meaning that I had not forgotten myself much – might easily have done more. She begins to stand closer to me. I might easily press queer to queer. Our liking each other is now mutually understood and acknowledged. I asked her this morning how much she thought I liked her. She said as much as contented her & that was not a little. She would not refuse sleeping with me if we could manage it well – & then – & then . . .*

Saturday 13 November

At 2–20 went down to Mrs Barlow, meaning to go out. She thought it would be too much for her. I therefore sat with her till 4–35. *Lovemaking, vindicating style of conversation respecting myself. A great pickle. 'Scaped my maid & got away among the workpeople. My father was one year in the Militia.*[2] *When my mother thought I was safe I was running out in an evening. Saw curious scenes, bad women, etc. Then went to the Manor school & became attached to Eliza Raine.*[3] *Said how it* [Anne's preference for, or sexual attraction to, women] *was all nature. Had it not been genuine the thing would have been different.* [I] *said I had thought much, studied anatomy, etc. Could not find it out. Could not understand myself. It was all the effect of the mind. No exterior formation accounted for it. Alluded to their being an internal correspondence or likeness of some of the male or female organs of generation. Alluded to the stones not slipping thro' the ring till after birth, etc.*[4] *She took all this very well. I said ladies could often hear from a man what they could not from a woman & she could from me what she could not from Mrs Mackenzie. She allowed this, saying it depended on how she loved them. Got on the subject of Saffic* [sic] *regard.* [I] *said there was artifice in it. It was very different from mine & would be no pleasure to me.*[5] *I liked to have those I loved near me as possible, etc. Asked if she understood. She said no.* [I] *told her I knew by her eyes she did & she did not deny it, therefore I know she understands all about the use of a ——* [The word is not entered in the journal]. *Alluded to self-pollution, how much it was practised. Thought my connection with the ladies more excusable than this. She declared she had never heard of this (I was incredulous at heart). From one thing to another. Got to tell her that the business of Thursday was exhausting beyond measure, as it always was to excite & then disappoint nature. Said if a man loved his wife as he ought, he could say anything to her & indelicacy depended on their own minds. Many things might pass between them without indelicacy that might otherwise be shocking. She agreed, tho' I hinted at things – sometimes having no night-shift at all for a little while. She said if I wore men's clothes she should feel differently. She could not then sit on my knee. If my father had brought me up as a son she would have married me as I am, had I stated my case to her alone, even tho' she had had rank & fortune & been nineteen & at that age she was well worth having. I thanked her. Happening to say I often told my uncle & aunt how I longed to have someone with me, she wondered what they would think of the person. I said my aunt knew nothing about it, nor would my uncle think anything. Then, expressing my wish to have her, she answered, 'But we have had no priest but love. Do you not know the quotation?' I did not yet I said yes. Kissed her repeatedly, rather warmly. We get on gradually. Perhaps I shall have her yet before I go.* [I] *told her, when speaking of Eliza* [Raine], *we had once agreed to go off together when of age but my conduct first delayed it & then circumstances luckily put an end to it altogether. Said I had never mentioned this to any human being but herself. At this moment* [of writing the journal], *I half-fancy I long since told it to Mariana.* At 4–35, ran off to the Rue St Honoré for some more flowers. The flower-woman gone, told the porter to get me 2 very pretty bouquets, one for Mme de Boyve . . . the other for Mrs Barlow. Did not dress. Sat down to dinner at 5. Immediately on leaving table went with Mrs Barlow to her room & sat with her from 5–50 to 8. Then dressed. Had the hairdresser after her & paid him 2 francs for making me a terrible grenadier-like looking figure. Mrs Barlow with me here ½ hour & we then went down to the party at 9–10. Perhaps about 70 people. They danced quadrilles (in the drawing room, we all sitting round – 3 card tables in the room next to us & all the gents who were not dancing) & waltzes. Mme de Boyve &

sometimes Mlle de Sans playing on the piano, which was all the music they had. The ladies looked by no means all of them first-rate. The gents appeared most the best of the 2. Mrs Williams, of ridiculous notoriety at Bath in 1813 for dancing cotillons with her monkey-faced husband, etc., formerly Mrs Briscoe, wife to the Governor of St Helena of that name – a dashing person risen, I fancy, from nothing – was here tonight & danced, too, at the close of the evening in the same set with her daughter ... Tea, bread & butter, & a few sweet cakes. Afterwards, tumbler glasses of common wine & what looked like milk & water. The cakes we had at tea – very indifferent. All the gents held their common round hats in their hands tho' it was professedly a ball – only putting them down while they danced. Mrs Barlow having asked me whether I would have her dance or not, I said no, & she refused, tho' I think with some regrets at doing so &, M. Bellevue, etc., quizzing her, at last I told him it was I would not let her dance. She had a daughter 14. It was time mama gave up dancing. It might do for a Frenchwoman but not for an Englishwoman. She and I left the room at 12–10 & I went into her room & sat with her ½ hour, *lovemaking. Kissed her neck. She would have me stay no longer. 'Go,' said she, 'remember the servants. Perhaps they do not love each other as we do.' I rallied her on having said* <u>*we*</u>*. 'Ah,' said she, 'I hoped you would not notice it.' I perpetually expressed my wish to stay all night with her. She says nothing against it. She said tonight, 'Now sit down & compose yourself. You look poorly,' meaning empassioned. She told me before dinner I had given her a warm look the first morning she had come to call on me & she had remembered it ever since & always liked me.*

Sunday 14 November

Mrs Barlow came to me & staid till 4–50. *Sat talking for some time. It did me harm to sit on my knee. It was all for my sake she refused. At last she consented. Sapphic love was again mentioned.*

I spoke rather more plainly. It was something Mrs Middleton had said that had made her comprehend what I had said about artifice [the use of a phallus?]. *I mentioned the girl at a school in Dublin that had been obliged to have surgical aid to extract the thing. Said boys learnt much vice, too, at school – the practice of Onanism, etc. She said the warm look she had said so struck her the first time she had called on me was directed to her bosom. From little to more.* [I] *became rather excited. Felt her breasts & queer a little. Tried to put my hand up her petticoat but she prevented. Touched her flesh just above the knee twice. I kissed her warmly & held her strongly. She said what a state I was putting myself into. She got up to go away & went to the door. I followed. Finding she lingered a moment, pressed her closely & again tried to put my hand up her petticoats. Finding that she would not let me do this but still that she was a little excited, I became regularly so myself. I felt her grow warm & she let me grubble & press her tightly with my left hand whilst I held her against the door with the other, all the while putting my tongue into her mouth & kissing her so passionately as to excite her not a little, I am sure. When it was over she put her handkerchief to her eyes &, shedding a few tears, said, 'You are used to these things. I am not.' I remonstrated against this, declaring I was not so bad as one thought me & injustice like this would make me miserable, etc. She blamed herself, saying she was a poor, weak creature. I conjured her not to blame herself. It was all my fault. I loved her with all my heart & would do anything for her. Asked her if she loved me a little bit. 'You know I do,' said she. I still therefore pressed her to let me in tomorrow before she was up, when Mrs Page* [Mrs Barlow's servant] *was gone with Miss Barlow to school. She would not promise. Asked me what I would do. I said teach her to love me better. Insinuated we had now gone too far to retract & she might as well admit me. In fact, she herself put this into my head by saying I had gone down this morning just before breakfast, when she would not let me in, because I knew Page was away, gone for Miss Barlow. I took the hint. Said I did not like Page's always being there. Said Mrs Barlow, 'When I am alone it is very well for then she guards me & nobody can say anything against me.' I took no notice but this speech struck me in consequence of all I have heard from Mme de Boyve. On leaving me, her face looked hot, her hair out of curl & herself languid, exactly as if after a connection had taken place . . .* [After dinner] met Mrs Barlow at the door [of Anne's room] . . . I saw Cordingley smile (but took no notice) when I said she [Mrs Barlow] must come for a few minutes. I said 10, & [she] replied, but my minutes were always so long. However, she came & staid 20 minutes with me – *of her own accord sitting on my knee. She looked low & said she was tired. She shed a tear or two & blamed* [herself]. *I said she would make me miserable & could she do so? 'Oh, no,' said she. 'I wish you were always quiet. I want no more.' I begged to be admitted tomorrow & she spoke as if, tho' she would not promise, she would not refuse. It came out this evening that she liked me for my pride. She used to have much. Now she ought not.*

Monday 15 November

Sat with Mrs Barlow till 1, when she went down to luncheon. *She seemed low when I first went in & shed a tear or two at the recollection of what passed yesterday . . . She said sitting on my knee was the first thing she had done wrong. I did all I could to reconcile her. She resumed her usual quiet, pensive cheerfulness & we talked of the goings-on there had been in the house since she came. A Mr Vale, who had been here a year ago, had left six or seven months ago. Had women in his room constantly & Mme de Boyve knew it. Colonel Wilson, here last winter, had Mme Chenelle, the housekeeper, & then her cousin whom she brought into him, with whom she might, perhaps, share the profits. Mme Chenelle intrigued with the menservants, too & others & gave a great many things away. Mrs Middleton & Mrs Barlow had once seen her in an odd situation with a man on the stairs . . .* Mrs Barlow came to me at 2 and staid till 4–45. We had a lit fire & sat over it very comfortably. Mrs Heath came for ¼ hour to say goodbye . . . She seemed to envy the sociable, comfortable manner in which we were sitting together, observing how independent 2 people who were very intimate could be of everyone else. *Mrs Heath being gone, Mrs Barlow for a while continued hemming my pocket handkerchief, then put it away to walk out, for the sun was shining, yet still sat still & I continued leaning over & talking to her all the time. I contrived to ask if I had no hope of making her dearer to me before I went. She said, 'No, never, till we are married.' 'Oh,' said I, 'can nothing persuade you to anticipate?' 'No,' said she, 'I hope not. You would then leave me very unhappy.' 'Why?' said I. She answered, 'Because it would be wrong. I should fret myself to death.' I had before said I wished we had to go to England together, that we must be five or six nights on the road & must share our room & bed. 'Then,' said I, 'would you not relax?' She had then said she hoped not. 'But,' I asked, 'if we were married or if we went to Italy together?'*[6] *it would be a different thing to this. She made no objection – tho' when I said were I now at liberty would she consent, she answered I was not at liberty & had no right to ask that question, adding* Mariana *would suit me much better, for she thinks* Mariana *likes me in spite of my having entirely persuaded her of my own belief that it is impossible.* Besides, *I always insist I have so long loved her in a different way, I could not perhaps change now. She owned it might be difficult . . . She began talking of* Colonel Barlow *in a manner which proved they had been happy . . . She said he was like me in disposition. He sang & played well & was a good sportsman & a fine martial man but he had not my talent . . . I told her how she* [Mrs Barlow] *had changed me. I used to think I could not choose a woman who had had any experience & at first I could not bear to hear her name* Colonel Barlow. *Now I rather liked both these things. She said I did not know her. She was affectionate but, insinuated, not passionate. She was leaning on my shoulder & said she was happy. She could sleep with me & be so. She liked to sleep in a person's arms but wanted no more. She smiled when I gently hinted I could sleep more placidly if lulled to rest by something dearer. She owned she had attached herself to me. She says she can never forget me and hopes I shall always have a little corner for her. I protested yes. Said our mutual circumstances were as new to me as to her. I had never before so loved & been loved so in vain. She indulged me to a certain degree but I found I had no hope of more till I had some better claim than now . . . Speaking of being together, said she, 'What would Mrs Lawton think?' & hid her face on my shoulder. 'Would that,' I said, 'be an objection?' She answered yes. I talked this off. She said she could live with my aunt. I said Mariana always said if I met with anyone I liked better, she would be no tie upon me. Mrs Barlow said that was only fair. It would be hard if she quite confined me.*

Wednesday 17 November

Breakfast at 10½. Read over my letter [written to Mariana Lawton] finished last night. The first p. very affectionate. *Pretty & sentimental – liked to have her always with me. When away from her, like a little skiff sent out to sea, nor hand nor helm to guide it thro' the trackless deep . . .* Mrs Barlow could not come to me till after 11. *Then read her the whole of my letter to Mariana, narrowly watching her countenance. I saw it fall to hear a style so affectionate, etc. She merely remarked it was so & rejoiced I had such a friend. Went down with her & sat from twelve till two, she having been away quarter-hour at luncheon. She thought the letter very warm enough from a husband to a wife but there was nothing beyond friendship. We then talked of my dress. My gown shabby, my lino-frills not fit for me to wear. I offered to give her fifty pounds with which to set me up properly but she dared not venture it . . .* Dinner at 5–30. *Mrs Barlow out of spirits. I saw it was about the letter. She owned she thought it foolish to make such a profession. Explained that it was nothing new to Mariana as the person pointed out as my future companion & whom I had never before felt a wish to change. Said all this was written last Sunday week, before last Thursday. If simple friendship must content me, why change Mariana? And how could I be certain Mrs Barlow felt anything beyond friendship till last Thursday? Made it appear impossible Mariana could love me. I once admired her but this was past & Mrs Barlow agreed it was more difficult for a thing of this kind to recur than begin altogether . . .* Had tea brought to us & sat quietly together till 11–10 when I came up to my own room. *She got into better spirits, kissed me two or three times of her own accord & I have never known her seem more affectionate. I said she was not calm at heart. No, she said, she felt too much. She liked to feel towards me as one of her best friends & should like to be in Mariana's place. I promised to be a good friend at all events. Leaned my head on her breast. Kissed the left one over her habit-shirt. Wanted to open that. She would not permit but closed her shawl. At last, however, she felt this open again. I said my mother had nursed me when my sister was born. She had too much milk. I liked it exceedingly. Asked if she, Mrs Barlow, would nurse. Oh no, she could not do this. Yet she said it without surprise or anger and as if I might attain this. At least, I fancied so. I put her hand to my left breast, saying she had called that her own place. Why should I not do the same to her? She said that was a different thing. Talked of the treadmill business. She said the people stopt to stare at me. She thought it was my gown, it was so tumbled & shabby.* [I] *explained that it was not that. It was common enough to be stared at on account of my walk, etc. . . . Told Mrs Barlow this morning I thought I should have two thousand a year. Asked how she could live on that – if it should be enough to keep her a carriage & satisfy her not to marry. She gave no very decided answer. Said the mode of living must depend on myself. But 'tis evident enough she would not refuse to try. We sat on the bed a little tonight. She said she was tired. I kept her feelings constantly excited & this tired her.*

Thursday 18 November

Went to Mrs Barlow. We went out together at 3 ... to Chez Baudry, Rue de Coq, to look at his Lord Byron's works, 12 vols. 18mo., printed for himself. 30 francs. Then went to Galignani's[7] (Rue Vivienne). His edition in 16 vols. 12mo., or small 8vo. on better paper ... We came away & got home at 4–50, *she talking whether to give me bracelets or a chain. The former would cost eighty-five franks* [sic]. *I foolishly told her I meant to give her Lord Byron's works. She mentioned Galignani's edition, which I knew not of, & I must give it.*

Friday 19 November

Went to the Institution Des Enfants Trouvés.[8] A very interesting sight. Evidently kept in beautiful order & very clean. 25 little iron cribs in 1 of the rooms. Curious to hear the mingled cries of 15 or 20 children & see them all wrapt up like little mummies & lying, for the moment, on a gently inclined plane before the fire to quieten them. All the healthiest children sent into the country. The more sickly ones kept here. It was about 3 when we were there. 15 children had already been received. They take all the children that are offered them. Never receive less than 12 a day & have received as many as 42 or 45, I forget which. At 6 years old, the children are taken away from their nurses & put into some way to earn their bread.

Monday 22 November

Breakfast at 9–50. *Waited, undressed, for the woman to try my stays on. She did not come till eleven instead of nine & a half & then they did not fit at all. Far too small ... At twelve, got into bed with my flannel waistcoat, chemise, drawers, night-things, dressing-gown, stockings & boots on. At first, Mrs Barlow, who never left me till five, sat by my bedside. I then persuaded her to get in. I got my left leg & thigh quite between hers. Held her fast on my right arm. Felt her over her clothes now & then with my left hand & pressed her close. I think we both slept for a considerable while. At least, I did. Not much said & nothing new* . . . I had my dinner in bed, then got up & washed & had my bed made . . . [She] returned to me . . . [She] *did not sit long before I persuaded her to lie down on the bed & lean on my shoulder. Whether* [she was] *really asleep I know not but she took no notice of my kissing her, making her lips quite wet & putting my tongue a little into her mouth, she having it rather open. At last, I fell asleep. She shot up a little before ten and had just got quietly seated when Cordingley brought us tea. After this she sat by me till eleven & fifty minutes. Lovemaking as usual.* [I] *said again & again I wished I could marry her. I would gladly do it at that moment, then I could have my own way. She blamed me for getting up to wash. I said I must do & made her understand that the excitement I had felt in the morning made it necessary. She knows quite well when this is coming on. She had said, 'Why do you trouble so? You are making yourself ill. I shall go.' But I always promise to behave well & she stays.*

Tuesday 23 November

Came to Mme Galvani. Spent the time in conversation. She offered to get me billets to see all I wish. *Said this pension* [Mme de Boyve's] *was very dear. I could live with my servants much more comfortably for the same sum in an apartment of my own, ready furnished & very pretty. I really think she likes me. I paid her, for thirty lessons, six napoleons.* Gave her a list of several books I wished her to get for me. She left me at 2–10. [I] went down to Mrs Barlow . . . *Loverlike as usual. Speaking of the necessity of Mariana's knowing the nature of our attachment if we were living together, she said she should not like this. She could not bear anyone to know but myself. Said I, 'Would you put my happiness in competition with this?' She made no answer & I came to dress for dinner. Thought I, 'She makes no objection but that of the thing being known.' . . . I had before all this asked her to take out the brooch on her handkerchief. She refused. I kissed her over it, warmly. She is certainly much attached to me. When I told her this morning I would try not to love, but would always like, her she said she should not think me right if my love dwindles to less than liking. Poor soul! I begin to feel that I have really attached her & that I cannot find it in my heart to deceive her more. I may be off with liking & I ought to give her my friendship in recompense. After all, she has behaved well & at present I see I have no chance of succeeding further. She says I never shall till I have the right to do so & she would not let me gain the right now even if I were at liberty for she would make me leave her & wait till I had tried whether I really know my own mind & could really be happy with her or not. I said this morning, if she were in Mariana's place she would not live with me. She would know friendship alone would not make me happy & she would not take me unless she loved me. She said, no, she would. Poor soul! How she is deceived. Why have I done this? I thought at first to succeed on my own terms, letting her know I was engaged. Then I could not acknowledge that Mariana loved me. I durst not say I was engaged to anyone else lest she should hereafter see me living with Mariana. For Mariana's sake I could not let her suspect anything & thus have I gone, from little to more, into this deceiving.*

---

1. *Queer* – (or 'quere'). Anne uses the word to denote the female pudendum. It appears to be a distortion of the word 'quim' or 'queme', a slang word used to describe the same area of the female body. It is derived from the old Celtic word *cwm*, meaning cleft or valley.
2. '*My father was one year in the Militia*' – In fact, the army career of Anne's father spanned some thirty-six years. He obtained a commission as an ensign in the 10th Regiment of Foot in 1770 and was still serving, as a recruiting officer, in 1805–6.
3. Eliza Raine – see Prologue, pp 4–5.

4. *Alluded ... to the stones ... till after birth* – Anne seems to be trying to present a rather garbled account of her idea of how the development or non-development of the genital organs can cause a confusion of sexual identity in a person. Her ideas appear to derive from reading the Classical works of the Ancients on anatomy rather than nineteenth century anatomists. Thomas Laqueur, in his article entitled 'La Difference: Bodies, Gender and History' (published in *The Threepenny Review*, spring 1988) states:

   'For several thousand years it had been a commonplace that women have the same genitals as men, except that, as Nemesius (bishop of Emesa in the sixth century) put it: " ... Theirs are inside the body and not outside it ... ". Galen ... in the second century AD ... could already cite the anatomist, Herophilus (third century BC) in support of his claim that a woman has testes with accompanying seminal ducts very much like the man's, one on each side of the uterus – the only difference being that the male's are contained in the scrotum and the female's are not ... Indeed, doggerel verse of the nineteenth century still sings of these hoary homologues after they have disappeared from learned texts:

   " ... though they of different sexes be,
   Yet, on the whole, they are the same as we.
   For those that have the strictest searchers been,
   Find women are but men turned outside in." '

5. ... *Saffic* [*sic*] *regard ... no pleasure to me* ... – Anne believed Sapphic love between women to be learned behaviour rather than natural. She says: '*The one* [i.e. Sapphic love] *was artificial and inconsistent* [presumably because Sappho married], *the other* [her own sexuality] *was the effect of nature ...*' [5th August 1823.] See p 296. Volume One *The Secret Diaries of* Miss *Anne \ister.*

6. ... *went to Italy together* ... – Although Anne genuinely wanted to travel to Italy, she also used the phrase 'going to Italy' as having a full sexual relationship with a woman. It is rather unclear here in which sense the term is used but I would think it is in the sexual sense, as she links it to the idea of being married.

7. Galignani's – now situated at 224 Rue de Rivoli, Galignani's bookshop claims to be the 'oldest foreign bookstore on the Continent'. The Parisian branch, then known as the Galignani Library, was founded in 1800 by Giovanni Antonio Galignani (1757–1829), in

the Rue Vivienne. After the fall of Napoleon in 1815, the influx of English visitors to Paris was so great that Galignani brought out an English newspaper, the *Galignani Messenger*, and the reading-room in Galignani's shop became a meeting point for the English colony in Paris.

8. Institution Des Enfants Trouvés – The Foundling Hospital. Louis Sebastian Mercier, writing between 1781 and 1788, in the first part of his book, says that: '… Eight thousand children are left at this place every year. They are taken in at any time, without inquiry as to whence they come, and the following day they are sent away to the country in the care of paid nurses, who take two at a time. About half die in the first two years …' (p 76, *The Picture of Paris Before and After the Revolution*). Jean-Jacques Rousseau (1712–1778), French philosopher and writer, whose works inspired the leaders of the French Revolution, consigned all five of his illegitimate children to the Foundling Hospital, even though he eventually married their mother, his housekeeper Thérèse Levasseur.

The Charm is Broken

One of the main reasons for Anne's prolonged visit to Paris had been to seek a cure for what she suspected was a venereal complaint. The infection had, as she thought, been contracted from her married lover, Mariana Lawton. The self-confessed libertine lifestyle of Mariana's husband, Charles Lawton, led the two women to suspect that he was the initial cause of the infection. Having gained little relief from her symptoms while under the care of English doctors, Anne had decided to explore the possibilities of a cure by French doctors.

The realisation that the growing intimacy between herself and Maria Barlow would lead inevitably to sexual contact meant that Anne felt compelled to confide her problem to her new lover, whilst making every effort to protect Mariana's reputation.

Friday 26 November

Letter from my aunt (Shibden). All well at home. [They] very kindly do not wish me 'to be particular to a week or longer about the time of my return home'. *On reading the 'glad I was better'* [to Mrs Barlow, I] *rattled off with, 'I came to Paris for my health' & afterwards* [said] *something of 'suffering for one's folly'. I saw*

Mrs Barlow understood me to allude to something venereal . . . She looked grave. She would not tell me what she was thinking. At last it came out . . . She said I had told her nothing new or that she did not know before. I expressed my astonishment. She declared she had made it out from my manner & what I had said before. Besides, she knew I could hardly have escaped it. I said there were those who escaped it always. Could the last four years be blotted out, I should have no reason to complain. She joked me that I wished to know everything. 'But,' said I, 'not that.' Asked if she forgave me? Yes, as much as she forgave everyone else. Did she love me less? No, she had no reason to do so. I said I was foolish to name it. She declared not. If I had had any guile in me I should not have told. She did not like me the worse for it. Would she still take me? She said I was not at liberty. I descanted, on my knees & leaning my head on her breast, on her being so much dearer to me since that Thursday. I was too much attached to her, she had often told me so. 'Goodness', she exclaimed to herself. The fact is, tho' she states objections against herself, having a child, etc., she is very fond of me & wishes to gain me. She is steadily particular in never allowing me to take further liberties.

Saturday 27 November

Went to Mrs Barlow in my dressing gown about 10¾ . . . *We got on the subject of yesterday. I had only confirmed her suspicions. Those pimples I lately had on my face might be owing to it & certainly the tendency to sore throats. She mentioned a famous man here*[1] *who had made some great cures . . . I determined to consult him on Monday. Said I had told my uncle & aunt. Left the former to his own conclusions but the latter was satisfied with my story of having caught it at a dirty cabinet d'eau at the inn at Manchester . . . Rather more than three years since I was infected.* [Mrs Barlow] *asked me what medical advice I had had. I said truly all about it & that I now used sulphate of zinc. She behaved so kindly & well about it I felt happy, tho' a little strange at the thought of the confidence I had placed in her . . . I was anxious to consult this man. It might alter my plans. I might stay to be cured . . .* [I] *said I was happy to have told* [her] *tho' astonished how I had done it. I should certainly have told her before we had come together, had there been any prospect of it. Convinced her I would never have done anything dishonourable to her.*

Sunday 28 November

Mrs Barlow & I reverted to the subject of my complaint. [She was] *afraid the surgeon should mention there being such a person in Paris as myself. She thinks me partly man. 'Oh, no,' said I. 'I will manage all that. No examination will be necessary & I shall call myself Madame.' Shall not give my address. She asked, if he ordered me baths, if I would go to Tivoli. There is a very good pension there but they only take those who use the baths. I said I would do all I was ordered but could not leave on her account. She said she never talked so on this subject before. Were it anyone else, she would dislike them for it. Thought I to myself, 'She is deeply in for it and much attached to me.' I said I hoped that, if possible, it would make the matter some little better to say I had not got it from anyone in low life. I never associated with people below myself. In this instance, far from it. Perhaps, had she been nearer on a par with myself I might have fared better. She was a married woman. Her husband was the origin of the thing. I had not got it quite fairly, meaning that she knew of it & ought not to have admitted me. 'Oh, yes,' said Mrs Barlow, 'it was fair enough if people will run the risk.' She asked how the person I had infected is.*[2] *I said I did not exactly know. I had been very uneasy. The case was mistaken for some female complaint & tonics, etc., prescribed . . . I said I had told the lady who gave it me & she only laughed. I had never been more shocked than by such an instance of levity. And this was the case when I first told Mariana when she was last at Shibden. How little Mrs Barlow suspects these two people are Mariana & Isabella. Could she know all, what would she think of Mariana? Could she know all fairly, from first to last, what would she say to all parties? Would she excuse me the most, or not? After all, I think I best deserve it. Tho' bad, the best. I have more than once thought this before & many notes scattered in my journal reflect no credit on Charles or Mariana ... What can I do about Mariana? If I should get quite cured I must have no further connection with her. She will certainly infect me again. I am convinced Charles is at the bottom of it. Can she come here & be cured & have no further connection with him?*

Mrs Barlow, in advising Anne on her choice of surgeon, had sent her to the top man in Paris, Baron G Dupuytren. Anne paid her first visit to his house at 4 Place du Louvre on Monday 29th November 1824. She had decided that, in the interests of propriety, she would pass herself off as a married woman, and she adopted Mariana's marital and medical history when she consulted M Dupuytren.

Monday 29 November

In twenty minutes, thro' the Tuileries gardens, got to M. Dupuytren's ... I went in when the door opened & sat down by the fire with M. Dupuytren. I said I could not speak much French *but hoped to make him understand. It was three years since I was first ill & one year since my medical man (he asked the name & I said Simmons)* [This was the name of Mariana's consultant in Manchester] *told me I was cured of that complaint. He then asked what it was & how caused. I said it was a 'case demonari'. I kept in mind Mariana & Charles & spoke all along as nearly as possible as if I was in her place. Tho' I was cured, or said to be so, there was a weakness left & a little discharge which was very uncomfortable. He asked how I knew it was a 'case demonari'. I said I thought so because he* [Charles Lawton] *had been very gay & had suffered much in his youth & had then des cicatrices* [scars] *in the groin. Had he been ill since marriage? I could not determine for he always denied* [it]. *Had I seen his linen? No, he always prevented this. Had he much intercourse with me? No, never since I was ill – not these three years. Why not? I could not tell. We never spoke on the subject. Was he gay with others? Yes, at first, with servants in the house & I was very angry but no, I believed not now. He had no desire. I thought him too feeble. He had wished much for children & had taken much medicine to invigorate him, which I thought had only had a temporary effect & weakened him & made him worse afterwards. But I thought he could not have children. He was malforme, the man who gave him all this medicine said. How so? I explained he had only one testicle. 'Ah,' said M. Dupuytren. 'Seulement le moitie* [Only half], *but that does not signify* [that] *l'autre est en dedans* [the other is not inside]. *That would not prevent him having children. Had he much difficulty when you were first married?' Yes, it was a fortnight before he could manage it. 'Well, but,' said M. Dupuytren, 'you were unusually stait*[?]. *Aviez-vous des rapports frequents?* [Do you have sexual intercourse frequently?] *Once a week? Once a fortnight?' 'Yes,' said I, 'about so often at first. Then once a fortnight & afterwards once a month, till I was, all at once, ill & since then, not at all.' 'How old are you?' 'Thirty-two.'* [Anne was, in fact, thirty-three.] *'How old is he?' 'Fifty-two.' 'How long married?' 'Eight or nine years.' He said I was young. It was very odd he* [Charles] *had been so – without any connection with me. Had he no inclination? He did not shew any. Did we sleep together? Yes. Had he no erections? No. Had I much pleasure with him? Pas beaucoup.* [Not a lot.] *He said he must examine me. I said it was very disagreeable. Could it be done without? He seemed a little impatient & said would I say yes or no. I very quietly asked if it was absolutely necessary. He said yes.*

'Well, then,' said I, 'It must be done.' My quietness made him more patient. (I was only afraid he should find out I was not married but he certainly did not make this discovery.)

Between November 1824 and her departure for England at the end of March 1825, Anne paid periodic visits to M. Dupuytren. He recommended on her first visit that she left off the vaginal douches of sulphate of zinc solution, and instead took regular warm baths and adopted a sparse diet. Her condition deteriorated so, on her second visit, he gave her a prescription for pearl barley and nitrate to dissolve in liquid and also, apparently, a prescription for mercury, which she began using on Tuesday 7th December. She also continued with the warm baths every other day.

Despite his great reputation, it appears that M. Dupuytren failed to cure Anne of her complaint. This could have been due, however, to the general ignorance which prevailed at the time. There existed a state of confusion about venereal disease. For instance, syphilis and gonorrhea were often classed as two different stages of the same disease. Vaginal discharges in women, such as that suffered by Anne and Mariana, posed a different problem which was not really solved until after the Second World War. Trichomoniasis[3] is the most common form of these discharges and is easily transmitted during lesbian sexual activity, whereas syphilis is virtually non-existent among lesbians due to the absence of penile penetration. The fact that Anne was technically a virgin would also have ruled out the possibility of syphilis. Anne's descriptions of her symptoms sound typical of trichomoniasis. There are no long-term effects from this type of infection and today it would have been treated quickly and efficiently, as would more serious venereal complaints.

The sad thing about this is that Anne, on going to Paris to

find a cure, was probably made worse by M. Dupuytren's prescriptions of mercury. Ingested through the pores of the skin, mercury was rubbed into different parts of the body each time it was applied, as too much rubbing in one part caused mercury dermatitis. Used over a long period, mercury produces toxic syndromes – mercury poisoning, loss of teeth, excess salivation[4] and a condition known as erethism[5] which causes the patient to display odd and eccentric behaviour patterns.

Anne, who had intended to leave Paris at the end of December, decided to stay longer in order to continue M. Dupuytren's treatment. The situation at Mme de Boyve's pension, however, was becoming untenable so far as Anne was concerned. Her relationship with Maria Barlow was under close scrutiny and the rest of the guests were becoming too knowing for comfort. Anne decided that she would persuade Mrs Barlow to seek a private rented apartment in Paris for herself, her daughter Jane, and her maid, Mrs Page. Then Anne and Cordingley could stay with her until Anne decided to return to England. Anne would, of course, pay for her own upkeep and that of her servant.

For the next few weeks the two women, with some assistance from Madame Galvani, were apartment hunting in addition to their usual sightseeing excursions in and around Paris.

Monday 6 December

Sat with Mrs Barlow from 10–40 to 11¾. *We talked of Mme de Boyve's worldliness, etc. I said I had now taken a dislike to her. Mrs Barlow always fancies she has said much against her to me. Of course, I will not allow this . . . She got to what she* [Mrs Barlow] *would not do for me. She had thought of this when waiting at the apothecary's door. When she used to hear a man was ill she would not dance with him. With me, how different, how strange, to do such a thing for a friend of hers – meaning how strange that such a person could be her friend. 'Ah,' said I, 'I feel this most keenly. You know not how you have touched a chord that will vibrate forever. It is this I mean when I so often tell you of my gratitude.' She saw that I had more sensibility on the subject than she had expected & said she was sorry to have made the remark . . . Poor Mrs Barlow. It is quite evident she loves me &, I begin to think, disinterestedly & for my own sake. She would do anything for me & I must be careful not to get her into any scrape.*

Tuesday 7 December

Ate very little dinner today, meaning to begin my meagre diet & rubbing with mercury, etc.

Wednesday 8 December

At 2¾, Mrs Barlow & I took Cordingley & went to the Bains Chinois.[6] Gave 15 francs for 6 tickets. Single tickets 3 francs each. Linen found for this. There were baths at 30 sols but no linen found for this price. Mrs Barlow promised to return in an hour. I got into my bath, 28 deg. Reamur, at 3. Staid in about 50 minutes. Felt myself very comfortable in it, tho' rather cold than hot. Dressed & walked back with Mrs Barlow, who had waited some time for me, & got home at 4–20.

Thursday 9 December

Got down to breakfast. Mrs Barlow & I chatted till about 2 . . . *We got on the subject of Mariana. If I behaved ill to anyone it was to her but I wished Mrs Barlow could know my whole life from infancy. I wondered how far she would always excuse me. Mariana's marriage had come upon me like a thunderbolt. I could never understand* [it]. *If she married for love, she could not love me, & why engage me? If not for love, it was too worldly – not romantic enough for me. Besides, she had once behaved ill to me.*[7] *I found I could never forget it. It always occurred to me when the least thing happened I did not like & there was many a note in my journal to her disadvantage. I was much attached. I loved her once, but this last was passé. The charm was broken. Yet* Mariana *was very good &* Mrs Barlow *would like her if she saw her. Said* Mrs Barlow, *'I hope I shall never see her. We three should not do well together,' & said she meant she herself loved me too well to like* Mariana. *I said I was not on speaking terms with* Charles. *It began on account of a gallantry of his & he afterwards got hold of a letter of mine,*[8] *not in his favour certainly, which finished the matter.*

Friday 10 December

Speaking of Mariana [to Mrs Barlow], *said her eldest sister & I were with her the first six months after her marriage. I arranged the time of getting off to bed the first night. Left* Mrs Barlow *to judge what I felt, for I had liked* [Mariana] *much. Resuming a little the subject of* [yesterday], *asked* Mrs Barlow's *opinion of* Mariana's *conduct in marrying & then engaging me, etc. She refused to give any opinion, saying she never would about* Mariana.

Sunday 12 December

Mrs Barlow came just as I was going to ring for Cordingley and told me she was ill and gone to bed but Mrs Page would do anything for me. Mrs Barlow helped me to finish dressing. I had luckily boiled my milk and sat down to breakfast . . . Got *talking about* Mariana *. . . Explained how her marriage had so surprised me . . . We had had a blow-up. All was settled to my satisfaction. She came and staid with me a long while and I staid with her. I left her father's home for ten days to pay another visit, supposing all was so far determined, that she would never marry, and that the thing was going on decidedly to all I wished. What, then, was my surprise to find on my return she had heard from, and written to,* Charles.

He was coming over at Christmas and it was then November and the match would be soon.[9] I said I had scarce uttered on first hearing this but on reflection had determined to make no objection. They were married. Miss Norcliffe had joked me and said she thought I should have been caught but I was now set at liberty again. I had told Mariana this and from that moment she wished to have me bound. I had resisted a long time but, at last, promised three years ago and had at times repented. Ever since, we had almost always something to explain whenever we met. Yet, when together, she always satisfied and reconciled me. Mrs Barlow said she had great influence with me, which I acknowledged but said I should leave hers for Mrs Barlow's. 'Ah,' said she, 'that is a different thing. My influence is of a different kind. Hers is from right.' I said I had once read [to Mariana] some of the observations I had made at the time of her conduct to me, her marriage, etc., and, not looking for a moment or two, found she had dropt at my feet, half-fainting. She had asked me to burn these papers, saying she should never feel secure till I did but I had refused hitherto. Before saying all this about marrying, I had told [Mrs Barlow] as one of the things we were always having to explain, that about a year ago [Mariana] had said, on lamenting some gaucherie or other, she would willingly have me different – to have me, my figure and appearance, more like other people. I had remonstrated, saying then I should be different altogether. There would be no making settlements [of money, on Mariana], etc. However, I so managed the whole that Mrs Barlow has no idea of our connection, of the real state of the case. In witness, see the distinction she afterwards made between her influence and Mariana's. But I know she thinks Mariana worldly. Indeed I said one of her sisters had told me she was and I often thought of this. Mrs Barlow was going to give an opinion and she stopt herself, saying, 'No, let me not speak.' But I know well enough what she thinks. Perhaps others, if they knew all, would think so, too. I said I would give anything for a really fair, impartial opinion. Yet, after all, I felt as if I had been talking treason to say all these things *and felt that if my changing my mind made her* [Mariana] *miserable, I could sacrifice much of my own happiness rather than do this.*

Sunday 13 December

I fancy myself better. I eat no meat and drink no wine and water at dinner to avoid anything cold. Take my soup and patties, if there be any, and sweet things as usual. Eat butter and take my boiled milk, as usual, at breakfast. I ought to drink beaucoup of my barley water nitre but I find no opportunity of drinking it till after tea and then, before bedtime, drink perhaps a tumbler full.

Wednesday 15 December

Have just had dinner. Twice soup, a little gâteau de pommes and a little chocolate cream, in my room . . . I begin to look pale and ill and always feel worse in an evening. *I feel rather more inclined to spit.*

Thursday 16 December

A great deal of conversation with [Mme Galvani] about Mrs Barlow having Jane herself and educating her at home. Could not have a very good music master – a bon marché [cheaply]. Must pay 8 francs a lesson and have 3 a week. Drawing good for, perhaps, 3 francs a lesson and 2 a week. Altogether, we made it out, music would cost £50 a year; drawing, £15; dancing, £10. Then, I thought to myself, Mme Galvani would perhaps undertake French and Italian for £25 a year.

Monday 20 December

[A] Mrs and Miss Canning come.[10] Miss Canning is quite a beauty. Covers up a good deal. [She] will cut out Miss Morse who walks about in a fantastical hat with her neck too much exposed and followed by a crowd of Frenchmen gaping for the £60,000 it is said she will have.

Tuesday 21 December

Mrs Barlow came to me at 10½ and sat with me an hour, *her shawl tightly and closely pinned up and she would not let me move a pin. I rallied her but it would not do. She* [said] *we were quite free from each other. She was not mine, nor I hers. I was another's. I said the tie to her might prove the strongest and I sometimes thought that, at all events, I would not have Mariana. At last, when nothing would do, I rose from my kneeling posture and sat down quite at a distance and then, after a little intertwine of legs in standing, let her go very quietly.*

Wednesday 22 December

Mrs Barlow came to me immediately from the [dinner] table a little before 7 and sat with me till 11–50, wishing to stay longer for my headache, which was <u>very</u> bad all the evening, seemed bilious and I was threatened . . . We had tea a little before 10. *Very soon after she came, she lay on the bed. This rather starved me for I would have my arms out to* [prevent?] *this. She got in and I had my arms round her, she lying* [with] *her back to me, my right leg under and left leg over, her. I got a hand towards her queer by degrees. She so turned round that my left hand got to her very comfortably and by degrees I got to feel and handle her. I got her gown up and tried to raise her petticoats also but, finding that this would not do (one of her hands prevented it), I was contented that my naked left thigh should rest upon her naked left thigh and thus she let me grubble her over her petticoats. All the while I was pressing her between my thighs. She just said once, 'Ah, you are doing yourself harm' and I gently replied, 'Oh, no. I am asleep.' 'No,' she said, 'you are not asleep.' I made no further answer nor did she but I went on grubbling for a moment. Now and then I held my hand still and felt her pulsation, let her rise towards my hand two or three times and gradually open her thighs, and felt her as well and as* [distinctly] *as it was possible to do over her petticoats, and felt that she was excited. I continued for, I daresay, quarter-hour more then, after being quiet a while, she half-sighed and said, 'Oh, I think I could do anything for you.' Then, by and by, she said, 'I once thought I could sleep with you. Now I find I could not.'* [This appears to be because of Anne's infection.] *I bade her not say this. I knew she could do it* [without fear of becoming infected]. *Were we gone to Italy* [Anne's euphemism for having a full sexual relationship] *it would be different but in my present state we were both quite safe. I loved her far too well not to be quite sure we were both secure.*

Thursday 23 December

We went out apartment hunting at 11–50. Were out on this errand all the morning and did not get home till 4–50. Went to about a dozen places here and there, from the Rue de Rivoli to the neighbourhood just near to and beyond the Boulevards ... The general run of a small apartment, only just enough for Mrs Barlow, seems to be, at the very lowest, from 200 to 300 francs a month. Mrs Barlow told me, while walking, her father had lost two brothers and a sister in the American Revolution. The sister was engaged to a major in our army. She, for the sake of a chance of seeing [him], would remain at a country house where she was on a visit, tho' the family had left it for fear of being near the contending armies. She was one day walking on the terrace when a party of Indians passing by were so struck with her extraordinary beauty they took her off and on quarrelling which of them should have the honour of presenting her to their chief, one of them, to end the dispute, struck his tomahawk into the back of her head and killed her on the spot ... *I took no notice of what had passed last night but I thought Mrs Barlow looked a little as if she remembered it but we were busy about other things and it passed off. Tonight, when she had crossed her shawl, I said, 'Now, as you have done it, I must do what no one else could and I must remove it for a moment.' I just kissed her neck where the handkerchief was a little open. She said nothing nor made any resistance, looking a look that seemed to say, 'It's too late to resist now.'*

Friday 24 December

Soon after 2, Mme Galvani came and sat with us till nearly 4½. She mentioned the following 11 streets as chiefly frequented by filles publiques and in which it was not, therefore, advisable for a virtuous woman to take lodgings. Rue Favart – de la Michodière – St Anne des Frondeurs – des Colonnes – d'Auboisse – St Marc-Feydeau – Richelieu – Pièrre l'Escant and de Chartres.

Sunday 26 December

Took a fiacre to Mme Galvani's . . . Monsieur —— happened to come in and said there were several apartments (good) to let – Quai Voltaire, quite a new house, where used to be a convent . . . Went to this new house (No. 15, Quai Voltaire). Quite charmed with an apartment au troisième. Salon opening on to a balcony terrace looking on the Louvre gardens, et salle à manger, deux chambres a coucher, cuisine and chambre de domestique en haut, 1500 francs per annum . . . Told Mme Galvani we had fixed on this apartment . . . and I am delighted to think the matter so happily settled. Mrs Barlow and Jane and I then had tea and sat talking till 10–30 . . . Jane fondled and kissed her mother, seeming jealous of me, yet still she behaves much better than I expected. I joked her and quizzed her about it, then talked gravely about her education and that she ought to like those who were her real friends – had a real regard for her mother. The child seemed to attend to this and likes me after all, tho' she does not quite like the regard her mother evidently shews me. Mrs Barlow appears quite satisfied about the lodgings and buying furniture.

Tuesday 28 December

On returning today from No. 15, Quai Voltaire, we sat a little while with Mme Portière [the porter's wife] who told us the proprietor of the house had been to ask what sort of person Mrs Barlow was. It is customary to beg people's characters of the porter. What an important person a porter is. Keep well in and you will do.

Thursday 30 December

Got to no. 15, Quai Voltaire at 3. There about an hour. Everything arranged to Mrs Barlow's satisfaction and she gave the porter 5 francs. (He always received a fee on these occasions by way of ratification that the apartment is taken.) Sauntered along our way home looking at the bookstalls and got home at 5.

Friday 31 December

Mrs Barlow came and staid with me ½ hour and we went at 12 [noon] to the bazaar to look at furniture; to the Passage de l'Opéra; Passage Feydeau; to my booksellers, 8 Rue Vivienne, where I bought Racine, vol. 4, 18mo., neatly bound. Charged 22 francs, gave 19 francs. Thence to the Palais Royal where Mrs Barlow and I bought each a workbox pour des étrennes [for a New Year's present] and Mrs Barlow bought Bossuet's 'Discours sur le Histoire Universal' . . . Tea between 9 and 10. I read aloud a little of 'The Pleasures of Hope'.[11] Mrs Barlow sat hemming one end of a tablecloth and we were very cozy and comfortable.

1825

Saturday 1 January

Could not have a bath today. The men were to have a holiday in the afternoon. Doubtful if I could have one at all because the bazaar was on fire (in fact, burnt down). The flames had communicated to the Rue Michodière & the police stopt all the men to employ them in getting the fire under . . . [I] remaining in bed all day, Mrs Barlow gave my five francs each to all the 5 servants & 5 francs to the porter, pour étrennes (or New Year's gifts) which all ranks give & receive from each other here. All your friends, but especially the people you employ, expect something. The bathmen would not be satisfied till they had an étrenne but for aught I know were satisfied with a franc between them. Gave Mrs Page a workbox, price ten francs, the same as Mrs Barlow gave Cordingley, to whom I gave the same sum in money. The people stay up the whole night always before New Year's Day, to sell things & people go to see the bazaar, Palais Royal, etc., at midnight. They look uncommonly well by candlelight but thus might accidents frequently occur. Jane gave me a bead purse tonight just before she went to bed, that she had made for her mother but as I admired it she will make another for mama.

Sunday 2 January

Breakfast at 10¼. We were going to Mr Way's chapel but the weather looked too uncertain. The fiacremen would grumble to go so far & cannot now be taken à l'heure [by the hour] unless they themselves agree to it. This is in consequence of their being in such request at this season, when all the world is paying visits & this lasts for several days. Mme Galvani says it is only on New Year's Day that it is not customary to take the fiacres a l'heure but that in point of law you have a right to do so if you choose to stand out against custom . . . Mrs Barlow has just told me that all the servants are dissatisfied at our having all given them only 5 francs each servant – for when Mme de Boyve engaged them she said every one in the house on New Year's Day would give them each 10 francs!!! Curious enough that Mme de Boyve should thus rate the sum each person should give yet never name it to any of us.

Monday 3 January

About 3 we set off. Sauntered along the Boulevards. A crowd about the bazaar & a large heap of the burnt timbers brought out & lying on the boulevard. Guards placed at the entrance & a box put up to receive subscriptions for the benefit of the sufferers. The building insured but none of the goods belonging to the different people. Fires, says M. de Boyve, so always got under in Paris, the people not afraid and never (speaking generally) insure their goods. He had once seen flames bursting from the Rue de Chaussée & entre-sol du premier while the inhabitants of du second were quietly looking out of the windows, watching the firemen, quite satisfied the flames would be got under without doing the 2d étage any injury. Sauntered to the end of the Passage des Panoramas very leisurely, looking at all the shop windows. The Passage crowded. The shops most gay. Got home at 4–40 . . . Felt a good deal fatigued. I am certainly much reduced in strength . . . *I had put on my dressing gown and had Cordingley to curl me immediately after tea & then sent her to bed & Mrs Page being also gone, Mrs Barlow & I seemed quite left to ourselves. She had had a little pain in her back as common after* [walking] *& had lain down but got up to tea, then had lain down again & I got into her about ten & three-quarters. I soon took up her petticoats so as to feel her naked thighs next to mine. Then, after kissing with my tongue in her mouth, got the middle finger of my right hand up her & grubbled her longer & better than ever, she seeming rather more at ease than before & taking it with more emotion & apparent pleasure, which made me keep dawdling there a long time. She seemed more moist than before but really very nice. She hid her face on my shoulder & we lay a good while silent & as if half-dozing. At last, said I, 'Have you not my affections & all my heart? How can I be more your own before we go to Italy?' 'Can you?' she answered, in a manner that seemed to say, 'If you can be more my own, do' or as* *if inquiring whether I could think of any way of being more hers at present or not. I had just before whispered to her, 'Oh, don't forget me when I'm away. Can you forget me now? Don't marry & forget me.' 'Ah,' said she, 'how can you talk so?' Just after Jane went this morning, she had said she thought Jane would know how to love. The child is a little jealous of me but it would not be gifts could bribe her, alluding to me having given her Racine. 'Yes,' said I, 'she is like you but you could not know so well how to love eighteen years ago as now.' 'Yes,' said she, 'I was better worth having then. I was plump & young & could love at seventeen as I do now' – instantly correcting herself & saying, 'as I could do now'. Just before dinner I laughed & said, 'But you did not like my nursing Mlle de Sans so well.'* [Alluding to an occasion when Mlle de Sans was ill and Anne had tended her in her bedroom.] *'Ah,' said she, 'you mistook me. I was not jealous, as you supposed. I had full confidence in you, for you seemed to like my being with you, but I think such things are better let alone. You know they excite feelings which I do not wish you to feel for anyone but me.' Surely she is very fond of me. She has told me more than once, any woman might deceive me. She always talks much of never being able to plan anything in her life, never could or would take the trouble. She never refused me so as to make me despair, yet since she has heard me talk of the tie of this thing* [Anne's infatuation with Mrs Barlow] *& the other* [with Mariana] *she has gradually indulged me more & more . . . If Mrs Barlow is really the very being she seems, I almost pity her & then I love her but alas, what shall I say of myself? In spite of all, I have no serious thoughts of her at present, tho' I am so far seducing her. Oh, this is terrible. It is the thought of her being so deep that has led me on. If I have really done her injustice in this, perhaps time will tell & then I shall make up my mind. What would Mariana say? Alas, she has not the nack* [sic] *of making me constant. The charm is indeed broken. I never have forgotten, nor can forget, the manner of her marriage, etc. I have thought her interested* [i.e. worldly] *& this has* *poisoned all my mind. Perhaps I am too sceptic now. If I am – poor Mrs Barlow! Yet, still,* [in] *spite of knowing me engaged, she has let me succeed with her. I know not what to think.*

Tuesday 4 January

About 5, Mlle de Sans sent up to say M. le Comte de la Marthony had sent her 3 tickets for the Théâtre Français, the Prince de Condé's[12] box ... The play, Racine's 'Phedre'. Mlle Duchesnois[13] very great in the character. So much so, one forgot her ugliness. Hippolyte well played by M. Firmin.[14] The performance altogether good. Our box – opposite the king's – too much on the stage. The theatre, newly done up since my aunt & I were there, looked clean & handsome. The duke of Orléans[15] has the 3 front boxes. He has now got the theatre with great difficulty but there is yet a great part of the Palais Royal he cannot get back again. The farce, Molière's 'M. de Pourceaugnac' (vid. Molière, vol. 5, p. 95). The consultations between the physicians capital – but the 20 or 30 apothecaries (men & tall boys) following the poor fellow with glyster pipes (large lead syringes) was beyond anything I could have imagined it possible to bring forward on the stage, particularly the Théâtre Français. Certainly not a scene for English ladies. Mrs Barlow looked at me & I at her. All the rest laughed heartily.

Thursday 6 January

We all set off to No. 15, Quai Voltaire to choose papers for Mrs Barlow's rooms. M. Vincent, the propriétaire, allows 25 sols for each rouleau of paper & six francs per piece for the bordering. Mrs Barlow's salon will take about 10 rouleaus. We chose papers & borders for the lodging rooms [bedrooms] at M. Vincent's price but for the salon nothing would do at less than 40 sols the rouleau. The additional 15 sols per rouleau must be paid by Mrs Barlow. Mme Galvani so much prefers a paper tout uni [all the same colour] for a salon & her taste in French furnishings must be so much better than ours, Mrs Barlow took it & chose a light-grey stone colour & a green border for her drawing room. This, which we should not have thought would look well even in a housekeeper's room in England, is much more comme il faut here, according to Mme Galvani, who says our papers in England are the ugliest things in the world & in the worst taste. She likes a paper tout uni, whose value depends on the fineness of the paper. We had almost chosen a very pretty paper (a blue star on a salmon coloured ground) at 6 francs the rouleau but Mme Galvani so much preferred the one tout uni, at 40 sols, we thought it best to take the cheaper.

Saturday 8 January

At near 2, we all set off together [to] Ausagne Petit (Rue des Moineaux), perhaps the largest, best & most honest shop in Paris, to buy curtains for the salon & bedrooms. Then went to Madame Davennés, Rue des Petit Champs, & chose a drawing room carpet (16 francs per aune), bedding & blankets ... Did not get home till 4–50 ... *While my hair was curled & just before, Mrs Barlow came in . . . I could have excited her if I liked. She has passion enough & would be a nice little bedfellow. She goes about her household concerns nicely. I said tonight what good order she kept me in, meaning that, after all, I could take no liberty – she had me at a word – & that I should love her always. 'Yes,' said she, 'as long as you can.' Has she a presentiment? For she often speaks in this way – that I shall, by & by, get the better of my fancy for her. She now begins to tell me anything. Said Mrs Cunliffe told her tonight, when Mr Cunliffe was once at Cheltenham, the whole inn was roused by the screams of a lady. All ran to her assistance. The joke was, the waiters had to stop them & say she was a bride of the first night. When Mr Hope, who wrote 'Anastasius'*[16] *was married, he passed the first night at his wife's father's & she jumped out of bed & ran screaming all over the house. The lady has now daughter sixteen.*

Sunday 9 January

Mrs Barlow met the Countess de Fumel at Mme Galvani's this morning, who asked her to a soirée chez elle [evening 'at home'] on Wednesday. She [the countess] said she would be glad if Mme Galvani would take [Mrs Barlow] with her ... For ¼ hour after Jane went to bed, Mrs Barlow & I were talking over her going with Mme Galvani to the Countess de Fumel's on Tuesday. *We seemed to be against it, not liking being taken by Mme Galvani. As she is now a teacher, we did not like her introduction &, however innocent, there are people who scandalize. Yet, at last, Mrs Barlow seemed to argue for the thing being well enough, saying I was no proper judge in this case.* At all rates, Mrs Barlow must now call on the Countess. By asking Mme Galvani to tell her how glad she had been to see her, she shewed a wish for Mrs Barlow's acquaintance & she, Mrs Barlow, according to French étiquette, must call. It could not be done here, in a large town like this, but in French country towns it was étiquette for strangers to call on those whose acquaintance they desired. Those people returned the call & then, if they too liked the acquaintance, they invited the strangers & a regular visiting was begun.

Tuesday 11 January

[Mrs Barlow] *spoke of what her aunt had written* [in a recent letter]. *It seems there was a paragraph about me she would not let me see. She* [Mrs Barlow] *had mentioned, without name, having formed a very agreeable acquaintance here & that we might eventually travel & then settle together, 'for I should not marry'. To which her aunt had sensibly replied she had better not tie herself to any woman, she had better marry, it would be more respectable. Besides, if I had less fortune than herself, the connection would be imprudent on her child's account & if I had more, she would seem like my dependent. Added to all this, I was younger than she, meaning that I might marry. I said I liked her aunt for all this. It was very sensible & proper. Then argued there was all the difference in the world between love & friendship. In a case of proper attachment there could be no such feeling of dependence, to which Mrs Barlow agreed. But, thought I, this is pushing the matter rather far. I do not much like this sort of communication to her aunt.*

Saturday 15 January

Finished packing & sent off my trunks at 11 . . . Went down to luncheon for a minute to see & take leave of Mme de Boyve but she did not make her appearance. Mrs Page had gone a couple of hours before. Mrs Barlow & I put the remainder of our things into a fiacre, took Cordingley with us & got here, no. 15, Quai Voltaire, about 2. *Page washing my room, where we were to sit as soon as it was done & then sleep, the other room not being ready. We were glad of the excuse not to send for Jane, & to sleep together. Sat for the moment in the salle à manger among all the furniture. Mrs Barlow looked so grave I asked if she was ill. Perhaps I talked too much. This overcame her spirits.* I had just gone downstairs on my way out when I met Mme Galvani. Turned back with her & she sat with us about ½ hour & left us at 4. [I] went immediately to the Cafe d'Orsai, en face du Pont Royal & ordered dinner at 5. Potage à la Julienne, omelette aux fines herbes & compote des pruneaux. Walked thro' the gardens ½ way along the Rue Castiglione, yet did not buy an almanac after all & got back at 5. Found M. le Comte de la Marthonie here, come to pay his respects to Mrs Barlow in her new house. He sat about ¾ hour longer. Dinner waited & we sat down about 5½. Tea a little after 8. *Mrs Barlow undressed in her own room, got into bed a few minutes before me & I was in bed* [with her] *at ten.*

---

1. ... a *famous man here* ... – This was Baron Guillaume Dupuytren (1777–1835), a French surgeon and pathologist, best known for his description and development of surgical procedures for alleviating 'Dupuytren's Contracture' (1832), in which fibrosis of the deep tissues of the hand cause retraction of one or more fingers. He became surgeon-in-chief at the Hôtel Dieu in Paris and also surgeon to Louis XVIII (who created him a baron) and then to Charles X.
2. ... *the person I had infected* ... – i.e. Isabella Norcliffe. See pp 188, 251 and 334 of *The Secret Diaries of Miss Anne Lister: I Know My Own Heart* (Volume One).
3. Trichomoniasis – A venereal complaint which was described by a man called Donne in 1836, in his early work in Paris on the microscope. Trichomoniasis causes chronic vaginal discharge. There is no long-term damage to the fallopian tubes. It is a common disorder which could be transmitted through heterosexual and also lesbian sexual activity.
4. Excess salivation – '... If you go to a patient for gonorrhea in the foul wards, at the end of his course [of treatment] and ask him how many times he has rubbed in [mercury], he will generally answer, "Twenty-eight times". If you ask whether he has salivated, he will tell you that he spits three pints a day. But ask whether his gonorrhea is cured and he will reply, "No. I have my clap still upon me." ...'

   Sir Astley Cooper. *The Lancet* Vol III, No 7. London. Saturday 15th May 1824.
5. Erethism – This condition is responsible for the origin of the term 'As mad as a hatter'. Hatters used to rub mercury into rabbit skins to 'fix' the fur before fashioning the hat from it. They ingested the mercury through the pores of their skin, thereby developing the condition of erethism, with its attendant displays of peculiar behaviour patterns. The sufferer becomes very shy and is prone to jumping about the room in 'bunny hops'. Other odd forms of behaviour are also manifested. The behaviour of the Mad Hatter at the Mad Hatter's tea-party in *Alice's Adventures in Wonderland* is a good example of the symptoms of erethism.
6. Bains Chinois – Chinese bath-house, so called because of its style of architecture.
7. ... [Mariana] *had once behaved ill to me* ... – See pp 300–307 of *The Secret Diaries of Miss Anne Lister: I Know My Own Heart* (Volume

One). Mariana Lawton had been ashamed of Anne's masculine appearance and had hurt Anne bitterly by placing fear of society's opinion of their relationship before her love for Anne.

8. ... *He afterwards got hold of a letter of mine* – See Prologue, p 9.
9. ... *The match would be soon* – Mariana was married to Charles Bourne Lawton on 9th March 1816.
10. Mrs and Miss Canning – The wife and daughter of George Canning (1770–1827), the then Foreign Secretary, later to become Prime Minister in the year of his death, 1827.
11. 'The Pleasures of Hope' – a poem dealing with human affairs, written in 1799 by Thomas Campbell (1777–1844). He was a Scottish poet, chiefly remembered for his sentimental and martial lyrics. *The Pleasures of Hope* was immensely popular and went through four editions in one year. In 1825, Campbell was one of the initiators of the plan to found the University of London for students who were excluded from Oxford or Cambridge for religious or financial reasons.
12. Prince de Condé – i.e. the Duc de Bourbon. See note 23, p 39.
13. Mlle Duchesnois – Caroline-Josephine Rufuin (known as Rafin), (1777–1835). Daughter of an innkeeper and horse-dealer, she made her debut as an actress at Versailles on 12th June 1802. Plain, mannish and undistinguished, she was not a success, initially. Eventually she became a much acclaimed dramatic actress at the Théâtre-Français, working with the great actor, Talma. She retired from the stage in 1833.
14. M. Firmin – Jean-Baptiste-François Becquerelle (1784–1859). Son of a Parisian vinegar-dealer, he began his acting career at the age of sixteen. Napoleon became his patron and placed him at the Théâtre-Français in 1811, much to the resentment of the company there. After Talma's death in 1826, Firmin became the great star of the French theatre, playing all the leading roles. He retired in 1845 due to his failing memory.
15. The duke of Orléans – After the restoration of the Bourbon monarchy, some of the aristocracy whose property had been confiscated during the Revolutionary and Napoleonic years had it restored to them where possible. Others were compensated financially. The Palais Royal, built in the 1630s for Cardinal Richelieu, became the property of the French Crown on the cardinal's death. Developed as a shopping mall under the Duc d'Orléans in the early 1780s, it became

a notorious pleasure place. The duke forbade the Paris police to enter its precincts. Gambling houses, brothels and political intrigues all flourished there and the Palais Royal became synonymous with all that was exciting and dangerous.

16. 'Anastasius' – written by Thomas Hope (1769–1831), English author and also furniture designer and expert on the Regency style of English decorative arts. His novel *Anastasius, or Memoirs of a Greek, Written at the Close of the Eighteenth Century* was written in 1819. It was at first attributed to Byron and it is thought possible that it had some influence on some of the later cantos of *Don Juan*.

Pairing Time Anticipated

The establishment of their all-female household at 15 Quai Voltaire meant that the growing intimacy between Anne and Maria Barlow was now safe from the more public arena of 24 Place Vendôme. Anne, however, began to entertain doubts about making any stronger commitment to the relationship. Although she was infatuated with Mrs Barlow, she had deep reserves about forming a life-long partnership with her. Mrs Barlow lacked any of the material advantages which Anne saw as desirable in the person with whom she chose to spend the rest of her life. There was no title which would gain Anne *entrée* into aristocratic circles; no fortune which would have enabled Anne to realise her ambitions of developing Shibden Hall and travelling abroad. Mrs Barlow did not even have any elevated social connections which could be of advantage to Anne. In addition, there was Jane to educate and launch into the world. So despite the obvious sexual attraction which Anne felt for Maria Barlow, she was forced to acknowledge to herself that the situation, from her point of view, was only temporary.

Maria Barlow, although she had acquiesced readily enough to the plan to move, displayed a great deal of insecurity once they settled at 15 Quai Voltaire. Prepared to be one hundred per cent committed to the relationship herself, she sensed Anne's readiness to 'be off'. Thus the uncertainty of her role in Anne's life, plus the financial worry of maintaining an independent household in a good Parisian quarter on a small income, rendered her nervous, irritable and tearful. Not the best qualities to induce a lover to stay.

Much of Maria Barlow's distress appeared to originate from a deep-seated guilt complex about her affair with Anne. It seems that the guilt was multi-layered. At the most superficial level, the level at which her contemporaries would have shared her guilt, perhaps, was the socially condemnatory act (for women) of sexual love outside marriage. Anne was sufficiently worldly to accept the fact that keeping a mistress was part of the accepted pattern in higher social circles. But Mrs Barlow's pride, self-esteem and awareness of the social gradations governing a woman's position in society at the more bourgeois level would not allow her to accept any status less than that of wife, or the equivalent of wife in this case, to the person whose life she shared on a sexual basis. Any deviation from that status was going to cause her deep distress.

The anxieties which arose from a deeper level stemmed from the fact that she was participating in lesbian sexual activity. Her marriage to Colonel Barlow had been a matter for social approval. Her conditioned role as a female had been played according to the expectations of heterosexual society. Prior to Anne's arrival at Place Vendôme, Mrs Barlow had had two serious offers, one from a Mr William Bell, from Guernsey, and one from Mr Hancock, a tea merchant in London who had visited Paris. Both men, according to her, were honest in their intentions. Marriage to either of them would have brought her an assured position in life, depending upon her husband's status. But it would also entail sacrifices – loss of her independent income and her Parisian lifestyle. It seems, also, that Mrs Barlow was not in love with either of the men, which begs the question – was 'being in love' a factor to which she would give priority? If so, can it be assumed that she was in love with Anne Lister? In choosing lesbian love, Maria Barlow may have been following her genuine desires but in the process of doing so she became a neurotically worried woman.

The third dimension of guilt inherent in the situation for her – though not for Anne who had long since come to terms with this aspect – was the reconciliation of her sexual love for another woman with the teachings of the Christian religion. Was her life as a Christian compatible with her new situation? In the moral and ethical climate of the early nineteenth century, there was no easy answer to this question. In the absence of any supportive structures or arenas in which the question was open to debate, Maria Barlow's journey from heterosexism to lesbianism was a very lonely one and it affected her profoundly.

Sunday 16 January

She nothing loth last night . . . Owned she loved me or she should not then be with me. If I knew her better I should know all this. Hinted at what she sacrificed. She meant virtue, I suppose, but I merely said I could sacrifice everything for her; Shibden, my friends, every prospect I had. I scarcely said it ere the feeling of insincerity on this point struck me. She shed tears as she said, if I knew her better, etc., & they continued to flow gently for some minutes . . . I had been thinking [while Mrs Barlow was out] *her temper would not quite suit me. Mariana better after all – more cheerful, more open. Yet I did not think so much of this when Mrs Barlow came back again.*

Saturday 22 January

We lay quiet this morning. She came to me very affectionately, saying it was so delightful to her to lie this quietly in the arms of those we love. We then talked a little of Eliza Raine & of her dislike to Mariana & my engagement. Said, as I had done once or twice before, that Lou [Mariana's sister] *told me Mariana was worldly. Mrs Barlow at last confessed that she thought she was, but perhaps she was wicked in owning this was her opinion, which she had always refused giving me before. She* [Mariana] *had two strings to her bow & she had great influence with me – she would change me when I was with her. I said no. 'Ah,' she replied, 'she may love you and were she hanging on your bosom you know not what she could do. She would not object to me. You might amuse yourself here with me. That would not hurt her cause.' Here I saw Mrs Barlow was affected. The tears fell fast. I was affectionate – said love was the strongest tie – I should always love* [her]. *'But,' said she, 'you can only leave me as you found me.' I said I really believed she loved me & perhaps none would love me better. 'No,' said she, 'I do not think they ever will. I love you for yourself alone, your mind & heart, not your person or situation at all.' I begin to be persuaded she really does love me & feel I cannot bear to give her uneasiness. My heart half ached for her. We both agreed we had gone too far but it was too late to recall the thing now. Talked a little on this subject just after breakfast & she was again low & thoughtful & the tears trickled down her cheeks . . . It was too late now but she would always think herself wicked for having so yielded to me. Agreed we should forgive each other . . . but still, she could never think so well of herself again. Said I, 'Circumstances alter* [cases?]. *As we cannot go & be married, what should we do?' 'Oh,' said she, telling me she quoted from Cowper, 'it is pairing time anticipated.'*[1]

Sunday 23 January

Letter from Mariana . . . *She now writes affectionately, seeming more than ever before awakened to a sense of sorrow at my suffering on her account & to the wish ' . . . it were in my power to make amends for all you have suffered & all your goodness to me.*

At this moment, my love, I feel as if I were more to be pitied than you. I have the pains of absence to combat with & the conviction of knowing that you are ill and I the cause – added to the reflection that a stranger is gaining the opportunities I am losing of endearing myself to you by numberless, nameless acts of love, gratitude and affection.' Read Mrs Barlow this last sentence & the one about Mariana's gladness I had found such a friend, her obligation to her & [her] *hope to acknowledge it sometime, but turning down the top of the page that* [Mrs Barlow] *might not see the 'and I the cause'. She did not like my hiding anything from her & had a little jealous fit, as she afterwards called it. I said Mariana's message, or rather mention of her, was very civil & I should say something equally so for her in return. She said it would not be true, nor her sending. She could not be half so civil. She 'could throw her into a ditch'. She did not want her kindness. However, I quizzed her gently & affectionately & she soon came round . . . She said Mariana had great influence with me. I said I had rather live with her* [Mariana] *en amie* [as a friend] *than anyone & what greater compliment could I pay her? I said I should do this from principle, but there was a wide difference between love & friendship. I was now more tied to her* [Mrs Barlow] *than ever. Loved a thousand times more since we came here. If she had never indulged me I should have got over it much better. Now it was too late. She seemed to think this might not be the case. I reassured her. Now I knew she loved me, this made all the difference in the world. 'Ah,' said she, 'I shewed my love more at Place Vendôme. Then I fought against it. Now I please myself.' I argued it could not be pleasing herself if she did not love me & this was more proof to me than fighting against it. 'Ah,' said she, 'you know what I mean. I gave much greater proof in giving myself up to you, in falling to you, than I give now & if you knew me, you would know this.' She is quite at ease with me now. Jokes about me having done too much & my being exhausted, & declares she will not let me, saying she is exhausted too. 'No, no,' said I, 'I am not, but certainly you are not. I am the most of the two.' She smiled. I blamed the mercury for weakening me. She can certainly bear all I can do well enough & she shall have it. I see she is fond of me but she would be desperately jealous, worse than Mariana, whom I could more easily cheat. She* [Mrs Barlow] *used to feel excited when she sat near me at Place Vendôme . . . often had great difficulty in resisting me as she did. But now, she has fallen.*

Monday 24 January

Mrs Barlow came about 11. *Got into bed & lay by me about a couple of hours & then got up & sat by me, or went backwards & forwards till I got up, when she sat by the fire watching me wash the mercury from my thighs & then wash & dress. She admired my figure, its masculine beauty, saying I was very well made. While lying by my side this morning, we somehow got upon Mariana's letter. She began crying. I asked why. She said no reason. It was Mariana who might cry . . . She would willingly exchange places with her. I said there would be no comparison between* [them]. *I should choose Mariana as a friend from principle & duty, not inclination. 'Ah, no,' said she, 'there can be no comparisons. She is better than I. I am fallen now.' She gently sobbed & the tears flowed fast. 'No,' said I. 'Judge not so. I do not, cannot, agree with you.' Thought I to myself, 'If you knew all, how you would change.' I mentioned Mr Hancock, entreating her to marry & consult her own welfare, hinting as gently as I could the uncertainty of my circumstances & that I would not for worlds be any tie upon her to prevent her marrying. In fact, I had been musing over Mariana's letter & had even before thought it would be best to prepare a little hole to creep out at. Perhaps she thought of this, but I denied it all when she asked me why I was so suddenly changed as to advise her so much to marry. Poor soul! The tears trickled quietly down her cheeks the whole time. She said she was quite altered now. She could not love two. She felt as if she ought not to marry. She could never think so well of herself again.*

How she was fallen! How unlike herself! How she used to talk – & now what could she say? She did not blame me. She was old enough to take care of herself. She did not now feel herself worthy of Mr Hancock. I was very affectionate. Threw all the blame on myself. Said it made me quite wretched to see her unhappy (and indeed a pang of remorse really did lie heavy at my heart). I would do anything in the world for her, etc., & on this, the tears really ran down my face too. 'Ah,' said she, 'perhaps I shall get over it in time, but never, never can I think so well of myself again.' ... Mrs Barlow read me several of her aunt's letters. *She* [the aunt] *is all for* [Mrs Barlow] *marrying Mr Hancock & seems to know how to calculate the advantage of his having a good income. His fortune, she says, is tantalizing – does not mind his being a grocer. Then* [I] *read her the whole of Mariana's letter, making, unperceived, as I went along, such alterations as hid all fault on Mariana's part. This seemed to satisfy her & she became a little more cheerful, having been very low the whole day. I was very kind & expressed much delight to have her back again to sleep with me.*

Tuesday 25 January

Writing the journal of yesterday made me 20 minutes *later in bed than Mrs Barlow. Saying I could not use the pot before her, she seemed a little vexed & said, 'Well, go out then. Do as you like.' On which, I did go out & on coming back told her that was not the best manner for her to shew to me. She argued the point that she was right & I had taken the thing wrong, as if I had been in a wrong temper. Thought I to myself, I was not tied to her, & thus went to sleep.*

Wednesday 26 January

She was low again this morning. The tears ran silently down her cheeks & she cried a good deal, saying she felt as if she should lose me. Could not love Mr Hancock now for she loved me too much. I really relented a little from my feelings of last night. Said I would do anything for her, loved her with all my heart, she would always have it, etc. She cheered a little . . . Just before getting up she said she only wished I could be her acknowledged protector. On questioning her I found she would be satisfied if we were what we call really 'going to Italy', that is, if I could acknowledge her as my own & give her my promise for life . . . She read me Mr Hancock's last letter, received just before leaving Place Vendôme. 'Tis evident he would have her if she encouraged him. I bade her consider her welfare & Jane's & act accordingly in whatever way that might be – to put me out of the question entirely. She said that could not be. It was too late now. I entreated she should think of me last. 'Perhaps,' said she, 'I should think of you first.' . . . Would wish me all happiness with Mariana. Had rather I did not come here at all. She should have one parting & did not wish for a second. I might not like her a few years hence. She knew I should take Mariana. What would friendship be after love? I had recommended York as a good place to settle in. She had fortune enough for that. She would be near me & would soon get into good society there. Oh, no. She would never go there. Why should she be near me? She cried a good deal & seemed very low. Fine day. Hard frost in the morning. The fountain in the Tuileries gardens frozen over but the sun had made the streets dirty.

Saturday 29 January

On the Terrace d'Eau, asked what she used to think of me when we at first used to walk there. 'I did not think so ill of you as to believe you capable of what we do now.' Yet she always excused me. 'The same excuse,' said I, 'there is for me is equally an excuse for you.' 'No,' she answered, 'the Almighty does not think so.' I looked grave – said she was very severe – she did not spare me. She saw I was serious & thoughtful. She explained when we got home she did not mean to say it would be wicked if we were really belonging to each other but only that she loved me too soon. In plain English, she was too much like a mistress. She was not my wife.

Thursday 3 February

We talked this morning more composedly than ever about Mr Hancock. I for her marrying him, saying I should always love her &, as we could not be together, at any rate perhaps for some years, she might marry him & be at liberty again by the time I was really ready to take her. She took all this better than I expected but shed a tear or two at last, saying that she must love me very much – she was not a crier in general, yet how many tears she shed for me. She often says our prospect of being together is not bright. What is seeing each other only once in two years? We had better not become so much attached. I believe she has not very much hope of getting me. She thinks of this engagement to Mariana &, after all, I should not be surprised if she marries Mr Hancock.

Sunday 13 February

M. de Lancy called a little after 1 & staid till 2¼, when he went out with us, thro' the Tuileries gardens & along the Boulevards to see the Carnival[2] which commenced today, to continue 3 days – today, tomorrow & Wednesday. Walked as far as about ½ way beyond the Passage des Panoramas to the Porte St Denis. The boulevards crowded with people & carriages but very few masks. It was chiefly children in the different carriages that were dressed up ... All Paris seemed afloat. We missed seeing the boeuf gras today. Gave 2 sols for 2 papers, each having a rude print of the ox & giving the 'ordré de marche et de la cérémonie du boeuf gras' [marching orders & the ceremony of the fatted bullocks].

Tuesday 15 February

Went out with Jane – Mrs Barlow not strong enough to bear the fatigues – to the Place du Carousel to see the boeuf gras presented before his majesty ... The animal was preceded by a party of gens d'armes on horseback & a band of musicians, then by the 'Messrs les garçons bouchers' [butchers employed by a master butcher] dressed like mountebanks & also on horseback. [The animal] was followed by a car in which were Vulcan, Venus & Cupid. The ox himself was covered with a scarlet velvet housing & had his head & horns covered with garlands. The cortège stopt for some minutes before the king's apartments. His majesty was expected to appear but did not. Of course, he gave money to the people who collected it for the animal, as it seems to be the custom for money to be given to the ox wherever he stops ... Several masks, carts & carriages full & a great crowd there, even on the boulevards. Much the best day. Almost all the masks in women's clothes were men.

Sunday 20 February

At night, we somehow got on to the subject of my not being here & her marrying Mr Hancock*. She said she could not act as if she had never known me. I had said I would always keep my promise* [to Mariana] *& when I afterwards tried to persuade* [her] *of my thought* [that I] *should, after all be hers at last, she said I contradicted myself – I had said I should keep my promise. She now saw it was time to lay aside all vain delusions to the contrary. The tears rolled down her cheeks. 'Well,' said she, 'my marrying would solve all this' – tho' I had plainly said I should love her nevertheless & should still seek her indulgence by every means in my power. She had said at dinner, the worst of it was she should not like to be incorrect herself & could not bear to see me another's. Surely she is fond of me. If she really is so, as much & as disinterestedly as she seems, I do indeed feel remorse at my conduct, for I have never seriously thought of having her. After all, I have always thought* Mariana *would suit me better. But I have suspected* Mrs Barlow *of being deep & thus have acted like a rascal in so gaining her affections. Surely it would be a more imprudent connection than with* Mariana*?* Mrs Barlow *has no friends whose acquaintance can serve me as an introduction. She has no money & there is Jane. Why, why leave Mariana in such a case? And yet, I now feel to like Mrs Barlow certainly more seriously than ever before.*

Tuesday 22 February

Lay quiet last night. On awaking this morning, Mrs Barlow did not like to put her face near me. She felt her breath [offended?]. *I said I did not perceive. I was gently putting my hand to her. She held it off. I asked her if she meant to be my friend only. She said evasively she hoped to be always my friend. I apparently took no further notice but somehow turned away my face a little & felt low & the tears* [began] *trickling gently down my face which I avoided her perceiving. I quietly gave her a kiss & got up as soon as Mrs Page had lit the fire & brought the hot water. On returning from 'my uncle'* [the water-closet], *opened her large cupboard door & washed behind it, instead of quite exposed as before, & used the seringue* [sic]. *She lay in bed, merely saying she would not interrupt me. Yet the thing struck her & when I had done washing, she got up & only did as much, as in general we both seemed to feel a reserve & I felt as if I had acted foolishly. Yet I had acted from impulse, feeling that from the moment we ceased to live together as we had done, a thousand particularities would come over. I should not be at ease & perhaps even my friendship would be formal ...* Breakfast at 12½ ... *Then sat chatting. She looked so triste I asked if she was ill. She said no in such a way I said we were both foolish to make ourselves unnecessarily unhappy. She said I had been so formal in my manner this morning, & the tears trickled down her cheeks. I said I had fancied she had meant to try to love me less, & now wished to act only as a friend & this made me reserved altogether. She said it was too late now – what signified it to change for the three weeks I should now stay? I declared I would have no more fancies. Apologised as affectionately as possible &*

became [friends?] *but, poor soul, she seems very low & thinks of my leaving her.*

Thursday 24 February

Slept in Mrs Barlow's room . . . She began joking, saying I had nothing to give, meaning I had no penis. Then declared she was the last to care for my having one. If I only wore breeches it would be enough. But if, in fact, I would really claim her as my own she would be satisfied. I said I often felt the want of breeches – the want of being a proper protector to her. At last I said I knew what always made her most uneasy. It was that, supposing a woman must be either wife or mistress, she felt herself most like the latter to me. She said I was right & the tears trickled down her cheeks. I consoled her. Said I would marry her if I could. Spoke of the purity of my affections – that a thousand circumstances might soon set me at liberty. She seemed in better spirits & a great deal more satisfied.

Wednesday 2 March

Mrs Barlow & I went thro' the Tuileries gardens to no. 20, Rue de la Paix, (à la Belle Anglais chez Mlle Dubos, Lingèrie) about a dressing gown (un peignoir) & staid there a good while. Then Mme Contant, brodeure, Rue des Moulins, no. 4. Looked at Valenciennes lace, etc., & there a long while . . . She was preparing a trousseau for a bride which consisted of 12 dozens of everything, 12 × 12 chemises, prs stockings, p. [pocket?] handkerchiefs, petticoats, etc., etc., & the bride would give 6 of everything to the bridegroom – 6 cambric shirts (at 17 or 18 francs the ell), 6 ditto cravats, p. handkerchiefs, prs stockings. 'Tis a very expensive thing for a man to marry in France. The cor-beille [presents offered by a man to his bride-to-be], consisting of trinkets, cachemere [*sic*] shawls, etc., costs a considerable sum – according to his income.

Friday 4 March

Breakfast about 12. For the sake of talking French, went & talked to the French girl who is hemming the p. handkerchiefs for my aunt, about an hour. She is a Napoleonist. They have it reported in her circles that the king, Charles X, had lately made it law that if anyone laughs or says a word at the church (à l'église), the person is to be punished with death. These people do not like the Bourbons.[3]

Sunday 6 March

Sat up talking to Mrs Barlow about her affairs. She has three hundred & eighty a year, including the eighteen annuity Jane has from the French funds for what was Colonel Barlow's prise [sic] money after his death. Jane's little fortune, which Mrs Barlow never touches, was twenty-two a year when she inherited it & it will be forty when she is of age. Mrs Barlow has four hundred & ten yearly but will now lose thirty by her under-tenant giving up her house in Guernsey.

Wednesday 9 March

This said casually, ''Tis the anniversary of Mariana's marriage.' Mrs Barlow said not a word but the colour instantly rose on her cheeks. 'Ah,' said I, 'I see, tho' you say nothing, you observed what I said.' She was still silent & I saw the tears starting. 'Oh,' said I, 'whatever I might think once, I now think it was a happy day for me,' and we then turned the subject.

Saturday 12 March

Breakfast at 12. I had just received, thro' Mme Galvani, a very civil note from Mme la Contesse de Fumel with 2 tickets for today for the Chambré des Deputies,[4] to admit us to the Tribune of the Duke de Bourbon, i.e. Prince de Condé.[5] We set off at 1. Got there at 1¼. Only the president & a very few there, tho' one member was speaking when we arrived. Saw all the rest come in & there were above 300 députés present.[6] The Law of Indemnity[7] to the emigrants was in debate. The discussion was warm. Every now & then the voice of the speaker drowned by the noise of no! no! – or other observations made by the other députés to one another, on which the president rapped on his table with the end of his ivory or, if this was not enough, rang a bell that stood by him, which procured silence ... Many of the members were in plain clothes but all those who spoke wore a single-breasted blue coat, a sort of livery, with gold or silver lace at the collar & cuffs which were sometimes also of yellow cloth or (I think) of white or red. M. de Villèle,[8] very grand with his gold lace, seemed more like a livery servant than Minister of Finance ... The Chambre is a very handsome ampithéâtre, lighted from a ½ circle window in the roof. The Tribune, red marble with low reliefs of white marble. Dinner at 6–20. Mme Galvani came before we had ½ done. Had her in my room – nothing but conversation – no reading. Consulted her about Jane's education, etc., & about the notice sent to Mrs Barlow of the marriage of M. de Glos. To all those qui font part du marriage (who inform the person of it) it is étiquette to send their card (but ladies never send cards to gents, only to ladies). After this, you wait for the new married couple to pay you a visit. If they do it, you return it & become, or continue to be, acquainted. But these notices of marriage are even sent to people whom the married pair do not know, for the sake of giving publicity to the thing, & are often sent to those whom they never visit, in which case, after having sent their card, no further notice is taken. On saying that Mrs Barlow knew nothing at all of the ladies qui avaient font part du marriage [who had announced the marriage], 'Ah, then,' said Mme Galvani, 'Mrs Barlow has only to send her card to the bride.'

Sunday 14 March

Mrs Barlow & I set off at 11–35 to see the Prison of the Conciergerie at the Palais de Justice.[9] It is only shewn from 10 to 12 to those who have tickets of admission. The chapel, behind which is made the entrance to the formerly dark, damp cells where Marie Antoinette & the Princess Elizabeth[10] were confined, separated only by a wall (tho' they did not know it), is therefore interesting & the cells themselves, now turned into an Expiatory Chapel,[11] are particularly so. Lighted & ventilated as they now are, Mrs Barlow could still scarcely bear the cold, damp floor. What must it have been during the Revolution? We next went to the Bureau belonging to the Ste Chapelle[12] & the archives, all which one of the clerks who was writing there very civilly shewed us. The fine old architecture of the Chapelle up to the window is entirely hid by the archives, beautifully arranged on shelves partitioned into little square compartments, having a remarkably neat appearance ... we ascended the winding staircase in one of the towers which brought us to the suite of apartments or galleries, whose walls are entirely lined with the archives of the parliament of Paris & the courts of the legislature & justice which succeeded it, from the time of St Louis[13] nearly to the present time ... [Our concierge] shewed us the proceedings against Joan of Arc[14] & the order of the pope to have the square or Place at Rouen planted with trees in memory of poor Joan. He shewed us also the collection of letters written by some of the kings of France to the parliament ... After this, our commis shewed us the oldest mss they have – 4 vols, 4[to] (in Latin), about A.D. 1240, du temps de St Louis. The writing of this period & for 2 or 3 more centuries [is] like that of our old papers in England of this time – but the writing we saw from A.D. 1600 & afterwards is really in what we would call a good, plain English hand of the present day. Much more like English writing than that what the French write now . . . All the proces verbaux [official records] of the Revolution are kept in cartons, arranged according to the dates . . . Anyone who suspected the loss of a friend during the Revolution might ascertain the matter here. Mr Edwards, the bookseller at Halifax,[15] might know whether his brother was guillotined here or not.

Wednesday 16 March

Just before getting into bed last night [Mrs Barlow] *read the letter she had from Mr Hancock on Monday – 3pp, the first two crossed.*[16] *Small, tradesman's hand. A love-letter in properly wrapt-up terms. Asks if, as he thinks of going to the king's coronation at Rheims,*[17] *he may call on her here. He writes as if she had given him no discouragement at Place Vendôme . . . His intentions are evident. His style not exactly that of a finished gentleman but well enough, all things considered. We sat up talking. She silently cried. I spoke as if I thought of her having him – as if I was not in a situation to ask, or wish, to advise her otherwise. She said she could not love him now. 'Oh,' said I, 'you do not know that.'*

Thursday 17 March

Lay in bed talking this morning. Somehow got on the subject of Mariana. I said I could not give her unnecessary pain. Owned that I always felt if I broke off suddenly she would take it to heart & might even never recover. 'Well, but,' said she, 'do you put her feelings in competition with what mine would be? But I see you always do and it is this that makes me dislike her. Can you compare the feelings of friendship with such as mine? Consider what I have sacrificed. She, at least, has always been correct. She has nothing to reproach herself with.' I said she [Mrs Barlow] *knew not my heart. I wished she could read all my journals, etc. Said she, 'There is something you have not told me.' I denied it in such a manner that she more & more suspected it & said she knew Mariana had been more to me than I had allowed. She asked if it was before or after her marriage. Said I, 'Oh, do not ask me. Never name the subject again.' Washed in a great hurry & returned to Mrs Barlow in little more than half-hour. Sat all the day talking in my night-shift & dressing gown over my stays & petticoat. Told the whole story of Mariana's marriage – everything correctly, only would not allow, that is disguised, that I had had any connection with her since her marriage. Said it was a match of convenience but she did her duty, etc. She* [Mrs Barlow] *got more & more satisfied – was glad I had told her, etc. She had cried much & I, too, a little. She said she saw I could not be hers, but we somehow got better reconciled & both seemed, after all, to have resumed the hope of being eventually together.*

Friday 18 March

It was evident all this morning she was pleased at what I told her yesterday. It satisfied her to find that Mariana, too, had yielded (but she had no idea of her having done it since marriage) tho' she said she saw us, Mrs Barlow *& I, further from each other than ever. Yet she knew I loved her from the confidence I placed in her & she would now be my friend always.*

Saturday 19 March

A strong excitement last night just after getting into bed. She said again this morning, it was the best she had ever had. Had a very good one an hour before we got up, slumbering all the while afterwards. In getting out of bed, she suddenly touching my queer, I started back. 'Ah,' said she, 'that is because you are a pucelle [virgin]*. I must undo that. I can give you relief. I must do to you as you do to me.' I liked not this & said she astonished me. She asked if I was angry. No, merely astonished. However, I found I could not easily make her understand my feeling on the subject &*

I dropped the matter altogether. Mariana would not make such a speech. This is womanizing me too much. Mariana will suit me better. I cannot do much for Mrs Barlow except with my finger. I am more sure of going on well with Mariana who is contented with having myself next to her.

Monday 21 March

Went to see the new Bourse[18] – the finest thing in Paris. Magnificent. May be finished perhaps in about a year. The iron rafter work to support the roof well worth seeing, as also the covered plafond of the grand salle which one walks round while passing along the iron rafter work of the roof. From here, went to Mellino, Rue de la Paix. Bought the Chrysofraes paruse (set of ornaments) for Mariana – necklace, bracelets and ear-rings (collier, bracelets et boucles d'oreilles) at 850 francs. Ordered a bracelet made of Mrs Barlow's hair.

Tuesday 22 March

Lay talking this morning. Foolish to be really connected [sexually] *now for fear of the possibility of doing her any harm. But she thinks when I come again we shall soon get accustomed to each other & do very well. 'But,' said she, 'if I do not fit you, you will not have me.' 'Oh,' said I, 'my little one' (as I always call her) 'there is no fear of that'* ... Went out. Mme Aucoq, Rue de Bac, no. 24 (our quincaillier) recommended me to M. Verni Layetier, Rue de Verneuil, for an emballeur, a wood box, etc. ... Then went direct to Hunaiker, Rue de Bussy, no. 22. Bought a pendule with a bronze figure of Minerva for Mrs Barlow for three hundred & twenty-five franks. Got home at 6. Dinner at 6¼. Mme Galvani came at 6¾. Had a fire in my room & had her tête-à-tête. Spent all the time in conversation ... *We all stood to see the pendule put up on the drawing room chimney-piece.*

Thursday 24 March

At the stand in the Rue de Luxembourg, took a fiacre, drove (along the Boulevards) to R. Mt Parnasse, no. 3 & took up Jane. Thence to the Institut Royal des Sourds-Muets[19] & got there at 1¼, ¼ hour after the séance had begun. The room was quite full but a gentleman of the Institution very civilly shewed us across the Tribune whence M. Abbe Serrier was speaking & we were placed close to it. I had, in fact, a very good seat brought from which I could see & hear everything. The answers, given in writing, by 3 of the grown-up pupils (quite young tho') to the miscellaneous questions asked them were wonderful, inasmuch they bespoke the writers as well-informed & having ideas on the subjects as just & clear as any of our senior wranglers at Oxford. The questions asked were numerous – moral, metaphorical, historical. What is eternity? This question, said M. Serrier, had been asked 20 times and the answer given had been always nearly the same. The definition was altogether precise, ending with 'C'est l'âge de Dieu.' [It is the age of God.] Ditto might be said of the definition of reconnaissance [gratitude], which ended with, 'C'est la mémoire du coeur.' [It is the heart's memory.] ... We all walked leisurely home ... & found Mme Galvani here. Sat with her tête-à-tête in [the] dining-room ... *On going into Mrs Barlow, found her quite grave. Saw something was not right – guessed she had not liked my being so long tête-à-tête with Mme Galvani. Could make nothing of her. Went out thinking, 'Fits like this will never suit me.' On returning, I myself was very grave. By after dinner she had come round. She had fancied Mme Galvani & I had ceased talking when she entered once. I knew nothing about it. Joked her. Said she was fanciful. She owned it & said she thought if she was mine she might be very miserable – I was so much admired & liked by the ladies in Yorkshire & they had such opportunities of besetting me. All this was because she loved me so much. I laughed & we got quite right. She lay down while I wrote all this page of today*. From 5 to 5–40, sauntered thro' the gardens to R. de Rivoli, no. 36, & bought a large plum cake for Mme Galvani to be sent tomorrow on her birthday.

Friday 25 March

Seeing a very great crowd along the quais & the Pont du Change & Pont Notre Dame, inquired & found they were watching the guillotining of L'Avoine, the man condemned for having murdered 2 children in the Bois de Vincennes. It was supposed he was hired to do it but he has never confessed. In the hope of seeing the guillotine (the man was dead, the deed was just done) we entered the crowd ... [Then] went to the Grand Bureau of the Messageries Royales in the R. Notre Dame des Victoires. 45 francs for an inside place from here to Boulogne – 40lbs of luggage allowed, the rest charged 4 sols a lb. Next Tuesday, Thursday & Saturday the Diligence will go by Boulogne & there will be a coupé. The intermediate days it does not go by Boulogne & there is no coupé, merely a cabriolet. They set off at 9 in the morning & 5 in the afternoon every day. Leave here at 5 pm & get to Boulogne the next day at 11½ pm. That is, they perform the journey in about 31 hours. 40 francs must be paid down to secure the places. I had not so much money. Had my name entered & left the matter to be settled tomorrow. *Mrs Barlow left the office in tears. Wanted me to stay till Thursday. I hesitated & am still undecided.*

Saturday 26 March

Lay quietly talking this morning about Mr Hancock & my own circumstances which prevented the possibility of my making any decided arrangements at present. The thing at present imprudent to us both. I could do no good in introducing Jane, etc. But Mrs Barlow loves me certainly very much. She says none will ever love me better & I believe her.

Sunday 27 March

Drove, for 3 francs, to the Bois de Boulogne, thro' the Barrière de l'Étoile. Paid off our fiacre & sauntered along the Grand Avenue (the road to Longchamp). A multitude of carriages, people on horseback (perhaps about ½ dozen ladies mounted) and on foot. Not a good horse there & a very shabby set of carriages but gay-looking. Sat down on one of the benches for some time. The air delightfully clear & light & refreshing.

Monday 28 March

In the evening, Mme Galvani sent me a ½lb tin box of her coffee, ready ground & a little note to say it was for myself alone, to be used on my journey. However, Mrs Barlow & I tried it & sat talking over it till late.

Wednesday 30 March

Packing. The emballeur packed all my gowns, hats & frill ... Packed my writing desk. While I was cutting open some of my books, Mrs Barlow gave me her sac de mint. Packing & fidgetting over 1 thing or other till one. Tea at 10 & then had my hair curled. Sat talking a little while.

BOULOGNE

Thursday 31 March

Cordingley lighted the fire in the drawing room about 9 . . . I in my dressing gown with nothing else but my night-chemise & stockings & slippers & in this trim I was finishing my packing. Paid the man for my front of false hair & did etc., till two when I half-washed, then dressed in a hurry . . . [Dinner at 3¾] Sat about ¼ hour afterwards with Mrs Barlow in the drawing room. Then took leave & off in a fiacre, which had waited 25 minutes . . . *In the morning I had casually said, 'Did you put all the lace in that little paper?' 'Yes,' said she, 'I have not kept any.' 'Ah,' said I, 'I did not mean that.' I looked grave & at last said, 'There are* [those] *who would not have said such a thing to me.' 'No,' said she, 'I know Mariana would not. You always bring up her name. She would suit you better.' I avoided saying much, thinking it was our last morning. At last she said she knew I thought her cross but she could not bear having Mariana so always mentioned. Her nerves were shaken – she was irritable. I must excuse her . . . She clung round me at the last & when I wanted to go, saying staying did no good, 'Oh, no,' said she, 'stay till the last minute.' She said she should go to bed immediately. She sobbed convulsively & as I went out of one door she hurried out of that into her own room . . . She said she would watch my pendule & think it spoke to her of me when it struck, particularly at the half-hour, that one little beat* . . . After leaving Mrs Barlow (Jane was to be with her at 5, for a few days, the Easter holidays) at 4–25, got to the Bureau, Rue Notre Dame des Victoires, only just in time to pay for my luggage & get comfortably seated in the coupé before we drove off at 5–05. I leave Paris, said I to myself, with sentiments how different from those with which I arrived. My eye was accustomed to all it saw – it was no longer a stranger nor found fault as before with all that differed from that it left at home. *Imperfectly as I speak the language, I felt almost at home in Paris & seemed to feel so in France. The parting words of Mary, Queen of Scots,*[20] *often occurred to me, 'Adieu, plaisant pays de France'* [Farewell, agreeable land of France]. *I thought over my whole acquaintance with* Mrs Barlow. *I was sorry to leave her but yet, somehow my sorrow was not so deep as I expected. I felt no inclination to shed another tear about her & I went along musing on the different manner in which things struck me from what they did at first. The towns did not seem shabby nor did I care for the want of hedges. In fact, I thought I could live abroad very well with someone I loved. But who should this be? It struck me not to choose Mrs Barlow. She does not satisfy me in several little things & the connection would be imprudent. Besides, she lets me see too much that she considers me too much as a woman. She talks to me about being unwell. I have aired napkins before her. She feels me, etc. All which I like not. Mariana never seems to know or notice these things. She suits me better. How shall I manage this thing with Mrs Barlow? She is surely attached to me. Somehow my heart is not so deep in the business as it ought to be & I scarce know why I have gone on, & led & been led on. Very strangely, it seems like a dream to me. The thing I regret most is the having owned Mariana's connection with me before her marriage. Thank heaven I have all that* [happened] *afterwards profoundly hid & Mrs Barlow's great curiosity strikes me in all its force. Surely it has exceeded all due bounds & this sticks in my throat. How will it all end? I cannot help thinking she has played her cards better than I have & yet she does not seem deep. She will not allow she has any vanity. I fear this is the worst scrape I have ever been in. How I have deceived her & myself, too, for lately I have fancied I liked her more really, merely saying to myself, would she not be too jealous for me?* Passed thro' Chantilly & thro' Clermont at 11½ pm. Beautiful day. The roads very dusty. Dusty & cold towards night. Slept a good deal.

---

1. '*. . . pairing time anticipated*' – From a poem or fable entitled *Pairing Time Anticipated* (1795) written by William Cowper (1731–1800), English pre-Romantic poet. Cowper was a forerunner of Burns, Wordsworth and Coleridge. He was one of the most widely read English poets of his day.
2. The Carnival – This was the Carnival of the 'Boeuf Gras', a three-day carnival which was traditionally held at the beginning of Lent, similar to the Mardi Gras in New Orleans. The parading of the bullock would be a symbolic demonstration of the fasting period to come, when the eating of meat was forbidden.

3. '... These people do not like the Bourbons.' – Some of the lower classes of Paris were still loyal to the memory of the Revolution or – especially in the lower ranks of the military – to Napoleon.
4. Chambre des Deputies – The Lower House of the French parliament, at that time under the ultra-right leadership of Villèle.
5. Prince de Condé – The Duc de Bourbon. See note 23, p 39.
6. ... 300 Députés ... – It is difficult to say what the total number of Députés was in the constitution of the Lower Chamber or Chambre des Députés of the French parliament at that time. The total varied with different electoral laws.
7. The Law of Indemnity – After the restoration of the Bourbon monarchy (1814), the aristocrats who had fled France at the time of the Revolution became an important force in French politics. Their claims resulted in the Law of Indemnity of 1825, whereby financial compensation was to be made to those who could not recover their lands.
8. M. de Villèle – (Jean-Baptiste-Guillaume), Joseph (1773–1854). French conservative politician and prime minister during the reign of Charles X. His reactionary policies on issues such as censorship of the press, reinstatement of the power of the Catholic church, and the Law of Indemnity in favour of the émigrés, were challenged even by some right-wing royalists. He resigned in January 1828 and his political career was then over.
9. Palais de Justice – Situated on the Ile de la Cité, the Palais de Justice was originally the meeting place of the Paris parliament under the kings of France – the High Court of Justice. In 1793 the Revolutionary Tribunal convened there, sentencing some 2,600 people to death by guillotine.
10. Princess Elizabeth – (1764–1794). Sister to Louis XVI and sister-in-law to Marie Antoinette. Her loyalty to them during the French Revolution led to her imprisonment and death by guillotining.
11. Expiatory Chapel – Danton and Robespierre were said to have been held in these cells also, prior to their execution. Although Anne here uses the term 'Expiatory Chapel', this is not to be confused with that of the same name which is situated off the Boulevard Haussmann attached to the cemetery in which the remains of Louis XVI and Marie Antoinette were interred until their removal to the royal necropolis at St Denis by Louis XVIII.

12. Ste Chapelle – The Ste Chapelle is the oldest part of the Palais de Justice. Originally it was built to house the Crown of Thorns and other sacred relics which Louis IX (St Louis of France) bought in 1239 from the Venetians for an enormous sum of money. The Crown of Thorns now rests in Notre Dame Cathedral. The Ste Chapelle was used as an archive between the years 1802 and 1827.
13. St Louis – Louis IX (1214–1270). King of France from 1226–1270 and the most popular of the Capetian monarchs. He led the Seventh Crusade to the Holy Land in 1248–1250 and died on another Crusade to Tunisia. He was canonised on 11th August 1297.
14. Joan of Arc – St Joan of Arc (1412–1431). National heroine of France who led the French army to a momentous victory at Orléans in 1429, which proved to be a turning point for them in the Hundred Years War. Because she claimed to act under divine guidance, she was condemned as a heretic by an English-dominated court in 1431. She was burnt at the stake in May 1431, in the Place du Vieux-Marché, in the city of Rouen.
15. Mr Edwards . . . – Thomas Edwards (1762–1834) of the firm 'Edwards of Halifax'. They gained fame in English bookbinding circles because of the quality of their work. William Edwards (1723–1808) allegedly invented the art of decorating the edges of the leaves of a book with landscape paintings. His sons, James and John, were set up in business by him in a shop in Pall Mall, London, named 'Edwards and Sons'. Thomas remained in Halifax. His brother, John, went to Paris during the Revolution for the purpose of acquiring some of the fine libraries available there, due to the dispossession of the aristocracy. He never returned home and, according to the family tradition, he was a victim of the guillotine. The story is feasible because, as an Englishman with money dealing within aristocratic circles, he would come under suspicion, at that time, as an enemy of the Revolution.
16. Crossed – The system of prepayment by postage stamps was not in force until 1840. Prior to this date, the recipient of a letter paid the postal charge on delivery. The charge was based on a number of things, e.g. distance, weight, number of pages, etc. To minimise the cost, friends used to write down the page from top to bottom, in the usual way and then turn the page sideways and fill it again over the original text. This produced a trellis-like effect, very difficult for the reader of today to decipher.

17. The king's coronation at Rheims – In the fifth century. Clovis, king of the Franks, was baptized at Rheims by Bishop Remigius (Reme). Rheims, which takes its name from the Gallic tribe of the Remi, thus became the traditional place for the consecration of French kings. Charles X was crowned there on 29th May 1825.
18. The new Bourse – The Stock Exchange. Occupying the site of the Dominican Convent of the Sisters of St Theresa, in what is now the Place de la Bourse, off the Rue Notre-Dame des Victoires, the erection of the new Bourse was begun in 1808, under Napoleon, and completed in 1826 during the reign of Charles X.
19. Institut Royal des Sourds-Muets – An establishment for deaf-mute people.
20. Mary, Queen of Scots – Mary (1542–1587), daughter of James V of Scotland and Mary of Guise, was sent to France at the age of five, by her mother, to be brought up at the court of King Henry II. French became her first language and she grew up a Frenchwoman rather than a Scotswoman.

More Than Ever English

When Anne returned to England, she found that little had changed on the surface. In 1825, Britain was enjoying a period of relative calm and mild prosperity. The reign of George IV was halfway through its ten-year span. The economic distress which Britain had experienced after the cessation of the Napoleonic Wars had abated somewhat and the government of the mid-1820s was thus less repressive and more open to the needs of the growing industrial classes, though this was not to say it was by any means liberal. The 1820s formed a period of what has been termed 'mild reform'.[1] Radical reform, as yet, lay over the horizon but the foundations for it were slowly taking shape during the reign of George IV.

That this climate of slow and thoughtful progress permeated Anne's Yorkshire background becomes evident from her journal entries. Her wide reading and interest in current events meant that she was always fully aware of the social, political and economic trends of the day. A Tory herself, Anne was unsympathetic to the radical temper of her home town, Halifax, and showed little sympathy for the problems of the poor *en masse*. To the servants, tenant-farmers and cottagers on the Shibden estate, she displayed in her dealings with them a certain amount of level-headed justice but she could never empathise with them fully. There are small, isolated incidents of philanthropy, such as taking on the cost of educating the motherless daughter of one of her workers but, mainly, the interests of the Lister family and the Shibden estate were the touchstones of her concern. Other issues had to fall into second place. At this stage, however, Anne was not yet mistress of Shibden and her concerns remained rather more on a personal level. Her real career as independent businesswoman, traveller, controller of her own destiny and that of Shibden, was waiting in the wings.

Meanwhile, Anne was relieved to be back in England for a while. On reaching London, she and Cordingley took rooms again at Webb's Hotel at 220 Piccadilly. Anne took the opportunity of a few days' stay in London to do some shopping and sightseeing. She also entered into a little escapade in order to satisfy her curiosity about Maria Barlow's beau, Mr Hancock.

Tuesday 5 April

Breakfast at 11¼. Looking over the map of London & dawdling over one thing or other till 1½, then took the porter with me to Hatchett's (White Horse [cellar?]) where the coaches stand that go to Kensington, Hammersmith, etc. (in Piccadilly, a little way from the Burlington Arcade) & got into one ... In returning along Cheapside, turned down Bread St.[2] (opposite to Milk St[3]) & went down towards the river as far as 18, Bread St. Hill. Went into the warehouse. Mr Hancock at dinner. He was called down. Asked if he would supply families in the country [with groceries]. No! Against the custom – they could not do it – it would interfere with the retailers whom they supply. Did not even supply his uncles & aunts ... He was very civil. Very good, white, clean teeth. Struck me as a handsome likeness of Mrs Cunliffe's cousin, the Mr Kingston we saw in Paris. A thorough tradesman ... *He had a black coat & waistcoat & fawn coloured trousers on. Clean neck handkerchief & looked clean & neat but thoroughly a tradesman. He was at dinner. It was quarter past five. His civility was that of a civil trades-shop tradesman. When I apologized for calling him down so unnecessarily, he said, 'Oh, no. Not at all. I am sorry you have come out of your* [way], *ma'am.' As I walked along the street I kept exclaiming to myself, again & again, 'God bless my soul.' Then, thinking of her aunt's letter, said twenty times over, in her own words, 'Il n'ya pas de choix.'* [There is no choice.] *Thought I, 'tis enough. How could she admire him? Could he, even at Place Vendôme, seem like a gentleman? How could she, then, think of him seriously? How can she do so now? She has owned she did not like the grocership before knowing me. Why lay so much stress on not liking him on my account? Said I to myself, I will see what sort of a place Bury Hall* [Mr Hancock's private residence] *is* . . . Just got home at 6. Washing my hands & waiting for soup, which they fancied I had not ordered, made me not have my dinner till 6¾. Gravy soup *&* haunch of mutton & a small batter pudding yesterday. Mock turtle soup & boiled beef & tarts today. I only drank about ¼ of my pint of wine yesterday. *I felt sure someone has taken at least a glass* . . . Very fine day & warm. Felt a good deal harrassed & unwell yesterday. Looked so ill & old & wrinkled under my eyes this morning, I was quite struck with myself . . . I had eaten no meat in Paris from the time of my consulting M. Dupuytren. This end [meaning England] I was taking meat – & wine may have affected me as well as the fatigue of the journey. I feel the blood in my head, swell'd & feebled.

Wednesday 6 April

Got into the Edmonton stage (2/– fare) & by giving the man an additional 6d. he set me down at Bury Hall about 3–10. Inquired for Mrs Hancock [Mr Hancock's mother]. She came to me in the breakfast room. [I] said I understood she was parting with 1 of her servants (thought of Molière's M. Porceaugnac[4] & the man who got all out of him that suited his purpose). 'Yes,' said she, 'my housemaid.' This luckily gave me my queue [*sic*] & my ruse answered so well & the lady was so communicative on the subject, I sat with her near ½ hour. Admired the house. She said it was rather a celebrated place. Judge Bradshaw, Oliver Cromwell's Judge Bradshaw,[5] had lived there ... In size & general appearance Mrs Hancock is not unlike Mrs Middleton [a former guest at Mme de Boyve's house in Paris] but more vulgar. She bears a strong, motherly likeness to her eldest son [presumably the Mr Hancock that Anne visited in London] with the exception of having a dusky, greasy complexion. She might have been a busy housekeeper just called off from her various employments, tho' with the difference of shewing all the mistress-ship of a rich, well-satisfied, tradesman's wife. Yet she seemed a very good sort of worthy woman ... Having been at least ½ hour there & having had some time to look about me leisurely, the 'footman', in his linen jacket & gray white apron, shewed a near way across the fields (perhaps nearer by about ¼ mile) to the village of Edmonton (Bury Hall is at Lower Edmonton). I hastened to the Bell Inn at the farther extremity of the place, got there at 4¼ & in just 5 minutes was off in a very good chaise ... My post-boy drove so well that I stopt 5 minutes at the Saracen's Head, Snow Hill, to inquire about places for Leeds. The Rockingham [coach] leaves there every day at 2 and gets into Leeds about the same hour the next day – inside places, 3½ guineas each. Extra luggage above the 20lbs allowed, charged 2d a lb. It is the Union that goes every morning at 7 from the Blue Boar, Holborn.

Saturday 9 April

Breakfast at 12¼. Repacked my basket – trunk, etc., & went out at 1–50 ... Sauntered all along Old & New Bond St., to Oxford St. & then along Piccadilly as far as Park St. Switch tails seem all the fashion for carriage horses ... Dinner at 6. At 6–40, took Mr Webb & set off in a hackney coach to Drury Lane to see

Freischuts[6] . . . The music certainly very singular & fine. The overture encored & played twice. The 1st appearance of 'Zamiel', the Devil, in his dark, brick-red, flowing mantle, hiding all the figure – his curling himself up in it & sinking thro' a trapdoor, was so inimitably done it really seemed as if the evil one had gradually shrunk to nothing & thus vanished, one knew not how. Caspar's sitting the Circle [*sic*] and forging the bullets, all hell let loose &, at the close of the piece, his falling down and Zamiel's dragging him away to hell, horribly well-represented, is altogether the most singularly terrific spectacle I ever saw or heard of as introduced upon a stage. To this succeeded the musical drama of 'Abon Hassan',[7] the music also by Von Weber.[8] The story taken from the Arabian Nights entertainments & made a pretty spectacle. Grand ballet in the 1st act. The dancing, or grace of the dancers, far inferior to that in Paris. The dresses good. The house looked clean & handsome. The large glass chandelier suspended from the top over the pit & lighted with gas, magnificent. On coming away, took a turn up & down the saloon – a very handsome oblong room. Recesses at each end & tea to be had at both. Mirrors between the pilasters on each side of the saloon. None but femmes galantes there – the room full of these & gents. The ladies very civil. Much quieter & more decorous than formerly. Not many [femmes galantes] in the house tonight but 1 or 2 very near us – not to be known but by the volumes spoken by their eyes when met by those of gents, & by their smile. In walking the streets the great sign is a white handkerchief peeping out a little from the top of a reticule. The old men much the worst. Men of 60 or 70 do things young men would shudder at. When Frenchmen are asked their opinion, said Mr Webb, of our countrymen abroad, they shrug their shoulders & say they seem what they are not. I owned there was often too much reason for this remark. Too many did abroad what they would not do at home.

Anne and Cordingley arrived back in Halifax on 11th April 1825. They were met by Anne's father, Jeremy Lister, who was staying, with her sister Marian, at Northgate House, a property in the town which belonged to the Lister family.

A small town in the West Riding of Yorkshire, Halifax was not a place for which Anne felt any particular affection. Originally a small medieval hamlet consisting of a few houses clustered around the ancient parish church,[9] the town had grown slowly over the centuries, drawing its sustenance from the woollen trade which had supplemented the meagre living to be obtained from the barren hillsides which surround the town. The many small streams and rivulets which ran freely down the hillsides into the valley bottom, wherein lies the town of Halifax, made it an ideal location for the setting up of small fulling mills[10] in which cloth was processed. Cottage industries related to the production of cloth, such as spinning, handloom weaving, carding and woolcombing, began to thrive. Merchants from many miles around would travel over rudimentary pack horse trails, bringing raw wool into the town to be processed by these industries. The finished cloth would then be taken back by them for resale at markets both at home and abroad. Daniel Defoe,[11] in his travels around England in 1724, passed over the Pennines and was greatly impressed by the industrious cottagers of Halifax and the surrounding areas. The culmination of such industry was the construction of the large and classically beautiful Piece Hall[12] specifically for the buying and selling of cloth pieces.

In addition to its lucrative woollen trade, Halifax also became a busy market town. Places such as Cornmarket, Swinemarket (renamed Upper Crown Street), Cow Green, Bull Green, Woolshops and Cabbage Lane (where fresh vegetables were once sold – now renamed St James' Road) indicate the diversity of produce and animal stocks which were bought and sold at Halifax markets.

During Anne Lister's adult life in Halifax, from 1815 to 1840, the town was in the process of transition, moving from a predominantly agricultural market town, with a woollen trade dependent mainly on water power and cottage industry, to a fully fledged industrial town based upon steam power and the organisation of labour into the factory system. The impact of the Industrial Revolution was as great in Halifax as in the neighbouring towns of Huddersfield, Bradford and Leeds, although in 1825, when Anne returned to Halifax, there were still pockets of resistance to the mechanisation of industry. Individual small farmers and cottagers still carried on trades such as woolcombing and weaving in their own homes in order to supplement their incomes.

Politically as well as industrially, Halifax was experiencing an exciting, albeit problematical, period of development. By 1825, the population of the town had grown from a figure of between 90 and 200 in the fourteenth century, to around 12,000 in the early 1820s. The disparate nature of industry prior to the factory system meant that the labouring classes of Halifax, as elsewhere, were not politicised to any great degree. The ideals generated by the French Revolution did give rise to sporadic outbreaks of democratic and republican sentiment,[13] the articulation of which were quickly repressed by the authorities. The Luddite movement, also, had active cells in and around Halifax.[14] On the whole, however, poverty, insufficient organisation, and the effects of repressive legislation kept Halifax radicalism reasonably contained. Redress of grievances through Parliamentary channels was not, in 1815 or for many years afterwards, an avenue open to the poorer classes. Yorkshire, the largest county in England, was represented by two MPs. Voting rights[15] were restricted mainly to the land-owning classes and the wealthier industrialists and tenant-farmers.

Commercially and socially, the town was run by a handful of large, energetic families, many of them inter-related by marriage, who had risen up on the crest of the Industrial Revolution. These were a new breed of wealthy people, distinct from the land-owning oligarchy which had so far dominated the town. Again, place-names in Halifax indicate the way in which the town was influenced by these 'new' men. Rawson Street, Waterhouse Street, Rhodes Street, Swires Road, Prescott Street and Edwards Road all bear witness to the influential families who combined to run the town's affairs in the eighteenth and nineteenth centuries.

These men also arrogated to themselves the roles of magistrates and justices of the peace, assuming the responsibility of ensuring that law and order reigned in the town. At night, only the streets in the centre of the town, ill-lit by flickering oil lamps, were guarded by one or two watchmen or constables. The outskirts of, and approaches to, the town were very unsafe, particularly in winter. There were many instances of highway robbery and of remote farmhouses being burgled. Self-defence, by means of carrying one's own pistol, was normal for those who had to use the roads at night, or as a means of protecting one's property. Felons were heavily punished, usually far in excess of the actual crime committed. Luckily, the infamous Halifax gibbet[16] no longer performed its grisly task but hanging and transportation were still on the agenda for offences which would now only merit fines or short terms of imprisonment.

The families of these wealthy Halifax entrepreneurs dominated the genteel social life of the Halifax well-to-do. The diary of Mrs William Rawson[17] of Savile Green, one of the most active of the Halifax hostesses of Anne's day, gives an insight into the round of polite entertainment enjoyed by the wives of these prosperous men:

> '... Dined last week at Stoney Royde [the home of Mr & Mrs John Rawson] with Mrs & Miss Stansfield of Leeds, & with the same [people] at Mr Waterhouse's [Well Head]. Had both these families to dinner & also Mrs Lees, Miss Lewthwaites & Miss Threlkeld & [the] Fergusons – & to tea, the same day, a numerous party.' [12th June 1821]

> '... Tea & evening at Mrs C. Rawson's [Hope Hall]. Tea & cards – Mr Waterhouse's ... ' [13th June 1821]

> '... Dined at Stoney Royde ... ' [16th June 1821]

> '... Dined at Mill House [another branch of the Rawson family lived there] ... ' [19th June 1821]

The diary continues in this way in practically every entry.

These gregarious hostesses issued invitations to breakfast, afternoon tea, card parties and evening entertainments at home around the piano. Occasionally there were much larger parties and balls given which could go on into the next day. Anne, although declining all invitations to larger gatherings, denouncing them as 'vulgar', would listen to the accounts of them from her gossipy young women friends around the town and then record them satirically in her journal.[18]

The old Assembly Rooms at the Talbot Inn were mainly used to provide a public introduction for socially acceptable newcomers to Halifax. A newspaper report in the *Halifax Courier & Guardian* in the 1880s tells us something of its history:

'About the middle of the eighteenth century a society was formed in Halifax with the object of providing innocent amusement & promoting greater social intercourse amongst the members of the principal families in Halifax. They met at stated periods – sometimes four times a year – & the evening was pleasantly spent in agreeable conversation, dancing, occasionally varied with a game of cards, & generally concluding with supper. These fashionable assemblies were very select &, at one time, the families represented might probably be counted on ten fingers . . .'[19]

Anne Lister provides us with an amusing insight into the social infighting of the day at what had become, by then, the 'less select' Assembly Rooms:

'. . . Went to Mr Saltmarshe's. Sat there a good while, listening to Emma's amusing account of the Assembly. Mrs Walker had the annoyance to see her daughter, tho' on her first appearance, stand the 7th couple, placed below the Misses Bates & Elizabeth Watkinson, who had precedence as being bridesmaid to the reigning bride, Mrs Turney (Miss Hannah Watkinson that was). Next to her, Mrs Frederic Norris, another bride, then Lady Radcliffe's sister, Miss MacDonald. Emma thought all the old Assembly-goers seemed like intruders among the new ones. A motley set . . .'

(Friday 3 December 1819. Halifax)

From Anne's final, withering comment it can be gathered that she was not an Assembly-goer!

To this vigorous, small town, with its mixture of bustling entrepreneurship energetically forming the future and its backward-looking agricultural and cottage industries; its Tory, Church of England, genteel society and its radical,

Nonconformist labouring classes; its multiplicity of inns, clubs and societies operating at all levels of the town's society, Anne returned in the spring of 1825. She was glad to be back in England, as she fervently told her friends, but the glitter and sophistication of Restoration Paris, the climate and culture of the Continent, had made a forcible impression upon her. She knew that she would, henceforth, be irresistibly drawn by the lure of foreign travel.

Meanwhile, there was her life at Shibden to resume and old contacts to be renewed. Anne settled once more into the even tenor of her day to day routine in the insularity of the Pennine hillsides.

Tuesday 12 April

Did not go into stables. (Saw Hotspur & Caradoc yesterday while my uncle & aunt were at dinner.) Went out at 9¼ ... Returned along a line of [our] new footpath and along the fields from Chas Howarth's. Looked about the sheds, etc., & at home and came into breakfast ... My father & Marian came about 7 & staid an hour. *Poor Marian disappointed there was no shawl for her.* [I] *said I had a friend in town (*Mrs Mackenzie *in* London*) who would get her one. The fact is, I see my aunt likes both the shawls I have brought. Keeps them both after many scruples & I have none for* Marian. *But who has so much right to be pleased as my aunt? I find all the money I have had, except fifty pounds, was hers & she has left herself without & will now give me more as soon as she can. She says perhaps she may not live to want the shawls but seeing her in doubt which to part with & liking both, I will have her keep them. She is very good to me. They say nothing is wrong I do & are delighted to see me back again.*

Wednesday 13 April

Mrs Bateman (from Hipperholme school) came just before I came away. She is much admired here, I understand. I scarcely saw her face but thought her, as I shall for a time think all the rest, dowdily dressed. The Parisian ladies spoil one for the dress of English ladies. I thought all the people I saw in London shocking figures. The common people quite louts after their compeers in Paris.

Thursday 14 April

In the evening talked to my uncle & aunt. The latter very rheumatic. Could scarcely move from her chair. Screaming with pain every now & then. I have never seen her so bad.

Sunday 17 April

Read over & sealed my 3 letters . . . chit-chat to Mr Duffin [in her letter to him]. The French manners & habits of thinking very different from ours. ' . . . Gambling, dancing, lovemaking, seem the prevailing tastes. There must, I suppose, be some novelty in the style of the latter to English people in general.' Would not change sentiments with any French person I have met. The liberty of their Chambre des Députés seems at least problematical . . . My being in Paris was a mere nothing. Scarce deserved the name of being abroad. Like a dream which I had already forgotten – but a pleasant dream, recalling every friend I had & making every person, thing & place [in England] more dear than before. Such, with a mind & heart in health, always the effect of absence from what we love. What, then, more wholesome than the occasional absence, if the memory of my friends was as faithful as my own? . . . Told them all I was more than ever English at heart . . . Dinner at 6½. Tried my cafetière à la Morize with success, taking poor Mme Galvani's coffee. In the evening, shewed the ornaments I had bought for Mariana, the French hand-screens, etc.

Monday 18 April

Could not sleep last night till after 1 – thinking about the new footpath ... Off at 10–40 (took George in the gig) to Haugh-end ... *Mrs W. Rawson & the whole set a vulgar-looking party. Mary Priestley much the best of them. I am much quieter & graver, I fancy, than they used to see me before I went. Vulgarity gravifies & sickens me more than ever.*

Thursday 21 April

Went out at 11–40, down the fields to the brook where Jackman was building the foundations for the new footpath bridge. 2 young men taken (while I was out, by George Robinson & his men) stealing the clothes off Thomas Pearson's hedges ... Taken before Stocks [the magistrate]. Thomas Pearson refuses to prosecute.

On Wednesday 20th April 1825, Anne had received a letter from Maria Barlow. It became apparent that the latter was not willing to accept that the relationship between herself and Anne was finished, despite the fact that her old Guernsey admirer, Mr William Bell, had reappeared in her life. She felt that because of the depth of her feelings for Anne, she had nothing of herself to give to any other lovers:

> '... *You have taught me much untaught before & surely I must strangely learn that hardest science – to forget – ere I can associate another with these sentiments which you have chastened & refined* ...'

Anne did her best to answer the letter in soothing and loving terms, while not giving Mrs Barlow any unfounded hopes for the future.

Saturday 23 April

Wrote [to Mrs Barlow] . . . *I have had no time to make extracts but it is very affectionate . . . Write as if having no wish to make her my wife, yet say she knows 'the hard necessity of circumstances that clings around me now'* [i.e. Anne's commitment to Mariana Lawton]. *Bid her do what is best for her own interest & Jane's. For her sake I can forget to be selfish. Nay, more than this – abhor the thought. Bid her ' . . . not sacrifice a certain good* [marriage to William Bell or Mr Hancock] *for the uncertain prospect of making happy one whose affections she had gained forever, but whose hopes of happiness had waked not from their sleep of years till roused by you to live & tremble once again'. All this brought on by my saying I had been taken by surprise altogether, tho' I ought not to have been, by the reappearance of her 'old beau', that is, William Bell. Said I had not the same feeling of repugnance towards him as Mr Hancock . . .* [Anne goes on to quote from Maria Barlow's letter, which she says was *'very, very affectionate'*.] *' . . . A diversity of objects & scenery save you* [Anne] *from the intense misery I have suffered . . . ' & she goes on to describe feelings much more intense than I had ever dreampt* [sic] *of her experiencing for me. It ended in her being ill & having a great deal of fever. ' . . . I became so ill, I had so much fever, that I compose letters in my brain to your uncle, telling him that your return alone could save my child from being an orphan. So thin am I that my rings are laid aside. I kept losing them every moment. Would that I had but one more day of your dear self in this salon. I have so many things unsaid which, perhaps, we may never meet with opportunity to express. But to tell you truly, I must have many days of your society to induce me to undergo the agonised feelings I endured the days which followed your departure. I thought I was near my end . . . I must stop my pen for I know not what my light head would scribble on to say. The best thing I could do with this sheet would be to consign it to the flames. My next, I trust, will be more rational. God bless & preserve you. You know all I would say. Adieu. M.B.' Thus ends the first page . . . In my answer . . . I slightly alluded to our connection. No-one could possibly understand it but herself.* [I] *said I still sighed after happiness gone by with a sigh more deep & long than she might think . . . I said my own room was perhaps the worst place in which to calculate my loss. In an earlier part of my letter, I had hoped that, at all rates, she would not be disappointed in me as a friend – would have nothing to regret but my misfortune (this 'hard necessity that clings around me now') – nothing to reproach but my loving her too well. This would be my only fault towards her, which I hoped she would forgive & even its very faultiness may wear away with time. ' . . . For time may come when my regard, without another voice to claim it, may be your own from duty as from inclination.'*

Tuesday 26 April

[Anne writes to an old friend in York, Miss Henrietta Crompton, who lived in Micklegate] – '. . . To believe the French ladies, or the ladies of any country, superior in anything to my countrywomen is not much my creed. But perhaps with all my Yorkshireism about me, I am not a fair judge. I grant the palm of victory in dress must grace the temples of the Gallic fair, but a well-bred, travelled Englishwoman who has caught 'the manners as they rise' is still my summit of perfection. The style of English elegance suits me better than that of French; it is more dignified & seems to me more purely angel-like than all that finished coquetry – that charm that lulls to sleep. French mannerism, French tact at conversation, are certainly striking but, taken nationally, give me the manners, customs, hearts & minds of our own country before those of every other country that the pen of Traveller has described. It would be invidious to particularize but I have seen many girls in our York Assembly Rooms who, after spending a couple of winters in good society in Paris, might not be deemed inferior in aught to your so vaunted rivals . . .' [All the French world] sighed for Paris. The Parisians would tell her, 'Il n'ya que Paris – demenser en province c'est une autre chose' [There is only Paris – to live in the provinces is another thing]. Concluded my letter with an account of the fashions – which my aunt seemed, last night, to wonder at my being able to give so well, never dreaming of my noticing these matters so narrowly. A lady's dress always strikes me, if good or bad. In answer to 'Had I read the Memoirs of Madame de Genlis[20] or the Visconte d'Arlincourt's[21] 'Ipsiboe'?' I said 'No!' The very little time I had for reading in Paris was not given either to memoirs or romances; but I think the readers of the former talked more of Madame Campon[22] than Madame de Genlis; & those of the latter talked more of Sir Walter Scott & Lord Byron (translated into French – the veriest curiosity you ever saw) than anything else.'

Thursday 28 April

Went out at 7–50. Saw . . . Thomas Pearson. Told him, before Jackman & his son, I was sorry to find my uncle had one tenant who would do so unneighbourly, so mean and so unjust a thing as to refuse prosecuting & thus turn loose upon us 2 such young men as were taken stealing clothes at his clothes-hedge. He looked small. Said not much but – he knew best what money he could afford to throw away. I said his landlord would have been the 1st to subscribe. He said he had children of his own. Knew not what they might come to. I told him a light punishment might prevent a greater & keep them from the gallows – he knew, perhaps, what he had saved but not, perhaps, what he had lost.

Saturday 30 April

Mark Howarth came to speak to my uncle & sign his lease (from year to year). Read aloud the lease to him, then witnessed his having made his mark, a cross. [I] wrote his name for him & signed my own at full.

Friday 6 May

Went to the workmen again at 11–30. Took up 3 young oaks & cut down 6 trees (2 firs, 4 larches, all large) to clear the way for the new footpath & the steps up the wood.

Saturday 7 May

Found a letter . . . from Mrs Barlow (Paris) on my desk . . . [She] *will not have Mr Hancock, nor will she marry at all. Says that even* [if] *I was free from Mariana, I should be at liberty to choose whom I liked.* The de Boyves [at Place Vendôme] have 23 people in their house. It is now visited by the police,[23] an Hôtel garni. They are obliged to send in the names of all who go to & leave there . . . Religion said to be all the fashion now in France.[24] Charles X to be crowned at Rheims on the 29th of this month. All the fêtes & rejoicings to be at Paris.

Sunday 15 May

Gave Hotspur oatcake. From 7–40 to 9½, reading aloud to myself from p.42 to 50 (very carefully) vol. 1, Rousseau's Confessions. I read this work so attentively for the style's sake. Besides this, it is a singularly unique display of character . . . At 5, went downstairs. Read aloud the evening service. No sermon, having got a little cold but, above all, feeling my chest a little delicate. Yesterday & Friday morning, spat a very little blood & felt a soreness as if my chest had been rather strained. *I think, or fancy, it may arise from holding the yard wand to put my shoulders back, for five or more minutes every morning. For this is worse than my umbrella, which I used to substitute for it in Paris. I have lately felt a sensation as if my chest had been too much stretched open. I shall cease this plan a little. I had better have a round back than a delicate chest.*

Monday 16 May

Went out at 7 to the new footpath ... levelled the old footpath & the new ... While the men had their morning drinking & dinners, [I] pulled ivy off the trees in the wood. Then, as before, stood over & helped James Smith – staking off & binding this side of the path at the bottom of the wood. Cut down one hard tree. I think we have cut down about 8 before & 4 Scotch firs.

There were times in Anne's life when she felt the need to talk as freely as possible about her dilemma over Mariana Lawton and her need for a woman companion with whom she could share her life. The need to preserve Mariana's reputation as a respectable married woman severely limited the circle of people to whom Anne could confide her most intimate thoughts. Mariana's sisters were fully aware of the nature of Anne's relationship with Mariana. Anne's advances, and successes, with each of them left them in no doubt about the situation. Uncle James and Aunt Anne, at Shibden, seem to have been the recipients of Anne's less intimate confidences. It seems they were well aware that Anne would never marry and also of her burning desire to live with a woman of her own choice. Aunt Anne appears to have accepted that strong friendships existed between her niece and the various women who entered Anne's life. She lamented the emotional disturbance such liaisons caused Anne but, so far as one can tell, the possibility of a sexual relationship between Anne and her women friends was never touched upon in the conversations which took place between Anne and her aunt. No doubt both aunt and uncle drew their own conclusions about Anne's sex life. Certainly no word of censor ever seemed to have been spoken to her. It seems that they were typical dour, albeit good-hearted, Yorkshire people who believed in keeping their own counsel. They listened to Anne when she was emotionally upset and gave her a great deal of silent, sympathetic support. It is obvious that they were very fond of their niece and very dependent upon her strength and commonsense handling of those business affairs which now taxed them beyond their own failing strength. They were anxious for her to 'fix' on her life companion before they died, so that they could feel she was secure. Perhaps their own lives as bachelor and spinster brother and sister had posed sexual problems of their own, thus giving them a sympathetic attitude to their niece's dilemma. Certainly Uncle James was an erudite man whose library shelves bore witness to his worldliness in these matters. The rest can only be speculation. What is certain is that Anne always found ready listeners when she chose to confide in them, particularly in Aunt Anne.

Friday 20 May

Told my uncle & aunt, this evening, Mariana married Charles without caring a straw for him. She might have married better but the man was younger yet Charles would not die to please anyone [i.e. to leave Mariana free to marry someone younger or live with Anne]. *Mariana had owned, since her marriage, she would rather have lived with me in a coal-hole. Say I, it is all chance whether Mariana & I are together. Should I find anyone who would suit me better, & should Charles live, Mariana will lose me. But pity does a great deal with me in her favour. Heaven only knows how it will be.* [I] *said Maria Barlow had said any lady who knew what she was about might easily gull me, & I thought Mariana had done it a little. I often thought of this.*

Sunday 22 May

Long letter from Mrs Norcliffe, Langton ... 'The plan I mentioned to you about having ice ... was 1st tried at Mr Duncombe's at Duncombe Park, his ice-house having failed. You dig a hole in the ground, the shape of an egg & then, with an iron bar, make holes in the bottom to receive any water & at the proper season fill it with snow & ice as an ice-house & cover it with straw, something like our potato-pies. 3 served Mr Duncombe the summer & he had one left over for another year ... '

Thursday 26 May

A little before 9, a letter from Mrs Barlow, Paris ... Her aunt & cousin arrived on the 7th. *Beset her about Mr William Bell. He, too, is laying close siege. She feels consideration for him but her affection for me is more strongly marked than ever. She does indeed seem deeply attached to me. I must be serious in recommending her to marry Mr Bell or make up my mind to have her myself. Her letter affected me much. Her aunt & cousin admire my character. She has written to Mr Hancock in such a way as to leave him no hope. If she had a little more money I should not hesitate a moment but, alas, it would be a bad connection for me. But my heart is somewhat won upon.*

Wednesday 1 June

Sent off my letter to Mrs Barlow ... *Tho' delicately & affectionately, yet plainly and decidedly advise* [her] *to marry Mr William Bell. The connection would not be a prudent one for me. I must break it off & yet I feel, at intervals, now the letter is gone, as if I knew not how far I had thrown away happiness or not, for I begin to believe she really loves me, perhaps as much as she says & I know I should not hesitate if she had more money & better connections.*

Friday 3 June

Having asked Mrs Saltmarshe on Wednesday to give a message for me to Dr Kenny to ask him to come here at 11 this morning, he arrived at the time. I saw him for a few minutes in the hall. He was above an hour with my aunt. To bring on a fit of the gout would do her most good – but she had no constitution to work up. The illness a break up of the constitution. Not much to be done for her by medicine . . . He agreed with me she was worse now than when he saw her last. Weaker. I asked if a change of climate would do her good. Yes. Much more than medicine. This might renovate her – warm mineral baths. Buxton would do no good. The baths there too cold – would be too great a shock. Bath, for 6 weeks, would put her in a better state for going to the Continent – the south of France.

Thursday 9 June

Went to the workmen at 7–10. Found them all there. Hurried them on to prepare for the magistrates coming to view the footpath at 11. Got the 13 topmost steps & the whole concern to look very decent. Our attorney, Mr Parker, came about 10½. Told him that if Mr L. Alexander, after giving notice to oppose us, really should do so, we should build a row of cottages close up to his garden wall at Belvidere . . . George had gone to the Stag's Head, Mytholm, in full dress to be ready to wait upon the magistrates . . . About 1, Mr Parker came to say Messrs Stocks & Bairstow [the magistrates] had viewed the footpath & were very well satisfied with it & seemed to think my uncle need not fear gaining his point . . . [I] went again to the workmen at 2. Gave Jackman 13/6, that is 9d each for 18 men . . . ale now being 3d a pint, the men would have 3 pints each, were to leave at 5 o'clock & seemed all highly pleased.

Thursday 16 June

Found a letter on my desk from Mrs Barlow ... An hour reading my letter & went down to breakfast at 11–20. Staid talking to my uncle & aunt ... Had told them of my having heard from Mrs Barlow & mentioned the real state of the case between us very honestly. *They both seemed very well inclined towards her. Were I really wishful to have her I am sure they would throw no obstacle in the way. On the contrary, they appear much in her favour. I told them she had four hundred a year & my aunt & I agreed this evening she might be better for me with this than Mariana with five hundred. But tho' I speak most highly of Mrs Barlow & that it would be my own fault if I was not happy with her, yet* [I] *owned I was very odd & perhaps I should, after all, like a person with more éclat about her. My aunt had talked my uncle over while I left them. They would like to see how & with whom they are likely to leave me. My aunt is for Mrs Barlow & I am sure I could have her here if I chose. But, alas, I feel it would not do* ... From about two to near five wrote 2/3pp, small & close to Mrs Barlow. My *own manner of writing affected me & I shed many tears. Yet, still, I know not how it is, there is always my old, lurking thought she wants to catch me & that it would be unsafe to take her till I have seen her home & friends in Guernsey & know more about her. From the very first I have fancied her hurrying me into the thing – see her first mention of our living together to her aunt. And even now the idea occurs to me of Mr Bell's being made a means of making me engage myself to her. How is it I have always had such a presentiment of suspicion towards her? Be as it may, I will not entangle myself & my letter shall urge her marriage in such a manner as shall be calculated to satisfy all parties. I shall keep this first draught* [sic] *as the copy of what I write. I like her more now than I did in Paris, yet I am determined to be cautious. I may hereafter choose better. I seem to have quietly made up my mind to give up Mariana. Let me keep free a while & look about me.*

Sunday 19 June

Read over all I had written to Mrs Barlow . . . The letter will do very well. I have shed many tears over it. I know not how it is, my own style affects me. Well may she feel it. Such beautiful sentimentality will probably not be addressed to her by anybody.

Thursday 14 July

Off in the gig at 8½ to Bradford. Got to the Sun Inn in 1 hour, 35 minutes. Saw Messrs Wiglesworth & Parker [Anne's attorneys] immediately, who told me Mr Alexander had just withdrawn his appeal [against the new footpath]. His son, Mr Edward Alexander, said he had not got his brief ready & Mr Lister had made a good road. Mr Parker asked why he had not withdrawn the appeal last night. It seemed they wished to put us to all the expense – they saying we had put them to expense before . . . Mr Parker called for me at 11 & we went together to the Sessions room. 'Tis the end of the Cloth Hall[25] fitted up for the purpose – too low & small. Sat at the end of the magistrates' box, heard the juries called. Near 12 before the magistrates came . . . the chairman said a few words of charge to the Grand Jury, then left his friend, Mr Dealtry, to address them on the subject of the workmen who have turned out [gone on strike] for wages. Spoke provincially & sometimes rather hesitatingly but the sense was good. Wished the grand jury to use their influence in spreading it abroad that the men had no right to intimidate those who were willing to return to their work & if they did, the magistrates would take it up – & the masters ought not to pay their men at public houses, or refuse them change & then compel them to seek it at public houses, which was a temptation to drink, & the whole of a man's wages were often drunk before he returned to his work. Nor ought the master to let small houses to people, who kept shops [in the houses?] &

oblige his workmen to buy all they wanted at these shops & be imposed upon in the price. Only one felon – found with a forged note in his possession – & he acquitted. Then Mr Maude, at 12½, brought forward our footpath business. He told Mr Edward Alexander his manner of proceeding had not been very candid, to which Mr Alexander seemed to acknowledge (I could not hear what he said) that they had put us to all the expense they could for the reason above given. However, the appeal being withdrawn, the order was ordered to be & we had gained our point in less than 5 minutes . . . The court being hot & crowded & being anxious to get home, left the court at 12¾. Everybody at the Sun Inn so busy (even the stairs crowded with a parcel of witnesses that were being drilled) went myself to seek George at the Bowling Green Inn, where all our witnesses were. Saw 3 of them. Ordered them to have everything good to eat and drink & plenty of it. Mr Wiglesworth just came in & said he would take care of them. Off from Bradford at 1½ & got home in 1 hour, 35 minutes, including a moment's stop at Northgate [where her father & sister were living at the time] while George ran in to say we had won the day.

Thursday 28 July

At 8–20, off in the gig to Lightcliffe. Stopt 2 or 3 minutes en passant at Mitholm. Sent for Jonathan Mallinson to speak to & told him my uncle would not allow him to sell off [surplus produce, at a profit to himself, from the land he farmed, which was rented from the Listers]. That if he had not cattle enough to consume his produce, he had too much land & my uncle would let it to someone. The man declared he had not sold off any part of the crop of his Yew Trees land but had conserved it all. But at last he owned he had sold off part of the crop of his land at Mitholm. [I] said there would be an end put to this selling-off system with all the tenants & Jonathan promised fair not to sell off without his landlord's leave, who would not give it without assurance of an equivalent quantity of manure being bought on.

---

1. . . . mild reform. – see p 781 of *The Making of the English Working Class* by E P Thompson.
2. *Bread St* – Formerly the site of the bread market in medieval London, the Mermaid Tavern (c1411–1666), and Saddler's Hall (c1454–1641). John Milton was born in Bread St at the Sign of the Spreadeagle in 1608. The street was burnt in the Great Fire of London in 1666 and is now occupied by a shopping centre which opened in 2010.
3. Milk St – Once the site of London's medieval milk market, St Mary Magdalene's Church was built here in the twelfth century and Sir Thomas More was born here in 1478. This street also suffered great damage in the Great Fire of 1666.
4. Molière's M. Porceaugnac – Molière (1622–1673) wrote this play, one of his best, in 1669, for Louis XIV at Chambord. Louis XIV gave his patronage and protection to certain writers, notably Molière and Racine, so long as they praised him in their works.
5. Judge Bradshaw – Judge Bradshaw (1602–1659) presided over the court that condemned Charles I to death in January 1649.
6. Freischuts – or *The Freeshooter*, an opera by German composer Von Weber (1786–1826), based on the German folktale of a legendary marksman who is given seven bullets by the Devil. Six of them will hit targets chosen by the marksman but the seventh is reserved for a target of the Devil's choice.
7. 'Abon Hassan' – A musical drama or one-act opera, also by Von Weber, about a young merchant of Baghdad, taken from a story called 'The Sleeper Awakened' in the *Arabian Nights*.
8. Von Weber – (1786–1826). Carl Maria Friedrich Ernst, Baron. German composer and opera director. His work was important during the transition from Classical to Romantic music in that it furthered the ideals of Romanticism, which place the heart's impulses above the head's rationalism.
9. Parish church – The Church of St John the Baptist, Church St, Halifax, which dates from the early twelfth century. Possibly there was also an earlier Saxon church on the same site. The greater part

of the existing church was built c1274–1314, when Halifax gained its first vicar, a man called Ingelard Tubard.

10. Fulling mills – The process of fulling (also called milling) was that of cleansing and thickening cloth by beating and washing with soap or fuller's earth.
11. Daniel Defoe – (1660–1731) English journalist and novelist, author of *Robinson Crusoe* and *Moll Flanders*. For his excellent description of Halifax and the industriousness of its population in the early eighteenth century, see pp 598–610 of his book *A Tour Thro' the Whole Island of Great Britain* vol II, first published in 1725.
12 Piece Hall – Built on a site known as Talbot Close, the Piece Hall was opened on 1st January 1779. It is a unique cloth hall, built specifically for the buying and selling of cloth pieces which were manufactured by the small industries in and around Halifax. The design of the Piece Hall is taken from Roman Classical architecture, adapted by a Liverpool architect of the day, John Hope. In Anne's time, Halifax's cloth trade was being overtaken by that of Bradford and the Piece Hall was used less for its original purpose and more for general public events, e.g. balloon ascents, celebratory fireworks displays and as a platform for political orators. Today it houses museums, craft shops and a busy weekend market. The uniqueness of its architecture makes it a great tourist attraction.
13. Republican sentiment – The years 1791–2 saw the publication of Tom Paine's *Rights of Man* and in Halifax a group of Paineite radicals met at the Crispin Inn, near the parish church. Their leader was one John Baines, a Halifax hatter, well-known for his republican views. (See pp 644–645 of E P Thompson's *The Making of the English Working Class*.)
14. The Luddite movement ... around Halifax ... – '... The Luddites had caused much alarm in these parts just before you left us ...' Letter from Anne Lister (senior) to her nephew, Samuel Lister, dated Shibden Hall, 16th Jan 1813. (Ref SH:7/LL/358, Calderdale Archives.) See also ref HT.Q42–74 (pp 101–105), Calderdale Reference Library, for an account of Luddite activities in and around Halifax. The Luddite attack on Rawfolds Mill in neighbouring Huddersfield was used by Charlotte Brontë in her novel *Shirley* (1849).
15. Voting rights – At this time (1825) the franchise was restricted to the forty shilling freeholder. Even after the passing of the Reform Act in 1832, when Halifax was made a borough and could return two

members to Parliament, the electorate of Halifax numbered less than 4%. The extension of the franchise still excluded most working men.

16. Halifax gibbet – The gibbet was used in Halifax for a period of almost four centuries, from the date of its first known victim, in 1286, to what is thought to be its last, in 1650. Halifax was the last place to relinquish the use of the gibbet – a fact which caused its inclusion in the old saying of vagrants: 'From Hell, Hull and Halifax, may the good Lord deliver us'. For a fuller treatment of this subject, see *Halifax and its Gibbet Law* by S Midgley and *Black Glooms the Gibbet* by A Wolfenden (1976).
17. The diary of Mrs William Rawson – The extracts here are taken from the Halifax Antiquarian Society *Transactions* (1958), pp 29–50. Mrs Rawson (1745–1837), *née* Elizabeth Threlkeld, was a remarkable woman whose impact on the Halifax social scene was impressive. An interesting glimpse of her is given in the story of how she took the young Dorothy Wordsworth into her Halifax home for a period of nine years, from 1778–1787, when Dorothy's mother, who was cousin to Mrs Rawson, died. (See pp 3–14 of *Dorothy Wordsworth* by Robert Gittings and Jo Manton. Oxford University Press 1988.)
18. Anne . . . journal. – See *The Secret Diaries of Miss Anne Lister: I Know My Own Heart* (Volume One), pp 90–91, 122–123, 127, 254.
19. See pp 68–69, *Social and Political Life in Halifax, Fifty Years Ago: Some Extracts from the Diary of a Halifax Lady*. Newspaper Cuttings Book (vol 2). Compiled by T Turner. (Ref Q070. TUR. Calderdale Reference Library.)
20. Memoirs of Madame de Genlis – Felicité du Crest de Saint Aubin, Comtesse de Genlis (1764–1830), French novelist and educator. Tutor to Louis-Philippe (who became king of the French in 1830) and mistress of his father. Both her husband and her lover were guillotined during the Revolution. She was exiled from France for seven years but Napoleon allowed her back in 1800. She became a successful writer, attempting to live down her scandalous past by writing religious works.
21. Viscount d'Arlincourt – (1788–1856). Born into a wealthy family of tax farmers, the title of viscount had no justification in fact. From being an ardent Bonapartist, d'Arlincourt became an ardent royalist under the Restoration. He translated the works of Sir Walter Scott and also wrote novels. *Ipsiboe* (1823) was a French satire about a

woman of that name who was an early 'bluestocking'. She flouted convention by giving birth to an illegitimate child. D'Arlincourt's most famous novel is *Le Solitaire* (1821), in which a man pretends to be a ghost.

22. Madame Campon – Jean-Louise-Henriette Berthollet, *née* Genet (1752–1822), former woman-of-the-Bedchamber to Marie Antoinette. During the Reign of Terror (September 1793 to July 1794), she left Paris and went to live in the country. In 1794, she returned and opened a highly successful school for girls in the old Hôtel de Noailles in Saint Germain. Her works, *Memoires sur la Vie Privée de la Reine Marie Antoinette* and *Correspondance avec la Reine Hortense*, were published in Paris after her death. She was helpful to Napoleon during his reign by advising him on points of étiquette at Versailles and providing him with skilled servants who had served under the Old Regime.
23. '... visited by the police' – an indication of the increasing efficiency of police under the reactionary regime of Charles X.
24. 'Religion said to be all the fashion now in France ...' – Charles X's reactionary rule, which eventually brought him down in 1830, included the restoration of the influence and prestige of the Catholic Church. This policy and the alleged power of the Jesuits greatly alarmed the now secularised bourgeois and lower classes of Paris. Maria Barlow is referring to the fact that many ambitious people were following the king's example and showing an enthusiasm for religion.
25. Cloth Hall – This would be the Bradford Piece Hall, which has been described as an 'excellent mart for stuff goods'. It measured 144 feet long by 36 feet broad and was divided into two apartments – an upper and a lower chamber. Occasionally it served as a court house and General Quarter Sessions of Peace were held there.

Taking the Waters at Buxton Spa

During the months following her arrival home from Paris, Anne had become increasingly worried about her aunt's state of health. Crippled with rheumatism and in great pain, Aunt Anne had become increasingly immobile. Following the advice of the Halifax medical men, Dr Kenny and Mr Sunderland, Anne had arranged to take a trip to Buxton in Derbyshire, to enable her aunt to 'take the waters' there in an attempt to alleviate her condition. Anne also decided that she herself might well benefit from the treatment. On 4th August 1825, Anne and her aunt, accompanied by their manservant, George Playforth, and their maid, Elizabeth Wilkes Cordingley, arrived at the Great Hotel, Buxton[1] where they were to spend the next seven weeks attending to their health.

Their stay there began on a note of gloom. The weather was unceasingly rainy and they knew no-one there. Anne was conscious that in dress and entourage they could not by any means compete with the best in society. She resigned herself to a quiet period of rest and medical treatment with only her ageing, invalid aunt for company. She was, in addition, made miserably sentimental by the music of the military band playing outside the hotel almost every day. Her aunt's illness, the poor weather and the lack of a loving companion with whom she could share her days and nights all served to deepen Anne's sense of solitariness and deprivation. We find her writing to a friend, Miss MacLean, from 'this most rainy, windwhistling and dreary of places, Buxton . . . ' about her need for a woman companion:

> '. . . Some companion I must have. I feel the want grow daily more & more into a strong necessity . . .'
>
> (Tuesday 9 August 1825)

As usual, though, Anne's strong spirit salvaged what it could from the experience. During the day she was an interested, albeit detached, observer of the passing social scene, writing up anything of interest in her journal. She mapped out a programme of solitary walking and driving out in the gig to places of interest around Buxton. She took out a month's subscription at the local library and embarked on long reading sessions, choosing amusing books to read aloud to her aunt in the evenings and more serious books for her own private reading. The receiving of and answering letters, and the supervising her aunt's medical treatment as well as arranging her own, were fitted into her daily routine. Anne's days were filled with constructive activity, her evenings quietly occupied with reading and writing, and she ate and drank well and slept soundly at night.

However, in contrast to the full cultural and sexual life she had led in Paris, and the succeeding months of involved physical work overseeing the workmen at Shibden, the enforced period of relative leisure at Buxton was tedious to Anne. It also gave her perhaps too much time for reflection which in turn led her into bouts of melancholy.

During the long evenings spent reading and talking to her aunt, she drew the older woman into her confidence, discussing the merits and demerits of both Mariana Lawton and Maria Barlow as possible life companions. Letters came to Buxton from both women and both declared their undying love for Anne. She found herself wavering between the two. On receiving a letter from Mariana, she writes:

> '… For the moment I thought more of Mariana & less seriously of Mrs Barlow. Too likely to question if Mrs Barlow has importance enough for me – if she thinks & calculates my fortune, etc., or if she loves me so much for myself alone. This evening relapsed into my carelessness towards Mariana & tenderness towards Mrs Barlow …'
>
> (Thursday 18 August 1825)

Meanwhile, unaware for the moment of any alleviation of the tedium, Anne provided a fascinating insight into the daily routine at the Buxton Spa by her regular entries in her journal.

Friday 5 August

Good lodging room & comfortable bed & slept well last night. My aunt, too, had a better night. *Thought I to myself at breakfast, 'What a dull lounge this will be if I do not get to know somebody.' What should I do without the gig. My poor aunt talking over her complaints, how she sleeps, etc., is not exhilarating – but I shall fend for myself somehow by & by* … My aunt & I went into dinner at 5–10. 14 or 15 of us. Mr & Mrs Christopher Wilson at table. Going away tomorrow. Mr Wilson seems a quiet sort of person. Mrs Wilson one of those rattling, good sort of persons whose gentility would be very questionable if one did not know who she was. She hardly looks as good as she should be. Her manner seems odd to a stranger. However, she offered my aunt & me some of her gingerbread & I took a little. Good dinner. Good mock turtle soup. Good trout & excellent mutton – a saddle and a leg & a loin together in one, roasted. It was just 6–20 as we came out of the dining-room. Sat on the sofa talking to my aunt till 8, having sent for Mr Flint, the apothecary. He came & staid perhaps 10 minutes or ¼ hour. A very vulgar man but my aunt was pleased we had sent for him & we hope he will do her good. He had just sent her an aperient draught & will order about her bath tomorrow. She is not to stay [in] more than 6 minutes ... Said I intended to bathe. How long should I stay in, who was not an invalid? ¼ hour. On saying I had been used to stay in an hour, he wondered that I should have tried my constitution so much. Did it not weaken me very much? I might drink the waters, only should take care of the state of my bowels. Wrote the last 15 lines. *Desperately dull. My aunt thought I was low this morning. Say I am anxious about her recovery but, in fact, if times don't mend here, I shall be half-stupefied. I see not much chance of having anybody to speak to but my aunt. I must drive out.*

Saturday 6 August

I set off (at 10) in the gig to Bakewell. Good road. The first mile or 2 thro' a ravine, the river Wye, which has its source in Buxton, running all along the bottom ... Bakewell much improved of late. Belongs almost entirely to the Duke of Rutland,[2] who has built an excellent new inn – the Rutland Arms – a very nice house to dine or stay all night at ... Found on the table at the inn (in no. 9, a very nice small parlour with a lodging opening into it), among several other books, Rhode's Peak Scenery, in 4, I think, thin 4to vols, with plates. Read there the account of Bakewell church, Haddon Hall, etc. Mrs Radcliffe (a native of Derbyshire) fond of the latter. Much there & there imagined much of the finest scenery in her 'Mysteries of Udolpho'.[3] ... The Wye runs along this vale (of Haddon). The Duke of Rutland generally comes down in the shooting season (not to Haddon

Hall) but a shooting box he has 4 miles from Bakewell. Ought to have seen the baths there kept by Mr White Watson,[4] a scientific man who has a good collection of minerals, but I had not time. Must stop on our way to Chatsworth. Only an hour at Bakewell & got back here in 2 hrs, 5 mins – 12 miles ... *Very dull today but my drive did me good. I shall get used to this sort of thing by & by* ... Came up to bed at 9–50. Read from pp 55 to 65, vol. 1. Rousseau's Confessions.

Sunday 7 August

Went to church at 10–50 ... The church well-fitted. Hot. Very neat, modern church.[5] Handsome, stone-faced walls within, not covered – not spoilt with any sort of wash. Got back at 1. At 1–10 set off walking. Went along the Crescent & old town of Buxton & a little way along the Derby road. Sauntered slowly & got back at 2. Sat talking to my aunt ¾ hour *then went to have Cordingley curl & pinch my hair & then slept in my chair till 4* ... Tea at 8. Read aloud to my aunt the 1st 31pp of Moore's Buxton & Castleton guide.

Monday 8 August

Tea at 8. A band of military music began to play in front of the Crescent & continued to play till about 9. My aunt, looking out of the window, saw the rooms at St Anne's[6] where she & my aunt Martha were this time (this very day, 8th August) 16 years ago, when the band played & my aunt Martha was so ill she could scarce bear it. The remembrance was so strong my aunt burst into tears & cried some time. *I could have shed tears at first but my aunt's crying prevented me. I sat & never uttered, thinking of Maria Barlow. The last time I had heard military music was with her in Paris. My heart turned towards her. I felt as if I could write instantly, 'Maria, live for me. Do not marry. Come what may, I will be yours.' A momentary thought of Mariana came. Then came the recollection of Blackstone Edge*[7] *& I said, 'I am or I am not throwing away my happiness in giving up Maria Barlow.' If I knew her family, her character, in Guernsey & found all right, should I not take her? Surely her attachment to me must be real & disinterested. But what could we do with Jane?*

Tuesday 9 August

At 2–30 went out to the library. Looked over the catalogue. Subscribed for a month. Sauntered to the top of St Anne's Cliff & walked about there & came in at 3½ . . . 3 Buxton guides came from Moore's & the 2 first vols of Amélie Mansfield.[8] Looked over the Buxton guides & chose one. Tea at 8. Then read aloud to my aunt the first 74pp, vol. 1, 'Saying & Doings'.[9] Excellent. Know not when I have laughed so much or so heartily. We both laughed. Came up to bed at 9–35. Sat up reading the first 79pp. & several pp. at the end, of Amélie Mansfield. The story interesting. How poor the language after that of Rousseau! This struck me instantly. I will keep to Rousseau to form my French style. How he spoils me for such language as Mme Cottin.[10]

Wednesday 10 August

Letter from Mariana (Lawton) about 1. *Too much interested in my book* [*Amélie Mansfield*] *to leave it off. Cried over it almost all the time. Read my letter just before dressing for dinner.* Mariana proposes coming over for a day. If the journey is too long (coming & returning), hopes to get a bed at Clayton's lodgings. Once thought of not telling me – then thought it best to tell me lest, as her coming was against my wish, I should frown too severely on her disobedience . . . *Told my aunt the contents of Mariana's pages then thought no more of them till the evening when the music played. Then Maria Barlow & Mariana jostled together in my thoughts. Somehow Maria Barlow is uppermost yet I shall tell Mariana we shall be glad to see her. I shall offer her half my bed.*

Thursday 11 August

Wrote 3pp & the ends of a letter to Mariana (Lawton) & sent it after dinner ... [Anne wrote] '... You were quite right to mention the thought of coming over or you might not have found me at home. My aunt would have been delighted to see you & I should have regretted every moment of your society that I had so foolishly lost ... You will be shocked to see me so much tanned. Should you stay all night, your thought of getting a bed at Clayton's lodgings rather surprised me. Should you come alone, you will find my room very comfortable ...'

Friday 12 August

Large party today ... Mrs Fitzherbert[11], (the Mrs Fitzherbert) & her sister, Mrs Smith[12] & one or two more. All in very neat undress morning gowns. Mrs Fitzherbert herself evidently as she walked out – in a large leghorn bonnet. In leaving the room got a full look at her en passant. A very handsome woman for her age, about 62? How strikingly handsome she must have been in days of yore. His present majesty had a good choice as far as beauty was concerned. Her complexion must have been very good. Rather aquiline nose. Dark blue [?] eyes. Good countenance. Very handsome. I have thought of her ever since.

Tuesday 16 August

The band began to play about 12 for above an hour. Musing & listening, *thinking of Maria Barlow & how much more I become attached to her* ... At 4, Cordingley brought me a letter from Maria Barlow ... *chiefly on indifferent subjects, except the first two pages. These very affectionate. Cannot bear the thought of my fancying she meant to reproach me. 'Excuse my lament.'* [Mrs Barlow writes] *'Sometimes it will break forth but if you could see my heart you could see no reproach. The spirit of love is all it wishes to breathe against you. Tell me you think this & remove this reproach from me.' She says before in her first page, 'Had I no Jane, a different path would I pursue. To hide myself from the world is what my soul sighs for. If a voice gone by, and duty, did not rouse me, mere maternal affection could not induce me to resume a place in society where happiness & I are severed forever. My heart, soul & spirit have been engaged in such affection as aught else would be tasteless & joyless. For my child only do I regret this apathy. For myself, I love to indulge it & to be quite alone is my greatest comfort, or would be, for her lessons perpetually call on me for my exertions which, in my present mind, I find a great bore. It costs me much to shake off my present thoughts. It is in vain I call myself continually to confess how wicked I am. I pray Heaven no mortal will offer to disturb this moody grief. In some hour of despair I may give my hand; be taken to the altar as an automatum; awake to wretchedness & have not only my own misery but another's to sigh over. Mr Bell's appearance is not what I lament. That matter could be settled. Difficulties & obstacles lie in another quarter for some all-wise & good purpose we mortals cannot foresee.' She concludes with, 'I hope & believe you will take my reproach from me. You may command silence but to bid me cease to love you is vain & surely it will harm no one. Divided as we are doomed to be, you may be happy in making others so & those who are blessed with your friendship & affection can never fail to be so. I may love you to the latest breath of my existence. That privilege cannot be taken from me, & that every blessing may attend you will be the often offered prayer of C.M.B.'* . . . Tea at 8. Talked all the evening about Mrs Barlow or Mariana. *Very candidly about both. Said if Mrs Barlow knew me well, she would refuse Mr Bell at all hazard & then she would certainly gain me at last. Mentioned her sentence that she might perhaps 'be led to the altar as an automatum', etc. Said I knew not what I should feel on seeing Mariana but if I knew I should never see her again, assured of her being well & happy, I should get over it without much trouble.*

But I, myself, could not calculate the effect of her presence now . . . I have even, since coming to bed, thought of ambition & said, 'Let her accept Mr Bell.' Alas, her letter arouses my affection. I love & can almost forget all else.

Sunday 21 August

Dr Scudamore paid my aunt his 4th visit today. Says he hopes to cure her. She has no gout – it is rheumatism. She was very weak this morning & would not dine in public.

Tuesday 23 August

On going into our parlour, Cordingley put into my hand a letter from Maria Barlow (Paris). [I] wondered what might be the matter. Opened it in trembling. *Was she beside herself when she wrote the first two pages? I sacrifice her happiness to my affection for Mariana & it is my heart that does it without commiseration. Had Mariana been my uncle's doing* [i.e. if outside pressure had been brought to bear upon Anne to retain Mariana in her life], *she could have borne it. 'Is it you who have set this rankling* [thorn?] *in my bosom forever? I may be hurt at the fate of my regard but you are not to blame. You but follow the fashion of the day & you unfortunately met with one not suited to it. In this the fault lies not more with one than the other. There is but one thing which stabs me to the heart's core – your renouncement of me without one word of pity & the incense raised to my happy rival for fear of her sorrow, without one thought of me. My injured feelings complain but of this one thing – this one act. I do doubt you & care not whether I do, when I find all is to be sacrificed to your sorrow for this friend.' Read this letter – my aunt in the room – & the last two pages twice. We talked of it all the evening but I said nothing but that I thought she would not have Mr Bell, hinting she was too much attached & saying I was to blame. I had left no stone unturned to make myself agreeable to her & I had indeed been all in fault. In silence I thought to myself, somehow I cannot get rid of the idea of her wanting to catch me . . . Has she ever used Mr Bell's name to spur me on? Surely she had hopes of gaining me? Is it not witnessed by the manner in which she takes her present despair? If she is so cool to Mr Bell will he ever offer to her again? But no more . . .* Came up to bed at 10–20 . . . I have just reread her letter . . . 'Nothing I can do for you is a trouble. Command me at all times & believe you will ever find me a most sincere, affectionate & devoted friend.' *This sentence moved me more than all the rest. The tear is starting in my eyes. Then read over the copy of my own last letter & wrote the rough draft of some empassioned lines, obscurely asking her, or hinting at her being my mistress, which took me till three & a quarter.*

Wednesday 24 August

My aunt went out in the gig at 11. I came upstairs . . . *Wrote three pages of a letter to Mrs Barlow, taking merely a few lines from the empassioned style of what I wrote last night. Kind & affectionate & moving . . . Insist that nothing can be done so long as my family circumstances remain as they are at present & I am bound in honour, etc., not to prevent her accepting Mr Bell by holding out a hope which it is still possible might be delusive. 'Must I then dare to ask if there be nothing you would refuse me? Will you take me, Maria, so long as one fold of uncertainty clings around me?' A distant, obscure question, would she be my mistress? Will she so understand it?*

Saturday 27 August

Went upstairs at 3. *Combed my head with a small tooth comb & brushed & dressed it for dinner.* Dinner at 5–10. *Talked a good deal, as usual, to Mr Picart. Caught Mrs Hartley's eyes looking at us. It struck me she might fancy me making up to him. The thought afterwards annoyed me for a moment. I have a wife & mistress of my own. How I seem to let myself down in talking pretty. I don't like dining in such public & all this thraldom . . .* Mrs Locke began to rub my aunt's loins at 8 this morning, for 1 hour, 25 minutes & came again for an hour at 6½ this evening. Tea at 8.

Tuesday 30 August

At 12¼, went out & walked 1½ hour along the front of St Anne's Cliff during the hour the band [played]. Afterwards walked on the top. Talked to my aunt a little. Went upstairs at 2. ½ sheet from Mariana – dated yesterday morning – to say she will be here today for 10 days, Mr Simmons having bled & blistered her & said the Buxton baths would be of service to her. Perhaps Miss Pattison [Mariana's friend at Lawton] will come with her but can only stay till tomorrow. *This note rather discomposed the quiet of my nerves for, after all, perhaps I know not whether I do not like her better than I have lately thought. She has been unwell it seems. Perhaps from fretting about me. Every carriage startled me & I got up to look, having first put on my new leather shoes & my pelerine to hide the tumbled frill of my handkerchief* ... Fidgetting now downstairs, now upstairs. Anxiously listening to every noise & looking for Mariana's carriage. Tea at 8¼. Still no Mariana. At 9, gave her up. Sent for George. Ordered the gig to be ready at 6 in the morning to go to Castleton.

Mariana arrived the day after and remained with Anne and her aunt for the rest of their stay in Buxton. The time spent there together was a physically and psychologically important period in the lives of the two women.

---

1. The Great Hotel – Built in 1784 by John Carr, the York architect, the Great Hotel formed the east wing of the Crescent. In the twentieth century it was converted for use as a clinic and geriatric annexe to

the Devonshire Hospital. In 1970 it came into use as a library and council offices.

2. The Duke of Rutland – John Henry (Manners), (1778–1857). He was Lord-Lieutenant of Leicestershire from 1799 until his death.
3. Mrs Radcliffe ... 'The Mysteries of Udolpho' – Mrs Radcliffe (1764–1823) was an important figure amongst the Gothic novelists of the Romantic period of English literature. Her novel *The Mysteries of Udolpho* (1794) is a typical example of the Romantic sensibility of that time.
4. Mr White Watson – White Watson FRS (1760–1835), a well-known geologist. Watson kept a museum shop where he sold fossils and minerals, in addition to working as a sculptor and lecturing on geology. In 1795, he was elected a fellow of the Linnean Society. In 1811 he published *A Delineation of the Strata of Derbyshire*, which was one of the first comprehensive works on the geology of Derbyshire. Watson is most famous for his work as a geologist.
5. Church – St John's Church, completed in 1811. This building was the last of the 5th Duke of Devonshire's improvements at Buxton. Its consecration in 1812 marked the closure of the old St Anne's Church in High Buxton.
6. St Anne's – Begun in 1780 and finally completed in 1789, this hotel formed the west wing of the Crescent, placing it directly opposite the Great Hotel in the east wing. The centre of the Crescent was originally the Duke of Devonshire's town house but, in 1804, he ceased to use it and it became the Centre Hotel. It is now a five-star spa hotel. See www.buxtoncrescent.com
7. Blackstone Edge – A moorland point between Yorkshire and Lancashire on what is now the A58 route over the Pennines. Anne here refers to a dramatic incident between herself and Mariana Lawton, which took place at this point. Anne, with a lover's impatience to see the beloved, decided to throw decorum aside and walk out to the isolated inn on the moors from which vantage point she could get the first glimpse of the coach bringing Mariana over from Lancashire to Yorkshire. She recounts the events in her journal as follows:

   '... I spied the carriage winding up the hill. It was a nameless thrill that banished every thought but of Mariana, and every feeling but of fearful hope. It was just 11–50 as I reached the carriage, having walked about 10½ miles in 3 hours, 10 minutes, i.e. at the rate of a mile in 18 minutes to the very top of Blackstone Edge. Unconscious of any sensation but pleasure at the sight of Mariana who, with Lou [her sister], had been dozing, one in each corner of the carriage, the astonished, staring eyes of the man and maid behind and of the post-boys walking by the horses were lost to me and, in too hastily taking each step of the carriage and stretching over the pile of dressing-boxes, etc., that should have stopped such eager ingress, I unluckily seemed to Mariana to have taken 3 steps at once. I had still more unluckily exclaimed, while the petrified people were bungling about the steps, that I had walked all the way from Shibden. What with exclamation and with stride, the shock so completely wrapt round Mariana's heart it left no avenue to any other feeling than joy that her friend, Miss Pattison, was not there! *She would have been astonished and Mariana horror-struck. Why did I say I had walked from Shibden? Never saw John's* [Mariana's manservant] *eyes so round with astonishment; the postboys, too; and how fast I talked!* [She had] *thought to have met me at Halifax. Why did I come so far? Why walk? Why not come in the gig?* I did talk fast. My words flew from me as though disdaining to touch on utterance. I expected them an hour earlier. Must either walk forwards or stop at an alehouse or cottage, when the suspense and anxiety of waiting would have been insupportable. The gig horse was taking diuretics. *But the poisoned arrow had struck my heart and Mariana's words of meeting welcome had fallen like some huge iceberg on my breast.* In vain the assurance of my talking slower when agitation had gone by. In vain the endeavour to excuse myself; to say I was neither really become ungentle in my manners, nor at all changed since she had seen me last. *In vain the gentle reproach that she was unused to me and had forgotten me and that this sort of reception was, at the best, unwelcome . . . The agitation of my inmost soul was met, not with any female weakness of sympathy but with the stronger mien of shocked astonishment . . . I felt – yes – unutterable things . . .*' (Tuesday 19 August, 1823.)

For a fuller account of Anne's reactions to this event, see pp 300–308 of the first volume of diaries: *The Secret Diaries of Miss Anne Lister: I Know My Own Heart*. The incident was instrumental in effecting a change of feeling, on Anne's part, towards Mariana.

8. Amélie Mansfield – A novel by Mme Cottin (see note 10 of this chapter).

9. 'Sayings and Doings' – by Theodore Hook (1788–1841), a popular English novelist whose early nineteenth century works presented descriptions of fashionable English life of the day to his readers. *Sayings and Doings* was a collection of tales based on proverbs put into fashionable setting. It became so popular that his original plan of three volumes had increased to nine by 1828.
10. Mme Cottin – Marie-Sophie (1770–1807), married Jean-Paul-Maire Cottin, of an aristocratic family, in 1789. He died in 1793. She turned to writing despite the fact that she was uneducated and barely able to spell. Her vivid imagination and romantic sensibility made up the deficit. Her greatest successes were *Claire d'Albe* (1799) and *Amélie Mansfield* (1803).
11. Mrs Fitzherbert – Maria Anne *née* Smythe (1756–1837), first wife of George IV, whom he married secretly, in 1785, when he was Prince of Wales. Under the Royal Marriage Act of 1772, the marriage was deemed illegal, as he had not gained the king's consent to the marriage. The fact that she was a Catholic also told against the marriage. Although the Pope decreed the marriage valid, English law did not recognise it as such and George married his cousin, Caroline of Brunswick. It was a loveless marriage and when George IV was on his deathbed, it was revealed that he had worn a miniature portrait of Mrs Fitzherbert around his neck.
12. Mrs Smith – This, in fact, was most likely Mary Ann Smythe. She was, officially, Mrs Fitzherbert's niece, the daughter of her brother, John. Gossip abounded, however, to the effect that Mary Ann Smythe was, in fact, Mrs Fitzherbert's daughter from her marriage to the Prince of Wales (George IV). There was also reputed to be a second daughter, whom Mrs Fitzherbert again passed off as her niece.

'What Am I?'

Part of Anne's propensity in her more mature years for flirtations with other women had stemmed from the realisation that Mariana was becoming increasingly settled in her Cheshire lifestyle. This had not been part of their original plan. The time between Mariana's marriage and the anticipated premature death of Charles was to have been a test of endurance, of strength – a trial of their love – from which they would emerge more closely committed to each other in the face of their ordeal of separation. What, in fact, had happened was that Mariana had become socially respectable, accepted by the comfortable Cheshire circle within which she moved. She appeared content with her domestic pursuits. Charles spent frequent periods away from Lawton Hall, so she was used to enjoying relative freedom, and during the periods he was at home he made few sexual demands on her. She was, therefore, quite content or had appeared so.

Two things happened which served to alter Mariana's complacency about her married state and brought her back to seek a renewal of love and commitment between Anne and herself. One was the dawning realisation that she was likely to remain childless. Ten years of marital intercourse, however intermittent, had not produced an heir to the Lawton estate. Charles Lawton's second marriage seemed likely to be as barren of children as his first. Mariana was aware that the property would pass to the next male heir in the Lawton line and that unless Charles made provision for her in his will, which he seemed strangely reluctant to do, she would be left destitute on his death. On marrying Charles, confident of his wealth, she had agreed to sign over her share of her own family's inheritance in favour of any of her sisters who remained unmarried. Now her mother was reluctant to allow her to reverse that agreement, believing that pressure should be put upon her husband to make provision for her in his will. If Charles refused, there was really only one person on whom she could depend financially and that person was Anne.

Anne was aware of Mariana's increasing concern about her financial future. In the past, Mariana had assumed the role of a wealthy woman, via the agency of her husband's money, and Anne had been virtually penniless, dependent upon her father and uncle for everything. One of the reasons for Anne's resignation to Mariana's marriage had been the recognition that she was in no position to offer Mariana a lifestyle, in material terms, comparable to that which Charles could offer. Anne had had to swallow her bitterness at Mariana's defection and try to concoct a plan to retrieve what she could at a later date. However, by 1825, the health of Anne's Uncle James was rapidly declining and Anne was due to inherit the Shibden estate, thereby becoming a relatively wealthy woman in her own right. She would have a substantial income without having to depend upon the whims of a capricious husband or the reluctant generosity of a grudging family. This change of affairs was not lost upon Mariana.

The second factor which caused Mariana some concern was Anne's affair with Maria Barlow in Paris. Over the years, Anne's light flirtations with other women, especially Mariana's sisters, had not given Mariana too much cause for concern.

On the occasions when she and Anne could steal a few days together, Anne would confess her little *amours* and Mariana would forgive them in the face of her own greater betrayal with Charles. The strong, passionate affair with Maria Barlow in Paris was, however, in a very different category. Mariana recognised that for the first time there was a serious rival contending for the role of life companion to Anne. She feared the effect such a serious love affair would have upon the commitment between herself and Anne. Knowing that with Anne sexual intimacy was a great strengthener of bonds, she hastened to Buxton to re-impose her emotional and physical claims upon Anne.

Wednesday 31 August

Off at 6¼. Took George in the gig & drove to the Castle Inn at Castleton in 2 hours. Ordered a little beefsteak, boiled milk, bread & butter & cold water. Off in ½ hour with Mr Ellis Needham of the Spar Museum, to the Bradwell mines. 2 good miles there. Very hot . . . A good deal of stooping – the cavern rich in stalactites. What the man called Paradise Grotto really very pretty . . . Got home about 6 . . . Had scarce been at home ¼ hour when Mariana made her appearance. She had had an attack of cholera morbus yesterday which had prevented her coming. [I] said how much I was shocked at her finding me in such déshabille after a fatiguing day of excursion. Went upstairs to bed about 10. Sat up talking, which kept us up so late. *Received her as well as I could but felt restrained. It was the second night of her 'cousin'* [menstrual period]. *Pretended it would do her harm to have a kiss*[1] *yet, at last, as if unable to resist, she not discouraging it, had one & fell asleep perhaps about four in the morning.*

Thursday 1 September

Affectionate to Mariana last night yet felt restrained. Glad to make the excuse of her having her 'cousin' & pretended to sleep, then to awake excited, she nothing loth, & we had a short kiss . . . She did not seem to find out that I was at all under restraint with her . . . About 12½, Dr Scudamore came for my aunt. [She] would have me consult him whether I should bathe or not & whether have my knees rubbed for the sensation of cold I am accustomed to feel in them. *Told him all this & also about what Dupuytren* [her doctor in Paris who had treated her for her venereal complaint] *had done for me, etc., only saying I had caught it from an unclean cabinet at an Inn. He wrote me a prescription for this complaint & said I should get quite well but might be occasionally subject to relapse.*

Friday 2 September

Had Mariana twice & about two kisses each time. Lay awake talking till six this morning. Told her honestly of the doubts I had lately had about her & of what I had said to Lou [Mariana's sister] *in York just before coming here.* [Anne had hinted to Lou that she thought it doubtful that Mariana and she would ever realise their hope of living together.] *She* [Mariana] *seemed deeply affected, giving me plainly to understand that she could not have long survived my giving her up. I reassured her, saying that my telling her all this was a proof I had changed my mind. She bade me do whatever I thought would make me happiest, in a manner that told what would be her anguish to lose me. I said I now found if I could not be happy with her, I could not without her & that, if happy at all, I must be made so by her. She seemed to wish I had not said what I did to Lou & I confessed I was now sorry for it but hinted not at* [Lou] *asking if I had transferred my affections to her . . . Talked of Maria Barlow. Owned we had slept together*

& the state of my health was the only thing that had prevented our nearer intercourse. Made her regard for me appear pure & beautiful. Made her to have most ingeniously proved to me, on my doubting the possibility of making a woman happy who had ever been happily married, that love with some depended more on mind than on exterior shape. In fact, even Mariana owned the justice of her remarks. [This was a reproachful reminder to Mariana of the time when she felt ashamed to be seen in public with Anne because of the latter's pronounced masculinity.] [Mariana] *said how interesting she* [Mrs Barlow] *must be.* [I] *owned I had done all I could to gain her affections – that I had taken her by surprise, etc., & had begun through being misled by* Mme de Boyve's *scandal* [about Mrs Barlow's flirtations with men and the admittance of them into her room at 24, Place Vendôme] *to think I might try her as fair game ... Read* Mariana *the copies of my last two letters to Mrs Barlow. She was almost fainting as I finished the last.* [I] *assured her my reading them was the best proof that I now knew myself better & was hers forever. She bade me take off her wedding ring, which had never been off since I myself put it on,*[2] *& put it on again in token of my return to her. I could not, but in agony of sobbing said it could only mark that there had been a time when my heart had left her, which I now felt had never been the case. She therefore bade me leave the ring undisturbed & I kissed it in proof of my re-promised faith. Asked if she forgave me. Oh, yes, yes, it was the thought of the fearful danger of losing me that she had escaped which so agonized her. We mutually professed our love, agreed we both wanted to sleep & therefore got into bed, lay quiet & went to sleep without attempting to have a kiss.*

Saturday 3 September

About 2 or 3, Mariana brought me a letter from Mrs Barlow (Paris). 3pp. & the ends. *Much more calmly written than the last & on the whole tolerably satisfactory. She owns that my uncle's wishes must be attended to & seems resigned to give me up, perhaps. She seems to insinuate that she will not take Mr Bell. Both my aunt & Mariana had been nervous at the sight of the letter & had doubted a moment whether to let me have it till tomorrow.*

Sunday 4 September

Had a kiss last night. Just before getting up this morning, talking of Mr Simmons [Mariana's doctor in Manchester] *having examined Mariana & his saying the womb had slipped too low, an inch & a half, said I should like to feel it. Just put up the right middle finger, brought it back bloodied, surprised to find no entrance into the womb. Said I really could not be quite sure but I thought Charles had never broken the membrane. It was very odd but I would feel again another time. 'Then,' said Mariana, half in wonder, half in joke, 'I am the virgin Mary still.' She said Charles had never gone higher, she thought, than an inch, if so much, & from her account I do not think he has ever been able to do the business.* [I] *asked if Mr Simmons had made any observation. 'No,' said she, 'none.'* Came down to breakfast between 12 & 1. Talking over 1 thing or other the whole day. *When with Mariana and speaking of Maria Barlow, told her I had begun to try her, fancying from what Mme de Boyve had said, I might have some fun.* Mentioned the time *I had made a sort of attack upon her one night, after which I had been obliged to apologize & change my manner in future.*

Tuesday 6 September

Gave Mariana the gold buckle I bought in Paris. I had before given her the tortoise shell fan & a bottle of eau-de-Cologne. We get on very well together. When walking, talked of my probable income, what we should do at Shibden to make it a nice place, etc. Should, without altering anything, have seventeen hundred a year – could make it two thousand.

Wednesday 7 September

Two good kisses at once last night & three this morning, after eight. At [9?] *we both got up together & washed before each other, naked, not pretending to take much notice but dressing as fast as we could.* I came down to breakfast at 11. (Mariana came down at 10½.) My aunt went out in the gig at 11–10. *While she was out, shewed Mariana Lou's note* [in which Lou makes an assumption that Anne wished her [Lou] to assume Mariana's role in Anne's life if Anne and Mariana did not realise their plan to live together]. *Mariana would not have believed it if I had not shewn it but was quite convinced Lou had no idea beyond friendship, & of mine she would be most glad.* [Lou] *would be flattered to have what she, Mariana, might have lost. Mariana talked of my powers to please & fascinate. She really loves me. I do now indeed believe she will come to me whenever I wish it. She could not long survive my loss & she will make me happy if devotion & love can make me so. We get on very well together & I am quite satisfied.*

Thursday 8 September

The Duke of Devonshire,[3] with a party of seven besides himself, came to luncheon. Mariana & I went upstairs at 3, then stood listening to the band till after.[4]

Friday 9 September

Soon after getting into bed last night had a very good kiss. Mariana went down to breakfast at 10–40 & I at 11. My aunt went out in the gig at 11¼. At 12¼ Mariana and I went upstairs. *Began to be on the amoroso. Pushed up my right middle finger.* Cordingley *interrupted us. At it again. Gave her a good kiss &, not pushing hard, merely pushing up & down – no blood followed – she was* [clean?] *even through her very gown, luckily – a white one –* [I] *said I believed I had done the business better than I had thought & she was now no longer a virgin, at which we were both well satisfied. My having had to do this for her seems to have delighted us both. It proves that Charles has had not much power & that she has never belonged but to me. She left me soon after one* ... Dinner at 6 ... Sat talking to Mariana. *If our time was to come over, she would not marry – she would never leave me. She seemed much affected – said she was sorry she had been so worldly but she knew not then her own heart or how much she loved* [me?]. *I had said, just before we got up this morning, I had often thought we were both wrong, & remembered she was another man's wife . . . She said she had never heard me say this before, & sobbed bitterly. She, too, had thought of it but hoped we were not so very wrong. She had done her duty to Charles. We had done no harm but to ourselves. My having found her still a virgin, in fact, was a great comfort to her. She would die as she had lived, mine & mine only. She really does seem devoted to me & will make me happy. I love her. We will understand each other better in future & I am satisfied.*

Saturday 10 September

At 5½, George rapped at the door to say Mr Lawton was come. *Mariana & I took it as coolly as we could. She went to see him in his room, close above us. He was not there.* [He] *dined in the coffee room, went to the play in the evening & we have not seen him at all, it being now near ten.* [He] has brought game & a basket of peaches. [We] *have talked about him, more or less, during the evening. Mariana will sleep with him tonight & we hope he will be off tomorrow.*

Sunday 11 September

Mariana came to me, washed, about nine & a quarter. Got into *bed & we had a kiss* ... [She] went down to breakfast at 11 & I got up ... *Charles not cross last night but said very little. Had never thought of the oddity of the thing but came over for amusement.*

Would not have come here had he had anywhere else to go. Never touched Mariana all night. Said he should return in a hack-chaise & leave her the phaeton. She asked him for five pounds & he left her ten on the table. He & Mr Harvey [his friend who apparently came to Buxton with him] *went to church. Left a message to say they would see Mariana afterwards. Mariana took Charles & Mr Harvey into my aunt & they sat with her a few minutes while Mariana came up to get ready to walk with me on the terrace. Charles turned very pale when Mariana mentioned his going into our room but* [she] *assured him there was no earthly reason why he should not & my aunt had sent a civil message to say she should be glad to see him. He went in & talked away composedly to my aunt. Mariana took two or three turns with me & they were off a little after two in a hack.*

Monday 12 September

Talked a little to Mariana ... *She told me how much had been said in York about my friendship for Miss MacLean* [a Scottish friend with whom Anne had been on friendly, but not intimate, terms for the past few years; they had met in York and had mutual friends there]. *Mr Lally had been visiting at Moreton last September & said he would as soon turn a man loose in his house as me. As for Miss Norcliffe* [Anne's former lover, Isabella Norcliffe], *two Jacks would not suit together* [Isabella had a gruff, masculine attitude, apparently] *& he did not blame* [me?] *there but Miss MacLean's was a last resource & therefore she took me. Mariana said Charles was very tipsy when he came home & had therefore told her all this, beginning with, 'You do not know what is said of your friend.' Mrs Ackers, too, had mentioned it. Mariana had turned it off by gravely saying I had been brought up by my brothers. Had a masculine mind – more sense than most people & therefore people said these things. What had, in fact, so annoyed Mariana at Scarbro'*[4] *was that which Lou had made her swear never to tell me, that Miss Morritt & Miss Goodricke* [who had snubbed

Anne at Scarborough by refusing to be with her in public and excluding her from their social invitations] *had told Eli* [Mariana's sister] *they wondered Mr Lawton would let Mariana be with me & that Mariana & Lou had quarrelled with Eli for listening to all this without defending me. Mariana . . . had often thought she* [Mariana] *was very foolish to care about* it [the effect of Anne's masculinity on other people] *but she should never do so again. For if we once got together the world might say what it pleased. She should never mind. At present I was safer with her than anybody but she dared say the world might talk if we were together but* [if] *I did not mind, she would not. Had she always talked this way I should have been satisfied but I am glad to see her in this mind now. All this conversation had been* [due to] *my having owned that, tho' I had never given any of the hair of my own queer to any one, yet I had asked for & received it from others. I had some among my curiosities now. She would know whose. Guessed everybody she could. At last guessed Mrs Milne* [Mariana's married sister] *& my blushing or looking conscious made her suspect. I saw she felt hurt & hastened to contradict. I had blushed at the thought of her guessing so nearly, for it was her sister Anne to whom I had alluded & I had last night said that Anne had made up to me & that we had gone far in flirting, tho' Mariana thinks not how far.* [I] *said I had completely persuaded Anne there was nothing more than friendship between Mariana & me.*

Anne and Mariana had now been together for twelve days. The knowledge, or assumption, that Mariana had remained 'unspoilt' during her years of marriage to Charles Lawton rendered the marriage all but invalid in their eyes. Mariana belonged to Anne as she had always done. The ritual of 'deflowering' Mariana was both a physically and psychologically important episode in their lives. For Anne it confirmed her possession of Mariana, and for both of them it was the final certainty that Mariana was not, in the spirit of the law, a true wife of Charles Lawton's.

The Buxton episode finally, for Anne at this point in her life, decided two issues: the status of the two women in her life and Charles' role in Mariana's life. Mariana was her 'wife' and Maria Barlow was her 'mistress'. Charles Lawton was a mere provider of material comforts and a respectable façade for Mariana in return for limited sexual access.

For Mariana, her mission to Buxton had brought about the expected results. The power of Maria Barlow had become vastly diminished and her own reinstatement in Anne's emotional life was complete.

The dismaying appearance of the cuckolded Charles Lawton only served to draw the two women together in defensive union. Mariana dutifully presented herself in his bed, a situation of which he took no advantage, according to Mariana's report to Anne the next day. His departure was greeted with relief and the two women were left to enjoy their idyll. They decided upon a few days away from the hotel in Buxton, and from Tuesday 13th September to Friday 16th September they left Aunt Anne in the care of her doctor and set out to explore the surrounding district.

Their renewed commitment and love for each other is apparent in Anne's accounts of their intensified lovemaking during the next few days while travelling together. There is a sense of closeness and companionship which depicts the rapport and completeness of the type of union which is eagerly sought after by most lovers, but rarely achieved, at least for any length of time.

Tuesday 13 September

Mariana & I took Christopher [Mariana's manservant] & were off in her phaeton ... at 7–35. So thick a fog the whole way we could scarce see ½ dozen yards before us ... Above an hour seeing Haddon Hall.[5] Very curious old place belonging to the Duke of Rutland. No fires ever made in the house because then, said the old woman who shewed it & lived in the cottage just below the great entrance, they would immediately charge window tax ... Got to Bakewell about 5½. Walked about in the bath garden. Very pretty. The grottoes in excellent taste ... Then sauntered along the town & along the beautiful walk by the water side. Pretty little town. Beautifully situated. Dinner most excellent. Capital mutton chop, a brace of partridge done to a turn. Dessert of Bakewell cheesecake, something like a raspberry puff, for which the person, Miss Hudson, who made it, had a particular secret receipt [*sic*]. Cheesecakes, preserved strawberries & apricots & a pint of very fair port wine, of which Mariana had five glasses & I four. Sat cozing over the fire, drinking our wine & eating excellent biscuits & went up to bed at 9.

Wednesday 14 September

Three or four all at once last night & one more, a good one, at four this morning. Pretended to be a little tipsy last night with my four glasses of wine. Breakfast at 10 ... Off to Chatsworth[6] (4½ miles, good but hilly) about 12½ ... 35 minutes seeing the ground, the fountains all playing, & 1 hour, 5 minutes seeing the house. A magnificent place. The kitchens & offices quite as well worth seeing as any part of the building. Surrounded with stoves à la Français. At one end a hot table for dishing up upon. A hot closet & steam kitchen, all heated by steam. An immensely wide, deep fireplace for roasting, full of burning wood ... Saw the Duke walking leisurely about, very like a gentleman – in a sailor's short blue jacket & white trousers, but stiff & set up like a Frenchman of the Garde du Corps. Returned to Bakewell. Just stopt to change horses & off from Bakewell to Ashburn at 3¾. Got out at the Green Man, Ashburn ... we found a far from civil reception from the pert-looking mistress of the house. The rooms, too, seemed close & dirty ... but the woman shewed us a good lodging-room & we consented to stay. Dinner at 8¼, very well cooked. Boiled fowl with white sauce, harico of mutton & excellent hot plum tart & a pint of very good port. Praised the cooking & the people became quite civil. We sat quietly over our wine & went to bed at 9–55 ... *Mariana & I quite happy.*

Thursday 15 September

Awoke at six o'clock this morning & had two kisses at once but fell quietly asleep on getting into bed last night ... We were off to Alton Abbey[7] at 12–10 ... Got out there at 2–10. The abbey not shewn. Lord Shrewsbury there now. There 9 months in the year. The house not finished ... Mr Orrell very civilly gave us his private ticket that he was allowed to lend to 'persons of distinction' & that would admit us to see both the gardens & the tower. Ordered dinner & set off to walk to the abbey ... Our first coup d'oeil of the gardens, on passing thro' the arched gateway that opened upon them perfectly [was] astonishment & we stood for a moment or 2 in mute astonishment at the most grotesque, unique & striking view we had ever beheld of this valley, of wood, rock & gardens. Chinese temples – gardens in all tastes – & a magnificent conservatory in the Chinese style. Fine views of the grounds & of the adjoining country from the topmost walks. We went everywhere but along the rock walk, which was too wet, the grass being rather long ... It would not do to admit the rabble to such a place. The gardener had asked us, as a great favour, to admit some respectable people – farmers, friends of his – along with us which of course we declined. Boards put up to say Lord S—— allowed none of his servants to take money from visitors – yet the gardener, who by the way soon left us to go to another party, took our ½ crown & the woman at the tower our 2/- & the man who chanced to shew us the way to the town took 1/-.

Friday 16 September

Two good kisses this morning about half hour before getting up. Breakfast at 10. Good bread & milk & butter & good fresh eggs. Off at 11¼. Some fine mountain scenery (rich-looking, verdant country just around Leek) & some fine grouping of hills as we came along. Got out at the Great Hotel, Buxton at 1–35. *My heart rather sank as we neared home. The thought that we were to take leave of our so perfect liberty & that my aunt might think of the expense, all which, on coming upstairs, I told Mariana whose pleasure is always deadened by the fear of being scolded, so generally has Charles scolded her on all occasions.*

Sunday 18 September

A good kiss just before getting up this morning. Mariana down at 10, I at 10–10. My aunt walked with us to church. Just before setting off, Christopher came to say Mr Charles Lawton was come. Would see her when she returned from church. A stranger [read] the prayers. Mr Spencer preached tolerably from Mark viii. 38. *I dozed, however, & knew not much about it.* On our return from church my aunt very nervous & lay down. The walk or the smell of mint water lozenges at church had been too much for her. I just got out of the room before Mr Charles Lawton entered it to see Mariana. He asked where the ladies were. Hoped he had not driven them away. Mariana lost her glass [her eye-glass]. In [my] coming downstairs with her to look for it, Charles came up to us at the bottom of the stairs. I turned my back. Stood looking for the glass a moment or 2 as if nobody but ourselves were there then quietly told Mariana she had better go & seek it in the arcade & walked forwards into my aunt's room. Mr & Mrs Charles Lawton [meaning Charles & Mariana] went to call on the Tryons. I took a few turns for ½ hour in the arcade . . . & I sat talking downstairs for some time while my aunt was lying down & afterwards [I] went to the Buxton baths for the 1st time since our being here. Mariana & I came upstairs at 3½. Talked some time. Mariana had her eyeglass cried [i.e. paged]. It was soon afterwards found in the house & brought to us ... Mr Charles Lawton went away about 2 pm.

Monday 19 September

Mrs Scudamore called at 2½, on my aunt & me & sat chattering incessantly ¾ hour. A *vulgar little personage who probably thinks herself very clever.* [I] went upstairs again at 3½. Sat talking some time to Mariana, who did not go down to Mrs Scudamore, not having been asked for.

Tuesday 20 September

At 12 [mid-day] Mariana & I went upstairs. She sat sewing & I reading aloud to her the first 3 or 4pp of the m.s. lectures on physiology Dr Scudamore lent me 10 days ago. The writing so bad we could not get on very fast. Both of us interested. At 1¾, went to call on the Tryons. Not at home. Left Mariana to wait there, when I went to the highest house on the hall-bank to return Mrs Scudamore's call. Sat about ½ hour with her. I had not much trouble in talking. She talked for herself & me. Then went to Mariana at the Tryons'. Sat there some time ... Mrs Tryon pleasant and ladylike. She & I walked together a little. She praised Mariana – said what a lucky man Mr Charles Lawton had been. I observed [it was a] pity he did not better appreciate his good fortune – but added he had a thousand good traits. She agreed. Seemed to insinuate that as for temper he might not always be responsible. *She said he was really attached to Mariana. I regretted he had not a better way of shewing it, as I believed his attachment* ... The shock of the Buxton bath had been too much for [my aunt's] nerves tonight. Sent for Dr Scudamore, who came about 8½ & staid ½ hour. He is giving my aunt lettuce-milk,[8] not to be got in the country – only to be had of one or 2 chemists in London . . . He, Dr Scudamore, recommended & has just sent me to look at Thomson's Conspectus of the Pharmacopoeias, a nice little 42mo. price 5/-, 5th edition.

Wednesday 21 September

Colonel & Mrs Tryon having called on us, we met them & walked up & down the arcade near an hour. I with Mrs Tryon *in close confab about Charles. I spoke handsomely of him & we both praised Mariana. Mrs Tryon had always wondered she married him, for she had known him in his first wife's lifetime. I explained gently how mistaken was Mariana's estimate of his character & vindicated her calmly and, I fancied, successfully. All the while, it seems, Colonel Tryon was praising me. Wondered I had never married. Mariana hinted at my having had a disappointment some years* [ago]. *Had then put on mourning.*[9] *Would never take it off & never marry. He asked if I was of a county family. Mariana said yes,* [I] *could count as many generations as most could & was very aristocratic.*[10] *The Tryons quite pleased with me, for Mariana & I mutually told all we had said & heard. We, delighted they did not come sooner. They would have had too much of our society and been a bore that we could scarcely have avoided* . . . We were just going up to bed at 11–05 when Dr Scudamore called & sat with us till 11–50. He had been at the ball (a very good one) & could not leave Mrs Scudamore & her friend [Miss Brevin?] or would have called sooner. Mariana had little to say for we talked on scientific subjects almost all the time, yet I learnt nothing save the repetition of his opinion that Dr Bostock's work on physiology is the best & will decidedly suit me best. He is certainly, as Mariana observed, very heavy in conversation. She says doubtless he is clever but it must be by plodding. He can have no genius. He has no conversation. He cannot talk on any subject. He is so slow & tedious & tiresome. I can't help thinking of the following observation of Swift in his thoughts on various subjects (vid. Johnson's Dictionary on the word Fluency), 'The common fluency of speech in many men, & most women, is owing to a scarcity of matter, & a scarcity of words; for whoever is master of language & hath a mind full of ideas will be apt, in speaking, to hesitate upon the choice of both.' Finding I had the new French stays I have never worn, Mariana tried them on & we had not done packing till near 3 [am]. Mariana put me on a new watch riband *& then cut the hair from her own queer & I that from mine, which she put each into each of the little lockets we got at Bright's this morning, twelve shillings each, for us always to wear under our clothes in mutual remembrance. We both of us kissed each bit of hair before it was put into the locket.*

MANCHESTER

Thursday 22 September

It was so late when we got to bed last night we had no kiss yet, not falling asleep immediately, we both agreed we had perhaps mistaken the way & might have slept sooner had we had a kiss. My aunt had breakfasted & was off in the gig with George at 10–20. We peeped out of the window & saw them drive off . . . Mariana & I off in the phaeton with Christopher & Cordingley in the rumble behind, at 11–40. Soon began to rain in our faces & we had the top up all the way to Manchester. Mariana was a little low. I endeavoured to talk as well as I could . . . At the Bridgewater Arms, Manchester at 2–50 . . . Went to Stoby (in St Anne's Square) & had my hair cut & dressed. Very nicely cut . . . *The moment Mariana & I went to walk about, the thought of having my pelisse & hat on – of Scarbro'* [when Mariana seemed not to want to be seen in public with Anne][11] *& of her being ashamed of me, threw a shade across me & Mariana observed it in St Anne's church. I* *was not at ease. The impression continued & I was queerish till after dinner, when I laughed & said I was better.* Went to our room at 8½. *Talked it over. Mariana declared she never thought of the thing. Certainly I did not look so well in my pelisse & in my French redingote & bonnet, but really she had not cared for or thought of it. As we returned from the old church, Mariana bought me a wedding ring at a shop near the Bridgewater. On leaving Buxton this morning, my aunt it seems saw nobody.* Mr *&* Mrs Muirhead [the proprietors of the Great Hotel] *came to the door to see Mariana & me off, doubtless on her account. On telling Mr Muirhead it was likely we should come next year & should like to have the same rooms, I thought he seemed to hesitate. I then turned & said the same to Mrs Muirhead. I thought she said, yes, if she could (that is, let us have the room), not with sufficient civility & not much anxiety to have us. I mentioned this to Mariana as we drove along, saying perhaps they did not like the cut of our establishment, which Mariana allowed was not improbable. I said I cared not. Would never bite my own nose off. If we wanted the rooms, we would have them if we could, repeating my maxim from Rousseau's Confessions.* 'Une mortel ne paut offenser mon ame' [A mere mortal cannot offend my soul].

The small party of three women and their three servants, having travelled from Buxton to Manchester and spent the night at the Bridgewater Arms in Manchester, now had to go their separate ways. Mariana and her manservant, Christopher, had to travel on to Lawton Hall in Cheshire, whilst Anne and her aunt, with Cordingley and George in attendance, set off on their trek over the Pennine border between Lancashire and Yorkshire to reach Halifax. On reaching Shibden Hall, Anne, as usual, confided her day's doings and her day's musings to her journal.

Friday 23 September

On getting into bed last night [at the Bridgewater Arms], *tried Mariana for a kiss but she was quite dry. Told her of it. She said I had set her wrong by being so queer while we were out. I said no more. Made no further attempt & we soon fell asleep. Awoke at two o'clock. A little play & two good kisses at once. She tried, she told me afterwards, to put the ring on but she could not & I was asleep & did not feel her. Awoke again at seven & then had three good ones all at once & she put the ring on & I promised not to take it off till Christmas. I may change my mind when I please. She will let me off whenever I like & when I wish it, I am merely to send her back the ring & she will understand me & give me no further trouble. She has several times at Buxton said she would then see me no more & should soon fret herself to death. We fell asleep again & slept till nine. Then talked of one thing or other. Recurred to my feelings yesterday. Explained, etc., etc. At last she said that she had only thought yesterday how changed were her feelings. Now she cared nothing about my pelisse & had often thought how foolish she was at Scarbro', but it was our peculiar situation that made her care so much. She could not bear to have our connection known or suspected & conscience made her cowardly. She shrank from having the thing surmised now, but declared that if we were once fairly together, she should not care about it. I might tell our connection to all the world if I pleased. I asked if she was sure this was really the case or she only said so to please me? 'Ah,' said she, 'do not doubt me. I could not say so if I did not feel it' & then gave me her word & honour of its truth. 'Then,' said I, 'Mariana, I am satisfied & perhaps you have hit upon the only means that could have made me so, for I am so now but was not before & I know not when I could have been. Scarbro'[12] & Blackstone Edge will now be as nothing. I will take care to keep all quiet while circumstances are as they are & I am & shall be satisfied. But would you follow me, Mariana, even to jail?'*[13] *'Yes, that I would.' I said she could not have been so devoted before she married. It was this want of devotion I had always felt so deeply. 'You are right,' said she. 'I could not then be so devoted. I neither knew myself nor you nor the world well enough. But I know the world better & can appreciate you better now.' I laughed & said perhaps I should try her one of these days as the duke had tried his wife in the honeymoon. Then joked & asked if she would be the nutbrown maid?*[14] *No, she would have no rival. I said I could name who had once promised me this & set her to guess. She named Tib* [Isabella Norcliffe] *& Miss Vallance.*[15] *I said it was her sister, Anne. She asked anxiously if I had really gone the utmost length & asked for my honour that I had not. I gave it. Could I do otherwise? But owned I had done all but absolutely 'kiss'. Had gone as far as possible* ... [Anne and Mariana parted and Anne got to Halifax by the early evening]. Got out at Shibden at 7½. My uncle looking well. My aunt [who had arrived earlier than Anne] in good spirits. Dinner at 7–55. My aunt a bit sickish & went to bed at 9. Could not resist unpacking my books from Paris. On seeing the purse sliders & map of the environs of Paris Mrs Barlow has given me, & on seeing the buckle she has chosen, my heart misgave me. *About ten, Cordingley came & curled my hair. Stood musing.* Peeped into some of my books. Vol. 1. Nouvelle Heloise.[16] Mrs Barlow had read it. On parting with Mariana this morning, I congratulated myself on being in the gig & having to drive. This, in some degree, occupied my attention and what was spared I could employ undisturbed in musing, as my mind loved best. I could have sat up all night but hastened into bed that I might not be up beyond 12. I had made a rule always to be in bed before this hour, to rise earlier than I have done these 3 months past & to try to make the best of my time. I have much to learn to make up for the lost time. Without some intellectual superiority over the common mass of those I meet with, what am I? Pejus quam nihil [A thing worse than nothing].

1. *Kiss* – In addition to the more commonplace and contemporary usage, the word 'kiss' was used as a euphemism for the sexual act. See *Shakespeare's Bawdy*, ed Eric Partridge (London: Routledge and Kegan Paul, 1968). The explanation given there states: 'KISS – n. and v. "A second time I kill my husband dead When second husband kisses me in bed" (Coits with me: it is a euphemism – cf French 'baiser'). *Hamlet* (III. ii. 203–204). Similarly, in defence of cuckoldry, the clown in *All's Well That Ends Well* (I. iii. 50) says: "He that kisses my wife is my friend".'
2. *She bade me ... I myself put it on ...* – Anne refers here to the occasion of Mariana's wedding to Charles. Apparently, Anne took Charles' wedding ring from Mariana before the ceremony and replaced it with another. Anne then wore the original wedding ring as a symbol of their eternal commitment to each other.
3. Duke of Devonshire – William Henry Cavendish (1790–1858), the sixth Duke of Devonshire. He never married and became known as the 'Bachelor Duke'. He inherited the charm and extravagant nature of his famous mother, Lady Georgiana Spencer, and entertained his friends lavishly. The superb gardens at Chatsworth House are due to his interest in gardening and the skill of his head gardener, Joseph Paxton (1803–1865), whom the duke appointed in 1826.
4. Scarbro' – This was a continuation of the humiliation suffered by Anne during the Blackstone Edge episode. See note 7, p 171.
5. Haddon Hall – A great mediaeval house which, in 1087, was occupied by an illegitimate son of William the Conqueror, one William Peveral. From 1567 the hall has been owned by the Manners family (the family of the Dukes of Rutland). It was left unoccupied during most of the eighteenth and nineteenth centuries, until the ninth Duke of Rutland, in the twentieth century, decided to restore it to its original splendour.
6. Chatsworth – Seat of the Dukes of Devonshire in Derbyshire. The original house, built in 1553, was demolished during the Civil War, in the mid-seventeenth century. The present house was designed for William Cavendish, the fourth earl, who was created first Duke of Devonshire in 1694. The sixth Duke of Devonshire (see note 3 above) extended it during the 1820s.
7. Alton Abbey – situated twenty-five miles from Buxton, the building

and gardens were created by the fifteenth and sixteenth Earls of Shrewsbury. Now known as Alton Towers, the place is an amusement park, open to the public. For a description of the original building and gardens, see *Buildings of England: Staffordshire* by Nikolaus Pevsner (pp 55–60), Penguin (1974). Also *Historic Places Around Buxton* by W Allan Milton (pp 164–169), Derbyshire Printing Co (1926).

8. Lettuce-milk – (lactuca) – the milky juice of the lettuce-plant. The juice of various kinds of lettuce could be used as an opium-type drug.
9. *Had then put on mourning* – This story was not true. In fact Anne had taken a decision to wear black clothes only as far back as 1817, when she was twenty-six. (See Sunday 1 June 1817 on p 18 of *The Secret Diaries of Miss Anne Lister: I Know My Own Heart*, Volume One.)
10. . . . [Anne was] *very aristocratic* – Anne's obituary, published in the *Halifax Guardian* of 31st October 1840, states: '. . . Miss Lister was descended from an ancient family in Lancashire, the main branch of which is represented by the noble line of Ribblesdale . . .'. The Ribblesdale line, which bore the surname Lister, ended with the death of the fourth Baron Ribblesdale in 1925. A paper held in Calderdale Archives Dept (ref SH:7/ML/B/30) shows a possible linkage of the Shibden Hall Listers with the Ribblesdale line.
11. Scarbro' – See note 7, p 171.
12. Scarbro' – Ibid.
13. *'Would you follow . . . to jail?'* – Presuming that Anne is here referring to the possibility of lesbianism being classed as an illegal act, see Lilian Faderman's *Surpassing the Love of Men* (Part II – The Nineteenth Century), published by the Women's Press Ltd, London (1985). There the legal attitude to lesbianism in the nineteenth century is discussed.
14. '. . . *the nutbrown maid*' – A reference taken from an English ballad circa fifteenth century. (See Thomas Percy's *Reliques of Ancient Poetry*, 1765.) It tells how the 'Nut-Browne Mayd' is courted by a man who pretends he is exiled from his country. Despite the hardships she would have to endure, the Nutbrown Maid remains steadfast in her love. Once the man finds her love has passed the test he reveals his true identity – that of an earl's son with a large estate in Westmorland.
15. Miss Vallance – Mary Vallance, daughter of a brewer from Sittingbourne, Kent, and friend of the Norcliffe family. She and

Anne had had a brief physical love affair when they were both at a house party at Langton Hall, the family seat of the Norcliffe family.

16. *Nouvelle Héloise – Julie: ou Nouvelle Héloise* (Julie: or the New Eloise), 1761. A novel by Jean-Jacques Rousseau (1712–1778), the French philosopher, writer and political theorist, whose writings and political ideas contributed greatly to the rise of the Romantic era in literature and inspired the ideals which helped to spark off the French Revolution.

The Hallowed Heart

The autumn of 1825 was to form the last period of Anne's life as a dependent niece. Her uncle's deteriorating health warned her of the changes to come. On her return from Buxton she quietly took on more of the burden of running the estate. In the face of her uncle's opposition to change, she was not able to have as free a rein as she would have wished but she was content to control her impatience until she was in sole charge.

Emotionally, Anne felt more stable. The closeness and intimacy which she and Mariana had enjoyed at Buxton had swung the balance of her feelings towards Mariana, as the latter astutely knew it would. Mariana, having known Anne since they were both young twenty-year-old women, had great psychological advantages over Maria Barlow. She knew Anne through and through and put that knowledge to dexterous use. She returned to Lawton Hall in Cheshire confident that her restoration as the most important person in Anne's life was complete.

Anne herself was always secretly relieved to retreat back into the safe haven of Mariana's love. The fixed 'engagement' or understanding between herself and Mariana gave Anne an excuse to philander without commitment, using the bond of honour with Mariana as 'a hole to creep out at', as she put it, when other lovers became too demanding or began to bore her.

Her affair with Maria Barlow was a classic example, although this time it had become almost too late for Anne to escape. Maria Barlow, for her part, was definitely badly hurt and, for a while, disoriented by the whole episode, which had not yet ended.

Once back in Halifax, however, Anne resumed the more even tenor of her life at Shibden. The new footpath episode was behind her, but the daily routine of work on the estate had to be carried on and it must have been a great relief to her tired, ailing, old uncle when his vigorous young niece returned to deal competently with the men and the business matters at Shibden.

Tuesday 4 October

Read over Mariana's letter of yesterday ... *Her pages strongly affectionate, all that an idolising wife could write. 'You may be tired of reading so I really will conclude with the assurance that, so long as life shall last, I will be your lover, friend & your faithful wife. If I can be anything more, teach me what it is & that I will also be, with all the truth & power of one who lives for thee & thee only.' She says before, 'Yours & only* [yours] *let me always be. That is, so long as it makes you happy to have me so. But one minute beyond this, one moment beyond the time that you can give me yourself in exchange & you shall hear of me no more. Yet I will never be another's – "True as the dial to the sun, altho' it not be shined upon" – this I will always be to you & this I have ever been. Believe it now if you ever doubted it before.'*

Thursday 13 October

Jackson began under the ale-parlour window, to dig the foundation for the nearside wall of our new cabinet d'aisance. My uncle had looked out of his window & stopped them. Went to speak to him. Got a reluctant consent, or rather presumed upon silence, to have it done my own way.

Saturday 15 October

Wrote a note to Whitley to order the student's manual (etymology of words from the Greek) & the sequel to it . . . Reading from pp.22 to 32, ii, Nouvelle Heloise. Stood over Jackman & the men digging for a foundation for the new garden wall next to our new cabinet. On examining the ale parlour closet, found there had been a cabinet there too, as well as above. Determined to make these old places do again. Removed the cistern & rebuilt the drain. Breakfast at 10¾. My *uncle in a great fidget, said we were pulling the house down.*

Friday 21 October

Chas Howarth, junr, came & shewed me a piece of old oak at Mr Carr's (the Swanyard) that would suit for the studding we want in the ale-parlour. Mr Carr had bought the old wood in the old buildings lately pulled down in the town. Large stock of old oak. Our piece had 12ft of wood in it. Old oak considered to be worth as much as new deal. Paid, therefore, 2/3d a ft, i.e. £1.7.0 for the piece. Paid Mr Carr himself. Speaking of building him an Inn & mentioning Northgate [a house belonging to the Lister estate] he was afraid it was too far out of the town. 'Then,' said I quietly, 'we must let it as it is. It will cost us much less money.' Thinking to myself, 'Well, perhaps it will be best', at the instant giving up all thought of its ever being an Inn . . . Fell in the wood & tore my old pelisse so that I cannot wear it again except a day or two more in the wood & in my own room occasionally.

Monday 31 October

I called at Lowe's, the umbrella-makers, & Whitley's. Bought 'Paul & Virginie'[1] in French, to send to Mariana & called at the

Saltmarshes. Sat 40 minutes with Emma Saltmarshe. [She] very civil & not vulgar this morning. She had seen Isabella Norcliffe at the Festival [the Music Festival at York][2] but did not know her now she is become so large. The Saltmarshes had taken Isabella's place at one of the concerts & she asked them gruffly for her fan & book that were left upon the bench. I turned it off with a laugh, thinking to myself I was glad I was not there.

Thursday 3 November

Sat down at my writing desk at 7–05. From then to very near 9, read over Mariana's last letter & wrote p.2 & the ends & finished my letter begun on Sunday. Small and close. *This ought not to be seen – not that there is anything in it flaming but some allusions to herself & others; telling her how much I am altered; to have no fear of me in future, etc., which might be ambiguous & turned against us. Yet there is nothing, I think, I could not manage to explain away to warm friendship if I had the letter before me & was obliged to defend myself* . . . Letter from Mrs Barlow, Paris . . . '*You seem to wish to impart something which you fear will wound my feelings but the surmises I am obliged to make torture my mind more than the reality. If it be that your friends wish you to cease all correspondence with me, pray oblige them & be happy in conforming to all you deem your duty. One seal is broken & the tie which still exists may live without being expressed by pen, ink & paper.*' Mrs Barlow has been ill but seems to be better. 'If I can last out 5 or 6 years longer, for my child's sake, I shall be thankful . . . My greatest wish would be never to be obliged to appear in the world again . . . but I cannot avoid going thro' this ordeal with my poor Jane. I never did care for fortune. The home of a heart in unison with mine is the only bliss I ever treasured . . . ' . . . [I] felt quite low.

Wednesday 9 November

Wrote . . . to Mariana . . . *Said there were many things about planting, fencing, the stables, etc., I thought it best to do quietly without saying anything. I found I should want more money than I thought it right to ask from my uncle. 'I spend more, too, in books & my postage is on the increase,' but said twenty-five or thirty pounds a year more would do for me. 'Consider this. Turn it over in all ways & tell me the result.' She will understand that I mean her to try & save this for me.* Said I had had a letter from Maria Barlow last Thursday. It made my heart ache bitterly. 'There is a settled sadness pervading her pages more melancholy far than if it was complaint.' *Said how much I was altered. 'My heart is fixed & sorrow & remorse have hallowed it.'* . . . The ground deeply covered with snow this morning.

Friday 11 November

[Wrote] *to Mrs Barlow . . . A long & very affectionate letter yet it will not quite please her. Poor soul! I am not hers & nothing can make up for this. Yet, I should fancy her a little bad-tempered from her letters. She speaks of Mariana & of my doing my duty as if she was. I have concluded with, 'I have only room to add God bless you, Maria. Surely you will never refuse the "home of a heart in unison with your own" so long as your charity in accepting it is so necessary to the welfare of your devotedly & unalterably attached A.L.' The 'unalterably' might have been spared but I had not another good word & I am always very conciliatory & respectful. Poor soul! If she really & disinterestedly loves me as deeply as she says, I pity her and will always behave as well to her as I can. But somehow I have always, now & then, fancied her knowing what she was about & wanting to catch me.*

Saturday 12 November

Box of game from Mariana (Lawton), sent off on Tuesday, unluckily by the new mail which never brings parcels regularly, which is the reason the box had been so long on the road. A hare & a leash of partridges.

Thursday 17 November

On horseback at 10–55. Went to Throp's (Shay Syke). Paid for the trees we had had – 2500 oaks at 30/- a thousand & 300 beeches at 35/- a thousand. Then ordered & paid for 300 more beeches myself without saying a word to my uncle who likes not so much expense. From Throp's rode to Huddersfield town end. Hotspur carried me exceedingly well & I found I had soon got back into the habit of riding &, perhaps, ride better than ever in my life before. Felt less shaken today than yesterday and not quite so stiff . . . Went to James Sykes in the Hall wood. Had him come to the house. Gave him the acorns I gathered & 7 quarts Chas Howarth's grandson (Charles Carter) brought this morning, to be planted in the ground at Wellroyde, about to be added to the end of Lower Brea wood.

Friday 18 November

On horseback at 10–25. Got off for ¼ hour at Mr Wiglesworth's to speak to Mr Parker about them having made 2 roads instead of one in Sutcliffe wood & getting more stone than they ought & whether raising Mark Hepworth's rent would not be the best punishment for his having let a cottage off the house (at Yew Trees).

Friday 25 November

On horseback at 11–10. Stopt at Wilson's at the top of the Hough (late of Godley) to say that if Rayner Wilson (the son) did not come here & let me see him before Monday, he should have a summons before a magistrate for shooting a stock dove in our grounds the day before yesterday. Then rode forward to Blamire's. Told him how ill he shod Hotspur the last time & that if he did not do it better I must try someone else. Will go with the horse myself, the 1st fine day next week, to be newly shod. Went along the road from Blamire's to Queen's Head – a bye-road which they, a few days ago, made a turnpike road – a chair across for the present. 1½d each horse . . . Letter, 4pp (widely written) in an envelope, with a brace of partridges & a plan of their coach house & saddle room, from Isabella Norcliffe (Langton) . . . Mrs Norcliffe 'has had a letter signed by the mayor of Leeds, saying they have had a meeting on account of the near approach of the dissolution of Parliament[3] & had unanimously agreed to petition Mr Fountayne Wilson[4] to stand for the county, & calling upon all Protestants to stand firm in support of their religion.'[5] Mrs Norcliffe sent the letter to Messrs Foulis & Bower, who will both support [Mr Fountayne Wilson] & they are going to call a meeting at Malton. They all hope Wortley[6] will not come in. Mr Bower says he 'is nothing but a shuttlecock'. To this, I write in answer, 'We are going to have a meeting here in behalf of Mr Fountayne Wilson & the Protestant interest. I heartily agree with you in wishing Wortley turned out. The sense of the county seems completely against the Catholics. The West Riding [of Yorkshire] is unanimous. They [the Catholics] appear to behave so foolishly about their Associations,[7] etc., they will lose their friends. That hint at appealing to the sympathies of Europe at large – that hint at foreign influence[8] will not go down with Englishmen.' . . . Breakfast at 11¾. My uncle out of sorts about stubbing the fence and making a wall between Chas Howarth's pea field & the calf-croft . . . I said quietly I would have nothing more to do with it. I really [am] in earnest. I shall think [no more of the] matter – tell my uncle quietly & give up troubling myself about things. It will save time & money. *I can do as I like when the place is my own. My aunt nervous. Wishes me to go from home & not pother [sic] myself. Thinks me all right. She shall be plagued as long as she lives. Knows my uncle better than I do. Said he sometimes got quite vulgar when he spoke of our not being able to have company.* Rainy, windy, stormy day. West wind drives the rain into my aunt's closet & into the water-closet. *It is a tumbledown place, my aunt says, the coldest house she was ever in. I believe it is the cause of all her rheumatism & will make me as bad if I do not take care. I will get away as conveniently as I can. Perhaps if I stay at home this winter, I may get over to Paris* ... I will try & study a little at home. Master French if I can.

Sunday 27 November

Rayner Wilson came (vid. Friday). Begged pardon for shooting the stock dove. Seemed very sorry, promised never to trespass on the grounds again & caution others against doing so. The young man was so civil, ordered him some beer. Read aloud the morning service & sermon ... Sat downstairs, talking about what my uncle would & would not have done. I am almost tired of interfering & mean to give it up as far as I can. There is nothing but nonsense about it. *My uncle is never right. I am wearied to death of squabbling* ... Dinner at 6–40. Did nothing afterwards. Talked about planting, walling, alterations & improvements. My uncle took it more patiently.

Monday 28 November

Came upstairs at 12. Rainy day. Enjoyed myself over the thought of having six hours for reading. Quite a treat to me.

Wednesday 7 Dececember

[Mariana had asked Anne for some advice concerning the arrangements for a winter house party Charles had promised to hold at Lawton Hall, without first consulting Mariana about it. Mariana panicked and wrote to Anne for advice.] Advised her, if possible to have some other room for dancing than the dining-room. The laundry or any other room that could be made to do. To ask her company, as she proposed, for 2 or 3 days – the house full &, if possible, let them have a quadrille each night. If this could not be managed, I should prefer having the dance the 1st night they came. No dining at 4 o'clock – to have the dining carpet taken up for dancing. But I knew not the localities sufficiently well to advise confidently. I knew not the people she would have. I could only judge as I should do for myself & this might not suit her case. 'I can only fancy myself Mrs Wilbraham, shrugging my shoulders a la Français at the rusticity of dining at 4 to have the dining room carpet taken up for a dance.' [I] said if she had any married people, she must ask the Wilbrahams; if not, she might ask the girls without them. If they were regularly introduced, must send her invitations to themselves. If not, she must write to mama to allow them to go. If Miss Rankin keeps house for her uncle, Mr Shackerley, she must not ask her; if she is in no wise chargée d'affaires, 'perhaps county étiquette may just permit it, for it is not a ball you are going to give.' But the best plan (the families don't visit) would be to tell Miss Pattison that if Miss Rankin would like to join the party, Mariana would be glad to see her & Miss Pattison might bring her.

Friday 9 December

On passing the Union Cross, George told me the living skeleton was there.[9] On seeing that he was only come for today, stopt, went up to see him. Took George too. Staid about 10 minutes. An appalling sight. The poor man came creeping from behind the curtain in the far corner of the room, just like a living death. The arm bone, from the shoulder to the elbow, only 2½ inches in circumference. The voice like that of any other man who spoke rather low. Addressed the man in French. Spoke better & with more ease than I should have expected. The man seemed pleased. Had his health very well. Did not suffer at all from the climate. Got home at 3¼.

Sunday 11 December

On coming in this morning, found on my desk a letter (3pp & the ends) from Mariana . . . 'You talk of a quadrille each night. What do you think they charge me for 2 violins, a violincello, & taber & pipe, for one evening? Seven guineas!!! Not a farthing less.' They are to have a man cook from Liverpool, while their house is full of company this Xmas, at a guinea a day & all his expenses paid.

Monday 12 December

Mr James Briggs came. He had come to see if we had any sovreigns [*sic*]. A great run on all the county banks.[10] Messrs Rawson[11] will have £50,000 down from London tomorrow at noon. In the meantime, Mr James Briggs collecting what he can. I saw a notice posted today in the town professing the stability of our 2 banks & signed by about 400 of the principal inhabitants of the town, who all engage to take their notes.[12] 7 banks have stopt around us [i.e. in other towns] . . . Said (to Mr James Briggs) we seldom saw any sovereigns here. We had little else than Rawson's notes unless we got Bank [of] England or gold from them, before going from home. My uncle happens to have 5 sovereigns. Gave them to Mr Briggs for a Rawson £5 note.

Tuesday 13 December

Went & sat in the drawing room & from 2 to 4, writing to Mrs Barlow . . . [Her] last letter made a deep impression on me. *I think Mariana will suit me better & I am fond of her. I think of Cordingley saying Mrs Barlow was bad-tempered & I think I could not have satisfied her as a husband. But yet, her last letter strikes me deeply. 'Whose you ought to be will never be adjudged but in another world.' & her remarks upon the sacredness of marriage affect & influence me, I know not how . . . I have shed many tears over my answer. The first day I made my eyes quite weak and even reading it over makes me weep, for it is beautifully written, very affectionately – & shews a mind, as I say, 'strangely bewildered between right & wrong'* . . . Felt so oppressed, *knelt down & said my prayers. Prayed sincerely for God to have mercy on me & cleanse the thoughts of my heart by the inspiration of His Holy Spirit, & the tears rolled down my cheeks as I prayed.* Then felt a little relieved . . . Yet, still, melancholy hangs over me. *I think of Mariana's marriage with unusual sadness. I am fond of her but she cannot be with me. She is another man's wife. I am solitary. I, for a moment, think how happily I might have met Maria Barlow again in Paris. We might have been happy there by & by. And yet – I know not. I am fond of Mariana. I could not make her miserable.*

Thursday 15 December

Finished my letter to Miss Marsh [Anne's old friend, in York]. Speaking of people's suffering from colds, etc., 'Ours is a glorious land; & we all agree with Cowper, "England! My country! With all thy faults I love thee still." But the climate frowns. 'Tis "fickle as the summer wind" & our neighbours across the channel have gentler airs & brighter suns than we. There is some difference between crowding over a sulphurated coal-fire whose lurid flame burns dully thro' the dampness & fog that clings around & sitting out beneath a clear blue sky & smelling violets in the Tuileries gardens. But don't mistake me. Ours is the land of righteous law & liberty; & I would not change my birthplace for all the loveliest spots that smile upon the god of day. But we may migrate now & then, & yet be patriot still . . .'

Friday 16 December

Went out at 8½ . . . to John Balmforth's. Said I should send him some notices & he must look after all trespassers. Told him, also, he should open his ditches. For want of this, soughing [*sic*] was of no use. I should advise my uncle to do no more. It was bad farming. The man seemed astonished at my telling him all this, for his neighbours seem afraid of him.

Saturday 17 December

Mark Hepworth came. Gave him a good jobation [i.e. reprimand]. Said he farmed ill. Must keep more cattle & farm better or ½ his land would be taken from him & if he did not still farm to please me, he should lose the other ½ also. He should keep more cattle. 5 horses & 1 cow were proper stock for that farm & he would not be allowed to sell off [i.e. any surplus crops, for private gain]. He said the cottage [that part of his farm building which he had sub-let without permission] had been in the house [i.e. had been sub-let] since March. [I] said he must pay after the rate of four pounds a year additional rent for all the time he had had this cottage. I found Mark telling a heap of stories to excuse himself but [I] told him it would not do for he could not deceive me . . . Young James Howarth told me there was a young man trespassing about the fish-pond but [he] would not attend to him [James] when he told him it would not be allowed. Sent James & Mallinson's cart-driver (I staid by the cart in the road & gave the man a shilling for his trouble) after the young man. They brought him to the house. Spoke to him. He said his name was James Wilkinson of Newton (the new houses by the Pine Apple). [I] said if he had been civil he should have been excused but that for his incivility (tho' it seemed he had now completely changed his tone) he should be made an example of & should be summonsed next Saturday . . . Dressed. Looking out my clothes for going to York.

Sunday 18 December

Wrote a few lines to Mrs Norcliffe to propose dining with her on Thursday & staying till Monday [at Langton Hall, Langton, near Malton, from which place Anne would then come back to York for a few days] & wrote to order a sitting room & lodging room & dinner at the White Horse, Leeds . . . Looking out my things. *Mending one thing or other. Trying on my lace frilled handkerchiefs.* At 5½, came downstairs & read the evening service.

---

1. *Paul et Virginie* – A highly successful novel (1788) by Bernardin de Saint-Pierre (1737–1814) in which the simplicity and beauty of nature is extolled and set against the corruption of civilisation. It is said that Napoleon slept with a copy of the book under his pillow. The Bourbons were also greatly impressed with it.
2. The Music Festival at York – In the year 1791, a festival was held in York Minster to commemorate Handel's music. From that there arose the desire to emulate the music festivals held in aid of charity at St Paul's Cathedral in London. The use of York Minster was obtained for this purpose in 1823 and the proceeds from this and subsequent festivals were distributed between York County Hospital and the general infirmaries of Leeds, Hull and Sheffield. (See *York Minster Historical Tracts, 627–1927* ed A Hamilton Thompson MA, DLitt, FSA London (1927).)
3. The dissolution of Parliament – Parliament was dissolved in 1825 and a general election took place in 1826 in which the issue of Catholic emancipation played an important role. Anti-Roman Catholic sentiment was particularly strong in rural areas at that time.
4. Fountayne Wilson – '. . . The candidates at the election in 1826 were Lord Milton, Wentworth House; Hon. William Duncombe; John Marshall, Esq., of Headingley; Richard Fountayne Wilson, Esq., of Ingmanthorpe, near Wetherby and Richard Bethel, Esq., of Rise . . . The election was fixed for the 21st of June, but between the day of the nomination and the polling, Mr Bethel retired, so that a contest was avoided. The requisition to Colonel Wilson was signed by 1,345

voters, which was said to be "an unprecedented circumstance in the annals of York electioneering".' (p 105, ref SH:7/ML/E/25, Calderdale Archives.)

5. '... all Protestants to stand firm in support of their religion ...' – i.e. against the bill for Catholic emancipation, which was seen as an insidious threat to the Protestant religion.
6. 'Wortley ... is nothing but a shuttlecock ...' – James Archibald Stuart-Mackenzie (1776–1845). First Baron of Wharncliffe. Grandson of third Earl of Bute. Tory MP (1797). Lord Privy Seal in Peel's ministry (1834) and President of Council (1841). Anne's reference to him as 'a shuttlecock' refers to the fact that he supported Catholic emancipation, which offended some of his party and his supporters. '... Just before the [1826] election he was elevated to the Peerage, under the title of Baron Wharncliffe, with a view, it was said, to deliver him from "the chances and cost of a discomfiture at the Yorkshire election".' (p 105, ref SH:7/ML/E/25, Calderdale Archives.)
7. Catholic Associations – formed in 1828 to bring pressure upon the British government for the emancipation of Roman Catholics in Great Britain and Ireland. It resulted in the passing of the Emancipation Act (1829), which allowed Irish and English Catholics to sit in Parliament and compete for most public offices. Daniel O'Connell, the most charismatic leader of the Catholic Association, known as 'The Great Liberator', became the first Irish leader to take a seat in the British Parliament.
8. '... that hint of foreign influence ...' – i.e. any intervention from the Papal authorities in Rome (as the supreme Catholic authority) in English affairs would have been bound to have caused a hostile reaction in England.
9. The living skeleton – Claude Ambroise Seurat (1797–?) was born at Troyes, in the department of Champaigne. At first a seemingly healthy child, his flesh began to waste away from his body as he grew in stature. Eventually he was left with a skeletal frame devoid of flesh or muscles. His condition excited great interest in France. He came to England in 1823. After touring in exhibitions throughout the country he retired on the proceeds, dying a few years later in his native town. (See *Tales of the Weirrd* by Ralph Steadman, pub Jonathan Cape.)
10. '... a great run on all the county banks ...' – Towards the end of 1825 and the beginning of 1826, there was a financial panic which

was felt throughout the country. The reverberations were particularly felt in the industrial north. '... In the autumn of 1825, overproduction caused a sharp drop in prices. Panic ensued, there was a run on the banks and seven London and eighty county banks failed ...' (*Nineteenth Century Britain, 1815–1914* (p 71) by Anthony Wood, Longman 1982).

11. Messrs Rawsons – Halifax bankers. For an account of early banking practices in Halifax see *The Genesis of Banking in Halifax* by Ling Roth (1914), and *Banking in Yorkshire* by W C E Hartley, Dalesman Publishing Co Ltd (1975).
12. '... all engage to take [the town's bank] notes ...' – Individual banks issued their own notes at that time but it could be a risky business, i.e. '... About this time [1781–1789] it would appear that Halifax traders were beginning to make use of the fatal power of issuing bank or promissory notes without an adequate backing of capital ...' (p 4, Ling Roth). Efforts were made from 1844 onwards to centralise the issue of bank notes by making the Bank of England the sole issuing authority but this was not achieved until the twentieth century.

A Winter Flirtation

Anne's periodic visits to her friends in York and Langton did a great deal to alleviate the loneliness of her years at Shibden Hall with only her ageing aunt and uncle for company. Travelling now in her own gig rather than by public stagecoach, Anne usually stayed with Miss Marsh or with Mr Duffin, visiting the Belcombe family daily and paying courtesy calls on other York friends and acquaintances. She would then go on to make a short stay at Langton Hall, the home of the Norcliffe family, coming back to York for a further day or two before finally departing for Halifax. This visit, in the winter of 1825, was no exception. Having arranged to take her horse, Hotspur, to be broken in by a Mr Briggs of Tadcaster, Anne decided to visit her friends whilst she was in the vicinity of York.

As usual Mr Duffin offered the hospitality of his house to Anne. He was now a widower. His wife had died in the August of that year and Miss Marsh, his long-time mistress, was anxiously waiting for him to announce the date of their marriage. He was seventy-eight and Miss Marsh was fifty-five.

Having deposited Hotspur with Mr Briggs and with her other horse, Caradoc, in the shafts of the gig, driven by George Playforth, her manservant, Anne arrived in York.

Tuesday 20 December

Got out here (Mr Duffin's, Micklegate, York) at 3. The Falcon full in consequence of the horse-fair. George took the gig & went to the Black Swan. *All very glad to see me & all in very good spirits.*

Wednesday 21 December

Half-hour with Miss Marsh. Mentioned [they say] *at Halifax she was to be married in March. She wanted to fight off the subject altogether. I would not let her – reminded her of all she used to say to me – that he* [Mr Duffin] *had given her a written promise, etc. She declared he had said nothing yet but they understood one another.*

Anne stayed with Mr Duffin for a couple of days and then, on the 22nd December, she went on to Langton Hall, where she joined the Christmas house party there. Anne was invited as the intimate friend of Isabella Norcliffe. The other guest was Harriet (christened Henrietta Willan) Milne, Mariana's married sister and a close friend of Isabella's sister, Charlotte. The four women spent the days in walking and driving out over the Wolds, shopping trips to Malton, paying a visit to Kirkham Abbey and, on Christmas Day, which fell on a Sunday, they all went to the tiny village church of Langton for the Christmas service. They whiled away the evenings very pleasantly, eating, drinking wine and tea, playing card games, gathering around the piano and indulging, long into the night, in gossipy, intimate fireside conversations. The closeness of the four women and their long involvement in the York social scene meant that there was always something or someone to discuss at great length.

Anne's time and attention was greatly taken up by Harriet

Milne. Harriet was married to an army officer, Lieutenant-Colonel Milne. The marriage was far from happy. Harriet's flirtatious nature had made her the focus of much scandal in York. She and Anne had had a relatively cool relationship for many years. In conversation with Isabella Norcliffe in 1818, Anne had commented upon the possible reasons for Harriet's coolness:

> '... Speaking of Harriet Milne, I owned she was no favourite of mine – that I liked her the least of the [Belcombe] family & that neither hers nor the character of her husband was much to my taste. I said I well knew she did not like me, for she could not bear anyone who had at all the character of being bookish. But that she was the best flirt I had ever seen – that I liked her well enough to talk nonsense to & thought she liked my society when I chose to conform to this rule & be very attentive. I mentioned a dinner-party at the Serjeantson's, just before Mariana's marriage, & said Harriet told me how agreeable I was ...'
>
> (Saturday 19 September 1818. Langton)

Two years later, Harriet's husband was taking strong measures to curb his wife's conduct, in public at least. On the 1st March 1820, there was an officers' ball at the Assembly Rooms in York. It was attended by all the higher ranks of the local military, their wives and guests. Anne and the Belcombe girls were there and spent a very enjoyable evening. Harriet, however, could not go. Mariana told Anne, confidentially, that:

> '... *Harriet's flirting was terrible. She would have gone to the ball but Milne would not let her. He was a miserable man & they had had a grand blow-up. He suspected her of a secret correspondence; had opened her writing-desk but had found nothing.*

Found, however, a letter in her trinket-box from a Mr Blake of the Guards, beginning, "My beloved Henrietta," speaking of the happy hours he had spent in her society & saying he should be at the Ball. The letter was directed to Mrs T. Boudwin & she [Harriet] *had herself secretly got it from the Post Office. He* [her husband] *could forgive folly but this was premeditated wickedness & she had promised, after that business with Captain Wallis, never to commit herself again . . . Milne says he has lost all his confidence in Harriet & will not take her with him – that she is to be left in Petergate when he joins his regiment & Dr Belcombe* [must] *tell her she must conduct herself more like a widow than a wife while she is under his roof. Milne will not have her with him till she is quite reformed. To keep up appearances he still sleeps with her but on condition she does not touch him. He is very domestic & has often given up his pleasures to hers & gone out more than he had thought right . . .'*

(Thursday 2 March 1820. York)

The following day, Mariana again confided in Anne:

' . . . *Mariana told me while I was dressing that Milne . . . wrote* [to Dr and Mrs Belcombe] *to desire they would not bring his wretched wife into his presence without his special leave. Mr Blake's letter to Harriet was abandoned. She, in one of her letters to Captain Wallis, had said she feared he loved his wife better than her . . . The woman has little heart or principle . . .'*

(Friday 3 March 1820. York.)

Anne, although superficially scandalised by such blatant behaviour, was nevertheless intrigued by Harriet's coquettishness. At a Christmas house party given at Langton Hall in the December of 1820, she found herself irresistibly drawn to the femme fatale:

'*... In the evening,* Mrs Milne *played. Hung over her at the instrument & sat next to her & paid her marked attention ... Said* [to Anne Belcombe] *I could not help it, etc.* Mrs Milne *was fascinating ...*'

(Friday 22 December 1820. Langton)

Now, in 1825, without the restraining presence of Mariana, Anne was thrown into close contact with the fascinating Harriet. It was obvious that the latter had lost none of her powers of seduction and Anne, ever the sexual opportunist, was not one to resist the spice of such a challenge.

Friday 23 December

Drove Mrs Milne to Malton ... [I] *talked rather cavalierly of Mariana. Said she must do as I liked or break with me at once, which last she might do if she chose. I must have my own way. Mariana had not that sort of indulgence to prevent it. Insinuated that* Mrs Milne [might] *succeed better. She might manage me. Ladies always ruled,* etc. [I] *said how dangerous she was. She said she could excite the feelings of others & keep her own calm. I said this might not always be in her power. Ended by shewing the highest respect for* Mariana *& not much for* Mrs Milne. *It was fascination* [that Anne felt for Harriet] *& not esteem. She had sense enough to see, & say, that I did not flatter her much. However, she seemed satisfied and praised my agreeableness ...* Dinner a little after 5. Talked away the evening ... *Covertly attentive to* Mrs Milne. *After we came to bed, had her in my room, trying on my French things – stays, petticoats, gown & bonnet, etc. I had made the offer – she willingly accepted it. Said I was very good-tempered about it. The girls so abused French things, & mine too, & me for, as they said, preferring everything French.*

Sunday 25 December

Went to church at 2 ... Mrs Milne & Charlotte Norcliffe loitered in the village. On their coming in [I] asked them to walk in the garden. Charlotte engaged with teaching children. Isabella would not put her things on again. Mrs Milne & I walked there, tête-à-tête, an hour before Charlotte joined us. [I] *made absolute love. Said Mariana was not warm & nobody knew her better than I did. Mrs Milne was warmer. I highly respected Mariana. My regard for Mrs Milne was quite different. Perhaps she, Mrs Milne, would suit me better, but I might never see her again. Why not? That depended on myself. No, I durst not have her at Shibden. Mariana would not let me. All would make a rowe* [sic]. *Some people might steal a horse while others might not open the stable door. Mrs Milne seemed to agree. This was her case as well as mine & here we sympathised. She said she liked me in my greatcoat & hat. 'No, no,' said I, 'not externally.' 'Well, but,' said she, 'at heart then.' I answered I should always have them* [feelings?] *at heart for her. I hinted at circumstances & inconsistent feelings. She received my advances well. I saw her feelings were getting a little interested. When Charlotte rang the garden door bell, Mrs Milne's cheeks were deeply suffused. She said, 'Well, well, I like you better than I did' & ran to open the door. She made the excuse of being out of breath. 'Twas well or Charlotte might have seen there was something more than common. We walked half-hour longer. I had long before said I would make an excuse & be off when Charlotte came but Mrs Milne begged me not. She said she was very fond of Charlotte but they went on humdrum. Her regard for me was very different. I behaved very properly before them all but Mrs Milne understands me.* Dinner at 5¼. Got, *as usual, near to Mrs Milne. She began pinching my feet upon which I became gradually empassioned. She saw this & went on, evidently pleased with the effect she produced, perfectly evident to, and understood by, her tho' not by the rest. Tho' Mrs Norcliffe kept talking to me, at last I got up & left the room. Mrs Milne thought (for I pretended a little more than I really felt, to try her) it was my excitement that was so strong I was quite obliged to go. I did go to my own room & take a little cold water & sat still for a few minutes, murmuring to myself, 'Well, they are all alike.' For I was a little taken by surprise, not expecting her to melt so entirely. I heard her on the stairs. As she was going down again I joined her. She looked tenderly & said, 'What are you?', evidently knowing what had been the matter. 'Oh,' said I, 'I had a little headache.' 'Are you angry?' 'Oh, no. How can I* [be]*?' & we walked into the room as if nothing was the matter.*

YORK

Monday 26 December

On going up to send all my things [back to York] *Mrs Milne came for a moment. I kissed her. She said, 'Don't forget me. Say "I love you, Harriet".' 'It is not love, it is adoration. But do you love me?' 'Yes. I do love you.' 'Well, don't look cross at me the next time I see you.' 'How can you say so. You have me quite.' She kissed me with open lips. I might have taken any liberty I pleased. 'You have me.' Yes, thought I. She would see us off & stood at the door in the cold. Whether she can love me or not, she has committed herself. We have both gone too far to retract. I thought & think of this. Poor Mariana!!! How can I trust myself? I know not yet how keen remorse will be or if I have too little virtue left to feel it deeply. I cannot, do not, respect Mrs Milne. I told her seriously she must not now be nonsensical with anyone else. I could not stand it. I should be desperately jealous. She has no conduct. She would intrigue with anyone. How can I trust such a woman?* … Isabella [Norcliffe] and I off in the gig at 1½, George riding Charlotte Norcliffe's pony … Set Isabella down at the Black Swan [York] & got out myself, here, at Mr Duffin's at 4½ … Went to my room at 11½. *Miss Duffin* [one of Mr Duffin's nieces from Ireland, who was staying with him at the time] *soon came to me & staid till near two, for I curled my hair while she was with me. Then latterly turned to obscure lovemaking. She said I was very odd. I said I was very foolish, she knew not how much, etc. She was evidently interested, she scarce knew why, & staid because she could not get away. Thought I to myself, 'Here am I flirting again, not contented with my folly with* Mrs Milne. *How can I trust myself?'* Very fine day. Beautiful moonlight.

Wednesday 28 December

Went to the Belcombes'. Tête-à-tête with Lou in the dining room near 2 hours ... *Talked of girls bringing me gauses* [*sic*] *to look at in Paris. My whole conversation odd & foolish & if Lou had a grain of nous, she must understand it. At last I said nothing was impossible. Perhaps I should fall in love with Lou. I never felt anything more like it. 'Why should you not?'* [asked Lou]. *I said, 'What! Engaged to one sister and in love with another?' 'Yes,' said Lou, 'with two of her sisters.' – alluding to* Mrs Milne. *Begged Lou, for* Mariana's *sake, always to stand up for me ...* Dressed & all went to Mrs A—— & Miss G—— at 7–50. Drank tea there & did not get home till 1½ ... Miss Duffin *came immediately to my room & staid till one. Flirting conversation. Rather made love to her. She said I was very odd, yet owned that nobody interested her so much. She seemed as if she could not get away.* [I] *said she should never see me so foolish again. 'Why not?' 'I will be wiser in future.' She hoped not. Surely she might almost smoke me. I went a little too far but tho' she is not at all yielding like her sister is, she did not discourage me. Were I at liberty to try, I might succeed. But 'tis indeed foolish to flirt in this way & shew myself for nothing. But somehow I seem as if I could never resist the opportunity. A woman tête-à-tête is a dangerous animal to me. What with* Mrs Milne *& my folly to* Lou *and* Miss Duffin, *what would* Mariana *say? 'Tis well she is in ignorance.* Packing above an hour then curled my hair.

Thursday 29 December

Off at 11½. Got to Tadcaster in 1 hour, 20 minutes . . . Drove to Leeds . . . Got out at the White Horse at 4¾. Mrs Turnbull very civil. Dinner at 6. Pease soup. Harico of mutton, hot minced pies & apple tart. Jellies & custard. Dozed a little after dinner. Good port wine. Drank the whole pint. Went up to bed at 9.

Friday 30 December

Off at 11–05. So slippery Caradoc could hardly stand. Got out & made George lead him for the last ¾ hour (about 2 miles) & got to Bradford at 1–10. At the Sun Inn, had the horses sharpened & baited . . . then off home at 3. Very cold. Got home at 4–55 . . . Settled with George, *after which I find I have just brought home twenty-nine pounds, seven & ninepence.*

HALIFAX

Saturday 31 December

Letter . . . from Mrs Milne (Scarbro'). *A regular love letter.* '*And we have at last met, for weal or woe – to one or both. God grant that the happiness may overbalance the pain but from my present experience I have little to hope & much to fear. Since I saw you last you have occupied every moment of my time. You dwell in my heart and in my head. In my waking & sleeping hours you are with me & to banish you seems so utterly impossible that my brain turns at the idea of the influence you have gained over me. Is it possible that I can have feelings which have never yet been roused into action? Affections that were dormant till you called them forth? You, dearest, whom I have seen a thousand times with such perfect indifference. Surely there must be some witchery in the deed, some magic spell that can last but for a certain period & will then vanish*

& depart like a dream. I cannot understand it. All I know & feel is that you have taken forcible possession of my heart & that there you have made yourself a permanent dwelling & abode. Should you think so pitiful a residence worth keeping, write & tell me so. Tell me all you would have said when we were together, all you well know I wish & long to hear. In short, write about yourself & your feelings & then I think I shall be quite satisfied. You owe me something, for I am not apt to be miserable & my mental illness has somewhat affected my bodily health. But I am better & when I hold a letter of yours in my hands, I shall be quite well. I sometimes fear that absence will now do for me what it has so often done for you formerly – send me from your mind without a sigh or a wish to recall. Yet I hope I do you an injustice. Surely you will & must remember for I think there is something written on your heart that cannot be effaced. If you would [remember?], whether for good to me I know not [sic], but love & friendship never despair. C'est l'amour which makes you overlook all these pretty little stories [about Mrs Milne's racy past] which my good relatives were kind enough to tell you and to forgive all the ill-natured things I used, in my folly, to say of you – & will it not make you my friend thro' life, willing to excuse errors which arise rather from a weak head than a bad heart, & in return, you shall have gratitude & love such as you never had, tho' lovers & friends have been round & about your path. I shall be anxious till I know you have received this. Today is Friday. Let me have a letter on Monday or Tuesday. Direct for me at the post office. Adieu, carissima. H.W.M. One thank you for the song – a thousand for the remembrance.' It is dated at the top of the page, Scarbro', December twenty-ninth. The above is the whole of the letter, verbatim . . . It rather excites me. I might have her on my own terms. 'Tis well I have not a penis. I could never have been continent. She wishes to lead me on . . . I must not get into a scrape with her.

1826

Sunday 1 January

From 8½ to 10¼, writing to Mrs Milne . . . At 10¼, sent down my letter to the post. *Troubled in my mind about what I had written. Could not say my prayers. The wickedness stared me in my face. The devil, rather than God, seemed nearer when I attempted to pray.* Dressed. Finding George had not gone (his bad cold had kept him from church) recalled my letter. *This was some comfort to me. Resolved to write another* . . . *Could think of nothing but Mrs Milne & my letter. Intently anxious – afraid of committing myself & of being in her power* . . . *Wrote the copy of another letter* . . . *ready to go tomorrow. Better satisfied with this. It does not commit me so much – makes it appear that she had led me away – that I could not resist her fascination. Saw the brink on which I was standing. Trembled at the sight & was wretched. ' . . . Accustomed only to your indifference, that sudden burst of kindness was more fatal than the electric bolt of lightning. You saw the nameless agitation of my mind. You saw that lapse of reason that, in her fall, threw back the curtain which had hidden me from myself* . . . *What have you done to me, Harriet? For I know not – cannot – tell, but I am wretched. I dare not see you again.'*

Monday 2 January

Reading & musing over Mrs Milne's letter. Said I to myself, 'She is a bad one. How lightly she mentions "those pretty little stories" [of her past]. *She would intrigue with me or anyone. What would Mariana say? Can one have any confidence in a woman like Mrs Milne?'*

Tuesday 3 January

Thinking of Mrs Milne. Fancying I had a penis & was intriguing with her in the downstairs water-closet at Langton before breakfast, to which she would have made no objection. I shall never forget her way of saying, just before we parted, 'You have me.' When she asked me to write I had the wit to ask her to write first, to which she consented at once & gave me a bit of her hair & cut off a bit of mine.

Wednesday 4 January

Ordered a chaise to be here (to bring up my father) & take my uncle to the Mitholm [Inn] to receive his rents. I offered to go with him but he did not wish it & I, of course, said no more. He strikes me as being much more nervous of late & perhaps more asthmatic & less & less fit for exertion of any kind.

Thursday 5 January

Letter from Mariana (Lawton). Have just read it aloud to my uncle & aunt. She is pretty well. Their dance went off uncommonly well – she not the worse for it. Had all her own way & nothing could answer better. *Very kind letter. It gave me a pang of remorse to think of my folly with* Mrs Milne, *but* Mariana's *affection consoles & fortifies me again. If* Mariana *was with me I should be better & happier. I could and should be content & secure against the blandishments of such a woman as* Mrs Milne.

Tuesday 10 January

Went into the stables. Went out again at 8–25, direct to Lightcliffe ... Mrs W. Priestley & I sat very cozily (Mr Priestley had had breakfast & gone out very early) till 1. We then went & called at Cliff-hill & sat ½ hour with Miss Walker. Mrs Priestley then walked with me almost as far as the turnpike. I returned with her as far as her own gates & then, leaving her at 2–25, came direct to the workmen. The Keighleys felling a large willow by the brookside. Young Chas Howarth & his son & Wm Green, with our cart horse, leading away the remainder of the wood reserved for ourselves. Jackman & his son, John, walling at the back of where is to be the rustic seat. Frank Oates digging the wall-race. James Sykes & John Booth taking down the old wall at the top of the hall-plantation ... Did not come in till 5–10. Mrs Priestley to come & look at what we are doing on Saturday, if fine & frosty ... [Her] *cook in a family way by John, the footman. Had them married by licence on Saturday. The woman sent off to her friends to lie in. The man keeps his place for a while. The Priestleys will afterwards assist them.*

Thursday 12 January

My uncle gave me my half-yearly allowance of twenty-five pounds.

Sunday 15 January

½ hour reading my letter (3pp, the ends & under the seal) from Mrs Barlow (Paris). *The first page was very religious. Prays for me every day . . . It won't do to introduce Mariana to her at unawares.* [Mrs Barlow writes] '*In answer to your Buxton letter, I spoke of a "fixed feeling" but I did not then understand that you had sworn fealty anew* [to Mariana] *& this, after having known me, makes the case absolutely decisive. There is no other form left to adopt but that of friendship. But I accept of nothing – then I shall have nothing to lose. You have acted as you thought your duty required you to do. Let your mind be at rest & never believe my forgiveness wanting. I have received my divorce! I am resigned & may you be happy with her destined for you. She is at present in the service of another but when she becomes yours, I tremble for the fate of my letters. You have no instinctive suspicion & if you had, you would contemn it. The sex are all angels with you . . .' She dwells much on her self-abasement & the wish that our connection should never be known to any but ourselves. ' . . . In charity to my deserted state, bury my error in your own bosom. The loss of my own self-esteem is sufficient punishment. If our secret was ever divulged, the tie which did exist would become perfectly hateful to me & have I not suffered enough? . . .'* It seems *as if she would not see me. ' . . . Never speak of forgiveness, Anne. You need not see me to know that no rancour has place in a heart which is only anxious for your welfare & happiness. Believe in the sincerity of this wish, & that I remain, your affectionate friend, C.M.B.'*

Thursday 26 January

Made my fire. Letter from Miss Marsh (York), 3pp & the ends. Chit-chat. Stood reading my letter. Was cleaning my teeth when (at 9½ by the kitchen clock) Cordingley rapt [*sic*] at my door & bade me go down directly – my uncle was laid on the floor. Ran to his room (my aunt almost in an hysteric of grief, supported by Cordingley, in the hall). Saw him fallen at the foot of his bed. He had evidently not hurt himself in the fall – the countenance calm, placid & unruffled, as if nothing had happened. The spark of life quite extinct, tho' Cordingley had heard stirring in his room not 10 minutes before. Getting up, as usual, he had got his smalls & stockings on. Nothing to be done. Alas! It was too late. All was over. Ran down to my aunt. Did all I could to compose her & she gradually became even better than I expected. George out with the horse. Sent John Booth for Mr Sunderland [the Halifax medical man who had attended Uncle James]. He came as soon as possible. Said there had been an aneurism of some great blood vessel near the heart – it had burst & death was instantaneous. Nothing could have been done. He [Mr Sunderland] did not apprehend danger. Had thought my uncle would rally again. Had he his attendance to begin over again, he could do no more. He had the consolation to think he had omitted nothing. Did not – could not – foresee this. It was a case in which medicine could have done no good. There could have been no suffering at the last. It was a very large vessel that was ruptured. Death occasioned instantly by the inward bleeding. I had noticed a swelling almost as big as my two fists on the pit of the stomach & my poor uncle complained of a little pain – tightness & heaviness here – yesterday evening & said he had it during the night before but it had gone off. Asked Mr Sunderland (thanked him for the brace of partridges he had sent my uncle yesterday) to call at Northgate [Northgate House, belonging to the Lister family and where her father and sister were staying on a prolonged visit to Halifax] – break the thing as well as he could to my father & Marian & ask them to come immediately. My aunt & I breakfasted. Sent for Matty Pollard. She & the servants did the last offices to my poor uncle. My father & Marian arrived at 11¾. We none of us spoke for some minutes. It was a melancholy meeting but my father bore it more, much more, calmly than I expected. Marian, after a burst of tears at first, was also calm. Both she & my father have wretched colds. About one, the corpse was ready for us to see & I took my father into the room. He lifted back the napkin for a moment; death was then stamped on the countenance. My father shed a tear or 2 & after I had opened my poor uncle's drawer & taken out his will (he told us where it was a day or 2 ago) we came downstairs. After waiting a little while, I read aloud the will. No one uttered a word. As soon as I had done I hastened up to my own room. Wrote to the editors of the Yorkshire Gazette, York; Leeds Intelligencer; Leeds Courier & Gentleman's Magazine, London – & to Miss Harvey, 17, Albemarle St, Piccadilly, London, to order mourning for myself, to be down as soon as possible. On sitting down to dinner, my aunt obliged to leave the room from a violent burst of grief. I went down to her in the drawing room. By & by, I left her tolerably composed & came upstairs again. Wrote a few hurried lines to Mr Duffin, York; to Isabella Norcliffe, Langton; to Mariana, Lawton Hall; to Miss MacLean, 15, Hill St, Edinburgh, to inform them of the melancholy event. Rayner, the undertaker, came about 4. My father & I gave the necessary orders. Sent off all my letters to the post office. Dressed. Went downstairs at 5½. A little while with my aunt in the drawing room. Then with my father & Marian, who had tea in the dining room. My aunt just came in to wish them good evening & they went away, a little after 6, in the chaise that brought them. My aunt had tea & I, dinner, at 6¾. We were best left to ourselves and talked of things as calmly as we could. The funeral to be tomorrow week. 8 tenants to be bearers, etc. My aunt is as well as can be expected. Everything reminds us of my uncle. How suddenly he has been snatched away at the last! It seems a frightful dream! *On coming upstairs to my room to dress, after seeing my poor uncle,* [I] *looked into my heart & said, 'Lord, I am a sinner. There is not that sorrow there ought to be.' Felt frightened to think I could think, at such a moment, of temporal gains – that I was now sure of the estate. 'Are others,' said I, 'thus wicked?' and knelt down & said my prayers. Oh, the heart is indeed deceitful above all things. He was the best of uncles to me. Oh, that my heart were more right within me. I shed a tear or two when my father & Marian came & stopt once in reading the will. I am grave & feel anxious to do, & seem, all that is decorous but there is not that deep grief at my heart I think there ought to be. Oh, that I were better. Lord, have mercy on me & forsake me not. Oh, cleanse my heart & forsake me not for mine iniquity.*

A Hard Mistress

Anne was, at least, honest in admitting that relief was her over-riding reaction to her uncle's death. She was now, for all practicable purposes, in sole control of the Shibden estate. Her uncle had bequeathed 'all his real and personal estates to his niece, Anne Lister'[1] on condition of making certain provisions out of the estate for her father and her aunt for the duration of their lives. To these provisions Anne dutifully attended, not without a wary eye on her father's over-readiness to step into his dead brother's shoes and assume control over Anne and her plans for Shibden. She sharply put a stop to this sort of ambition on his part. One reactionary, grumpy, old man had gone. She was not going to allow another one to take his place! Also, Anne had inherited the estate for her lifetime only. Her duty lay in passing on the estate in an improved condition to her future heirs. There is no doubt that, while not neglecting her own needs and priorities, she took this duty very seriously.

The management of a landed estate[2] had become a very complex business in the nineteenth century. New methods of farming, introduced during the agricultural revolution of the previous century, meant that a world of mechanical expertise was beginning to be formed, the application of which greatly altered the level of skills needed both from owners and tenants.

The rapid acceleration of the Industrial Revolution meant that entrepreneurs were seeking more and more ways of tapping the mineral resources of the land. In Anne's case, coalmining, albeit on a small scale, was to provide a way of raising extra revenue from the estate. She also held shares in canal development and turnpike trusts, which paid half-yearly dividends. Rents from farms, cottages and any other buildings, such as inns and the rent from Northgate House, when her father and Marian moved out of it, formed her main source of income. In order to keep the estate in good repair and thus maximise her income, there was a plethora of duties to carry out. In addition, detailed accounts of all these activities and of income and expenditure had to be kept if the estate was to be efficiently run, even a relatively small one such as Shibden.

Anne, however, was a competent and demanding taskmistress who would stand no nonsense from the people she employed. If the workmen thought they had a soft option when a woman inherited Shibden estate, they were quickly disabused by Anne of such fanciful thinking. She kept a much tighter rein on them than her uncle, on whom age, illness and a sort of fond familiarity with some of his old tenants had taken their toll, causing him to adopt a lenient approach to the backslidings of some of his tenants. Estate owners were not, in the main, running their estates for philanthropic reasons. Anne had the aristocratic concept of estate management in which motives of self-interest and the perpetuation of the estate for future generations of the family were paramount. Occasional philanthropic gestures were made – careful subscriptions to one or two charitable causes or paying for a basic education for the motherless daughter of one of her old and valued tenants. Certain ritualistic payments were made – a meal for the tenants when they gathered at the Mytholm Inn on rent-day, twice a year, to pay their dues; beer money for the workmen when the foundations of a new wall or building were laid, or when the project was completed. Apart from these instances, Anne's main concerns were to generate income for her personal use, sufficient for her lifestyle – in particular her travels – and to allow for a degree of capital re-investment to increase that income and ensure that the estate was handed on in an improved condition.

It seems that little innovative change was seen at Shibden. The property was not large enough to warrant the introduction of the new, large-scale farming methods introduced in the late eighteenth and early nineteenth centuries. Much of the land was parcelled out in small farms and individually rented fields. It was still possible, therefore, for Anne to deal personally with her tenants' affairs and methods of farming. It is true that Anne did find it difficult to maintain this sort of intimate day-to-day involvement, mainly because it interfered with her passion for travelling abroad. She became, for some years, an 'absentee landlord' and such absenteeism meant employing a paid agent to ensure the smooth and profitable running of the estate in the owner's absence. Anne's worries about choosing the right man for the job are understandable. Stories of dishonesty amongst stewards and paid agents were rife throughout the landed gentry and it is true that there were many opportunities for making illicit gains at the expense of absentee landlords. Anne also knew of her father's chronic inability to handle money wisely and did not feel happy about the fact that he and Marian would be installed at Shibden Hall for long periods while she was away. The chances for her father to indulge in back-door deals with her steward were only too obvious.

However, there were some months to go before she could put her travel plans into action, and she took advantage of that time to make her presence felt and enforce her way of rule upon the workmen and tenants of the Shibden Hall estate.

Saturday 4 February

Letter from Mariana (Lawton) . . . This letter upset me more than anything. I did not expect so much real feeling on this occasion [of the death of Uncle James] from Mariana. She had kept her room ever since she had got my 1st letter & was far from well even on Thursday. Would continue in her room till yesterday, when she would get her mourning. [She] would wear bombazine & crape 6 weeks & then second mourning six weeks longer. '. . . This tribute to your uncle's memory, Fred, is no more than I owe him & less would not satisfy the feeling I have for his memory. It would be injustice on my part if I failed to tell you that no person could have been kinder than Charles on this occasion. Tho' Messrs Powys & Cholmley are staying in the house, he wished to leave them & dine tête-à-tête with me. Sent to Manchester for woodcocks & all sorts of things he thought likely to tempt my appetite. Indeed, he has shewn much more feeling than I expected.' I did not expect so much either from Mariana or Charles. I shall not forget it. It has endeared Mariana to me more than she can be aware. *As to Charles, my first impulse was to write & make an opening for our reconciliation – to write the letter of that proud & haughty spirit that cannot bend to menace but yields to kindness at once. His letter to me was ungentlemanly.*[3] *If he will apologize for this, I will apologize for the sentence in mine that gave him umbrage. It was wrong in me & I am ready to say so handsomely if he will satisfy me as to his letter.*

Monday 6 February

Wrote 2 & ⅔pp. to Mariana. Made what I consider a very handsome offer of reconciliation between Charles & myself, tho' without any 'constrained or uncomfortable compromise of my feelings'.

Saturday 11 February

Got home at 5. Found Isabella Norcliffe (with my aunt), who had arrived at 1½, looking very well. Dressed. Dinner at 6–10. Tea & coffee at 8¼ . . . *Tib* [Isabella] *seems inclined to be very accommodating & really begins well, having coffee so late. She is to have no suppers.* [She] had 2 or 3 bad headaches just before she left home, with numbness creeping up the arm. Mr Cobb said she must be particular about her diet. Give up suppers or he feared the consequences.

Sunday 12 February

Isabella came & sat with me. *She asks what I shall have. Will it be three thousand a year? I said no. 'Well, but would it be two thousand?' 'Perhaps,' said I, 'it may eventually.'* [I] *said my aunt & I would have about a thousand a year of which I should only have about two hundred or less. Said I should have money to borrow, the funeral expenses would, from first to last, be five hundred, I expected, & one thing or other – workmen, purchases of ground, carriages, etc., – might take a thousand or more to meet,* [of] *which I could not calculate on more than five hundred till the next rent day.*

Tuesday 14 February

A kiss last night of Tib [Isabella]. *Perhaps I may never have another.*

Thursday 16 February

Read Mariana's letter immediately on receiving it yesterday. My last [letter] 'was a comfort to her' but Messrs Cholmley & Powys being still in the house, she had made no use of it with respect to Charles. [She] could not calculate what would be the result but thought of shewing the letter to him. 'It would certainly be desirable if some sort of reconciliation could be affected between you & Charles. It might seem better to the world & we might enjoy together some additional hours of happiness.' My feelings at the first moment of reading this, & now, is – I like not this calculation. I want no worldly good in this business. I am too proud to value it & have more than once thought to write & say I acted only from the impulse of my heart but, now that I find the thing can seem to have any worldly interest in it, I scout it altogether & beg Mariana will not, to Charles, take any notice of my letter but let us remain for ever as we are. *Tib said, this evening, Mrs Milne had more feeling than people gave her credit for. She* [Mrs Milne] *had written a beautiful letter to Mrs Norcliffe* [Isabella's mother] *& been very much affected on leaving Langton (that was the day but one after Christmas Day & after I left there). Charlotte had never seen her so ill & was quite frightened. She fainted in the evening (of the day I went away) & alarmed them all, & was very ill afterwards at Scarbro'. I never thought, when she told me in her letter that she had been ill, that there was so much truth in it. Surely it could not be on leaving Charlotte & Langton. She cares not enough for them. I wonder what, that is, how much I had to do with it? Of course I took no notice to Tib but the story struck me forcibly.*

Saturday 18 February

Tib and I sparring, after we got into bed last night, about French-made dresses . . . I can less & less tolerate her society. I fear we should quarrel seriously if long together.

Wednesday 22 February

Tib annoyed with me at dinner about not liking to do things abroad for my friends [i.e. smuggling contraband goods in and out of Britain]. *Called me a fool & an ass before George. I took it ill & hardly spoke afterwards but came upstairs.* Wrote the journal so far of today. *She came to me to make it up & we have just got right again* . . . Letter . . . from Mariana (Lawton) . . . She has shewn my last one to Charles who, it appears, does not trust himself to talk much on the subject (nor she either, for their communication has been chiefly by note from her) but he says he will do as she likes and adding [that Charles said] ... 'I never felt any ill-will towards Miss Lister. I was hot & angry at the time but I have never thought of it since.' 'Then why did you not speak to her at Buxton?' 'I never saw her at Buxton.' 'Yes, you met in the passage.' 'I don't know that I did, & was not likely to put myself in her way. I should have no objection to shake hands [*sic*] with Miss Lister – but don't talk any more. I want to go to sleep.' This, Mariana observed, began & ended their conversation. It is my present mind to give myself no further trouble on the subject but let it rest forever. I care not about it. Charles' manner is not enough conciliatory for me, whatever it may be for him. I shall take no more notice of the thing. Poor Mariana! She would muse over my letter [which] she would get this morning.

Saturday 25 February

George went this afternoon to a man in Shelf (with a note of recommendation from Mr Sunderland) & brought us back a nice brown pointer (which the man is too poor to keep himself) for a house dog instead of Con. We have renamed the dog Peiro, instead of Jack.

Monday 27 February

Dinner 6¼. Staid talking to Isabella made me so late. In spite of the rain she went in the gig to Northgate [House, in which Anne's father and sister, Marian, were living at that time] after her luncheon. Marian went with her to the library & to see the new Assembly Rooms.[4] *She, Marian, had a long & foolish talk with Tib. Said she was eight & twenty, had never been at an Assembly & never had any society. She was stupefied to death. Must go out more – should like to go to the Assemblies here, with Mr Rawson, for instance, but I did not wish it. It was hard upon her, etc. My aunt & I were laughed at for our pride. Mrs Veitch had told her so. The only people here – Miss Saltmarshe & Miss Catherine Rawson – I liked her to be intimate with, she did not like.* [She] *would never live with me. Could never have any of her friends to see her. My aunt was my echo. Marian does not like* [it]. *Would do anything to please me but must have more society. Tib, it seemed, had agreed with her cordially. I explained. Said I had always promised to bring Marian into proper society if she would wait patiently. She would be impolitic not to wait now. Associating with those I would not was foolish. It was not my fault she had had no society. I could not help it. It was my father – had thrown himself & his children out of it* [society] *& all I had, I owed to myself. Marian could not have done like me. She had not the nous.*

Tuesday 28 February

Glad to have got rid of poor Tib. Would not travel with her on any account. Ashamed of her & besides, she talked of our going abroad – asked what gown I had taken with me – hoped we should take George, etc., all which, tho' I took no notice, I much disliked. My aunt, I know, was tired of her but behaved very well & did not shew it. Her habits are altogether – her voice – too loud for my aunt & I myself have soon had quite enough of poor Tib's society. I would not live with her for all the world. She talks of coming to see us abroad. I shall say nothing to a soul but get out of her way, if possible. What with wine & snuff & want of judgement & temper, I could not stand it. She is boisterous & not always like a county gentlewoman in her choice of society. I could not help thinking to myself, how times are changed. Her family importance, etc., used to please me. Now I am ashamed of her. In fact, it has been of use to me to know the Norcliffes & being intimate at Langton does very well. I like poor Tib & her family. I like Mrs Norcliffe but Isabella's manners annoy me & here the matter rests.

Tuesday 7 March

Went out immediately. Had all the men (George too) to say I would have my orders obeyed, & inquiring why John had not dined here yesterday. Knew it was on account of James Smith's grumbling at it. Poor John durst not own the truth but George had told me before. [I] said if I heard anything more of this sort, he, or any of the rest of them being guilty of it, should lose their place altogether ... Spoke to young Chas Howarth's son about getting rails cut by Thursday. Taking him by surprise & making him say how many roods' length of railing they cut in a day, the lad said he thought seven. Now his father had asked me 3d a yard for cutting them on Saturday & when I said Mosey would cut them at 1/- a rood & I would send the wood to him, 'Well, then,' said Charles, '& we will do them for the same' – to which I agreed. That is, he [had] asked me 1/9d. a rood & finding I could get the job done for 1/-, would take 9d. less. These people want looking after. To saw up 7 roods a day at 1/9d. a rood would make good wages!

Friday 10 March

About 1½, set off to Lightcliffe ... Sat talking to Mrs Priestley till 5 ... said my residence here for some time to come was uncertain & would be till I could settle, which would not be till I had some friend ready to settle with me. Wished I had one now. It would be a great comfort to my aunt as well as myself. We might remain abroad some time. [I] did not think my aunt could get over another winter here nor could she do very well anywhere in England on account of the dampness of the air.

Saturday 11 March

Hinchcliffe's son came between 2 & 3. [I] said my uncle had thought it high time they should pay for the coals they had, the bed of which was under water. They ought to pay £30. The times were bad. I did not wish to distress them but they must fix a day for paying this money & keep to it. I hoped they would always be punctual in their payments. If not, I would stop the pit & [I] was not very fond of getting coals at any rate. Young Hinchcliffe said they should go on better now for he was appointed receiver of the money.

Sunday 12 March

Letter . . . from Mariana (Lawton). She is nervous at the thought of coming [to Shibden] as the time draws near . . . *'Oh, if you knew how perpetually, how constantly, how entirely, my every thought is yours, you would be sorry for me often, when your heart knows not how mine is aching.' 'Tis plain enough she would leave Charles for half a word but I will not give it. She must weather it out. I am attached to her & have no thought but of being constant – but she must wait. I like not the idea of having another man's wife.*

Monday 13 March

Great deal of conversation with Mrs W. Priestley. [I] said she should have a key of the walk-gate & come & bring anyone she liked . . . *The people think I shall not live much here. Perhaps not, after all, for I have felt a little rheumatism in my right knee today & anything of this kind will soon drive me off. I see too much of my aunt* [in pain from rheumatism] *& like not to be always wearing leather kneecaps & woollen ones at night in bed, as I have done perhaps these six months. Perhaps when I once get away, I may care little to return.*

Tuesday 14 March

Came upstairs a little before one. Calculating what money we should probably receive & probably spend before the next rent day. The receipts ought to be about £300, the expenses will be about £2,000. I hope we can do with borrowing £1500. If this be the case, I think we shall have about £950 a year ... On coming in from Halifax, found a letter from Mrs Milne (Langton). Read it at the breakfast table ... My *heart misgave me. I did not expect such an answer & yet she was right* ... [Harriet Milne writes] '*Langton. March 13th. Strange & inconsistent* [meaning Anne's behaviour]. *But I have done. Never more shall a letter of mine hurt your eye or wound your heart. You have indeed, with a ruthless hand, snatched & destroyed the blossoms you yourself planted in my bosom. But it is ever so with me. It matters not however. A few short moments of weal or woe & this scene must close for ever on the wretched & on the happy. I have it under your own hand, otherwise no power could make me believe that my friendship & love could make such desolation. Forgive me. The mischief was unintentional. Your happiness, not your misery, was my hope & prayer. But I have done. Best loved tho' latest known, farewell for ever.' The copying this letter makes me feel a strange sinking at heart. How pathetic brevity affects us. I know her – all her scrapes with others – & have been taught she has no heart nor principle & yet my heart is sad & her lines affect me. She is indeed a dangerous woman. At this moment I could kneel to her yet I have before said to myself, she is a bad one. She would only make a fool of me, or Mariana has often told me so, so it must be true* . . . *I will take no notice of this letter, the matter shall rest where it is* . . . *this will be best for us both. Surely there is not much harm done, yet I catch myself sighing deeply. What means it? I will quit the subject, & my journal, for the present.*

Wednesday 15 March

In anxious expectation of Mariana. The blood rushes to my head. I will go out for a few minutes. Went out for ¾ hour along the walk ... Came home at 6. Dressed. Sat down to dinner at 7. In a minute or 2, Mariana arrived with [her maid, Watson] ... They had very bad horses at the Wellington Arms, Rochdale, &

been above 4 hours coming from there here. Mariana very low – much affected. Some time before she could seem comfortably composed ... [She] looked pale & thin & ill.

Thursday 16 March

Slept very little last night. Talked almost the whole time till about 4 in the morning. *Went to Mariana four times, the last time just before getting up. She had eight kisses and I counted ten. Charles worse tempered than ever. He had not spoken to her of four days before she set off & she had scribbled & left two or three lines to say he was aware of her having left him on a journey of one hundred & fifty miles there and the same back, with twenty-four pounds in her pocket (he knew not of her having more) & she did not, at that moment, know if she should ever return. Half a word would make her leave him but I urged her going* [back], *at least for a time. My uncle's death was so recent it would look as if she took this opportunity of parting from him to come to me. She was for going back to her own family* [in York]. *I objected to this. Charles might not live long & then all would be right. Just before getting up, mentioned the subject of Harriet Milne & how I had committed myself on the Sunday, but declaring I had gone no farther. Mariana had suspected it & the assurance things were no worse was a great comfort to her.*

Friday 17 March

Sat up reading Mariana the copies of my letters to Harriet Milne & her last but one (to me). I had only read about half the copy of my last letter when I thought Mariana could bear no more & I stopt. She seemed for a while quite insensible, then a little incoherent for a moment or two, as if wandering. I expressed my deep sorrow. 'Is it,' said she, 'because you will never see her any more?' I noticed the cruelty of the remark, then became so agitated with weeping that it recalled Mariana to her [senses] *and she said she could do anything if she might see me calm. She forgave me but was horrified at Harriet*

Milne's depravity. She had no principle. She had tried to make excuses for her. Did not think her so bad as this. She now believed that business about Mr Meeke [Harriet's former lover] *solemnly as Harriet had sworn against it. But Mariana promised me her manner should not betray what she felt. Harriet should not find out what I had told her. But she hoped she would not go with her to Scarbro'. She would no more ask her to Lawton – she would make Charles an excuse. Then she told me of Harriet trying to intrigue with Mr Hugh* Cholmondeley. *She saw her take a rose from her bosom & give it him. I would ask to have my letters returned. She said Harriet would refuse. Her desk was full of such. She would declare she could not bear to part with them – must have them as a remembrance of me. I said I would anticipate this by offering her a better remembrance – a diamond ring or something with my hair in it. Mariana would not hear of her having my hair. Could not bear the thought. I never said she had got some already & I some of hers. I said the letters would be cheaply bought at any price. Mariana agreed. Said they were far too flattering. Would not for worlds have them seen. But she would not let me give more than six or seven guineas & if she saw a pair of ear-rings, for instance, at Barber's in York, she would buy them for me to give. We mutually professed our love & she her entire forgiveness, saying I was more sinned against than sinning.*

Saturday 18 March

A few minutes before 10, Watson brought in a letter for me from Charles, Lawton Hall. 2pp. to say I had some time ago done him the honour to make an overture of reconciliation, which he regretted he did not directly accept as then he might not have had to apply to me on this present occasion – insinuating that his not accepting my offered reconciliation, & that circumstances respecting her (Mariana's) own family, had been the cause of her leaving home. If I was still inclined to hold out the hand of friendship he would meet me in all sincerity of heart. What he wrote was in perfect confidence – I knew not how much he wanted a friend. *If all was known, he might not seem so much to blame. Mariana looked over me while I read it but, dwelling on his having written in perfect confidence, we agreed I was to consider myself not at liberty to shew her the letter & she was to know nothing of the contents. We lay about quarter-hour, talking & chuckling over the thing. Whatever happened, his writing to me & the way in which I would behave, would acquit me to the world.*

---

1. A rough draft of James Lister's will can be seen at Calderdale Archives Dept under ref SH:1/SH/1822.
2. The management of a landed estate ... – I am indebted to J V Beckett's book *The Aristocracy in England: 1660–1914* (Basil Blackwell, 1986) for much of the information in the introduction to this chapter. See in particular Chapter 4 (Part II), 'The Aristocratic Estates', pp 134–156.
3. Anne refers here to the letter she received from Charles Lawton shortly after his marriage to Mariana, when he had found out that Anne and Mariana hoped for his early death so that they could live together.
4. New Assembly Rooms – The New Assembly Rooms, built in 1828, were demolished by 1898, along with the adjoining premises of the old infirmary. The site was then used for the building of the Halifax Borough Police Court, which was opened in October 1900.

The Tyranny of Feelings

Charles Lawton's capitulation in the face of his wife's threatened desertion of the marital home was a triumph for Anne. Her view of the marriage as a purely business arrangement, on Mariana's and her family's side at least, had been vindicated. She had tried to keep silent on the issue in front of the Belcombe family for, as she told Mariana's brother, Steph Belcombe:

> '*They* [the Belcombe family] *had first blamed me for preventing her marrying, then for making this match but I had done neither one nor other. Her father & sisters had made the match. He* [Dr Belcombe] *always not knowing what would become of them* [his unmarried daughters] – *they must get their bread, etc. They* [her sisters] *all anxiety for her to make so good a match & she was not happy at home. But the match, I always thought, ought not to have been. It was mercenary & did not deserve to answer. It was a mere legal prostitution & tho' I would not prevent it, would not mar what was deemed Mariana's interest, I never did & never could approve or think it was right. I knew Mariana had done her duty to the utmost that she could but the match was too mercenary . . .*'
>
> (Saturday 15 April 1826. York)

This speech was an attempt by Anne to preserve her own and Mariana's reputation for, now that it seemed that Mariana's marriage might founder and their dream of living together become a reality, Anne began to be concerned that Mariana's current behaviour should not scandalise society. Anne would have preferred to wait for Charles' death so that it would seem more socially correct for a grieving widow to take refuge with her lifelong friend. This running off from her husband and joining her lesbian lover as soon as Anne was financially independent smacked too much of a scandalous escapade. For the people in Anne and Mariana's 'set' had ample foundation for their gossip about the relationship between the two women. Anne's own exuberant, loverlike manner towards Mariana had caused scandalised comment in their younger days, and her physical lovemaking to each of Mariana's sisters on different occasions left them in no doubt as to the true nature of the bond between Anne and Mariana. Now, however, with her new-found respectability and position in society as a landowner, Anne was anxious to keep things under control and act within the bounds of propriety so far as it was possible. She had no intention of letting Mariana take the initiative in this matter.

Mariana was thus despatched to York to stay with her family. She then went on to Scarborough with them and Anne gave her strict instructions, which were endorsed by Steph Belcombe, to return to her husband when her visit was over. Anne needed time to think. She fully intended to carry the war into the enemy's camp. The chance to score over Charles was irresistible, as was also the opportunity to put herself into the respectable position of family friend, welcomed at Lawton Hall by both husband and wife. This would dispense with the reliance on furtive, clandestine meetings with her lover which had hitherto been necessary. But Anne needed a plan of campaign. There were also a few business matters to be dealt with at home.

Between the end of March and mid-June 1826, Anne paid two or three flying visits to York in order to arrange for the sale of her horses, Hotspur and Caradoc; to visit her York dentist, Mr Horner; and to supervise the building and buying of a new travelling carriage. During one of these visits she inadvertently met Harriet Milne:

> '... Miss Duffin & I went to the Henry Belcombes' [Steph's house] ... Whom should I meet in the dining room, on her legs coming away, but Mrs Milne. She shook hands with me, merely added, "We shall see you at our house" & calling her son, Duncan, walked out as we walked in. *I fancied she coloured. Did she see my agitation? I felt to turn pale. My legs trembled under me excessively but I sat down. Miss Duffin talked away to Mrs H.S. Belcombe & I think no one guessed what was passing within me ...*'
>
> (Tuesday 6 June 1826. York)

It was very apparent that the affair had died the death and neither party cared to resurrect it. Anne's mind was firmly set on the new developments between herself, Mariana and Charles. She was also engrossed in setting affairs at home in order and, in particular, engaging the right man to act as her steward before she set out on what was to become a lengthy period of travel abroad.

Monday 27 March

I learn from Mariana's 2d letter that she did as I wished at Langton. *She suffered much from seeing Harriet Milne but hid it entirely. Harriet was not ill at Scarbro'. '... She did not speak of you quite as I liked – told me you had sat up with her & Charlotte*

[Norcliffe] *three hours one night, telling them indecent stories. Fred, this should not be.*' Harriet is to go to Scarbro' next Saturday & share Mariana's room and bed ... Mariana has had 2 more letters from Charles. [She writes to Anne] ' . . . *I was sorry to say I could find it in my heart not to go back but you say I must. Well, Fred, your will must be done.*'

Friday 31 March

Letter on my desk, 2½pp. from Charles (dated Lawton, 29 March, 1826) thanking me for my last but not in any way authorizing me to say anything to Mariana about his letters. He seems to hope she will return thro' the influence of Steph when she 'has given herself time for cool reflection. *I cannot, my dear Miss Lister, believe you would consider me so faulty as I may appear & wish you, knowing all circumstances fairly, were left to judge between us.*' *Declares he has always felt the sincerest regard for her & wish to make her happy . . . I will wait to hear from Mariana before I do anything more. She must go back. It will be best on all accounts.*

Sunday 2 April

Letter ... from Mariana, Dr Belcombe's, King St, Scarbro' ... 'I *sent my letter to Charles on Monday. It was not decisive but sufficiently so to leave it in his own power to recall me or not. I told him, Fred, that my affection was gone, my esteem shaken. That I had no feeling left that could support us under a repetition of the annoyances I had had to contend with. Consequently it was not likely that I could meet them again with calmness. That, thro' Steph's & your interference, the present disagreement might be made up but that I felt convinced in my own mind it was but for a time, for I feared I know us both too well to expect on either side the bearance or forbearance which I knew it would require to ensure our living together . . . I have not allowed my own opinions to have any weight. You said I must return & Steph said so too. It was the remembrance of what you said that made me listen to his arguments, that were strong &, perhaps as far as the world was concerned, convincing. But I am no longer a servant of the world further than is consistent with religious or moral duties.' . . . She told me when here, if it had not been for me she should not be with him* [Charles] *now. But did she deceive herself, for is she not minded to leave him chiefly to be with me? I do not think she calculated on my opposition. To the world she appears exemplary. Alas, the world knows not our connection or how we have always cheated Charles. Our intercourse is – what? Adultery. And when she leaves him, it is to come to me. I am attached to her. She has my heart & faith. 'Oh,' I last night said to myself in bed, 'I would rather go abroad without her.' Wished to be a while at liberty & have my fling in Italy. It is a bad business. She ought not to have married . . .* Wrote the whole of the journal of today which took me till 5–25. Writing my journal always does me good. I am always more composed.

Monday 3 April

It is my birthday & I have completed my thirty-fifth year. I am my own master. What events have happened during the last twelve months. Maria Barlow does not write to me. My last [letter] *went the twentieth of February. No answer. Mariana has been all but leaving Charles & probably will leave him soon. My aunt & I are going abroad. Perhaps she will not live many years. I have much to reflect on.*

Wednesday 5 April

My long-expected letter from Mrs Barlow . . . Great deal of useful information respecting our journey . . . *'Should I be in Paris when you visit it, you will call on me or not, just as you please . . .' Her letter is mere chit-chat & about our travelling & as cold or, rather, indifferent as possible. Never once addresses me by my name. Pointedly avoids any address at all . . . What a letter!*

Her style – how altered! Is she, then, going to be married, that her being in Paris in the autumn is uncertain? My heart misgave me as I read her pages – I felt I knew not what. My aunt asked if I had had a letter from her. She wished to speak of her. I said her letter was deadly cold. I knew what she meant – did not blame her. It was my then mind not to call on her [in Paris] *& I turned the subject. I could not speak of it. My heart was full. Tears were almost rushing to my eyes & all my blood seemed in my head. Perhaps she will not write to me. There will be little more intercourse between us. A feeling of desolation came over me; tho' I thought of Mariana, she must go back to Charles. We will hurry thro' Paris. I will see no-one there. My mind seemed unstrung, unable to attend to anything. How can she be so cold so soon? . . .* [I] *have just written all the above of today. It has done me good. My mind is more calm. I begin to feel as if I could care less about it. I will not write to her from the impulse of the moment. I begin to reason on the altered style of her letter. The change is too sudden. The last was all religion – this all indifference. I cannot help returning to my old thoughts – she is deep, she wants to catch me. Is it not possible the change in her manner is studied? She expects and means me to notice it. I will take my time & muse upon it & play cautiously . . . Poor Mariana! I can trust her & she will suit me best, perhaps, after all. I have known & tried her long. My journal has indeed done me good. The tyrannous feeling of the moment of mortification & I know not what, is passing by, God be thanked. Oh, that I was better in the eyes of Heaven!*

Friday 7 April

[Anne paid a visit to the Priestleys at Lightcliffe] . . . *Speaking of Mr Briggs* [as a possible steward for the Lister estate], *Mr Priestley said he* [Mr Briggs] *would see a good deal of my father. I too hastily said I did not think that a good recommendation. Mr Priestley looked & said no more. I just observed, 'You do not quite understand me.' 'Yes,' said Mr Priestley, 'I know you act quite independently of your father . . .' I assented, not choosing to explain what I really meant, which was my father's being too familiar with my steward. I felt sorry I had said this. In short, I came away out of love with my visit, thinking I shall be glad to get away abroad, out of the way of all of them. If I ever come back to settle here, I shall begin anew & hope to be more guarded & to do better. I mused on all this.*

Thursday 20 April

Sauntered up & down the walk. Fell almost asleep under the sycamore I call my summerhouse, overhanging the brook. Warm but plenty of air or wind. Thought of our journey & of Mariana – *to tell Steph . . . that if Mariana cannot stay with Charles, I wish her to have a small lodging & live quietly in York where all the world can see her good conduct. I will make business to come back to England at the first succeeding rent day & take her back with me.*

Saturday 22 April

At 10, James Sykes came. Has walked all the way to & from Pontefract. Got the 1,500 hollys yesterday at the nursery of Messrs Oxley, Thomas & Scholes & got them (by 3 waggons) brought as far as Archard moor last night & expects them here at 11 this morning. Throp [at Halifax] had written for them [the holly trees] but they (the people) would not let him have them. 'They are very dear.' £3 per thousand, but Throp charges me £4 per thousand, i.e. takes 25 per cent profit. Probably he may have done this on all he has sold to me. Nothing like experience. I will always in future send to Pontefract at once. Asked James what his expenses were on the road. A shilling for beer & for the rest he had lived on penny cakes. I am pleased with the man. He said he had his wages (3/9 per day) & thought he ought not to want anything more. Gave him 4/6 (with which he seemed much pleased) which, including mat [*sic*] & package & carriage to Archard moor, makes £5. I shall have to pay carriage from

Archard moor here (one shilling), that these 1,500 hollys will have cost me (including James Sykes' 2 days wages) just £5.1.8 ... settled with all the men up to Saturday the 18th ult. A balance due to me from James Smith of £9.16.2. which I agreed to let him pay by ½ yearly instalments of £1 every rent day for [which] he said he was much obliged to me. A balance due to me from John Booth of £2.16.2. Gave him this balance & promised to give him £1 towards his rent due on May day. Poor John! His heart was lightened. I believe the man really did feel grateful. What a pleasure it is to give judiciously!

Sunday 23 April

Letter from Mariana to say she should leave Scarbro' on Thursday ... begs me to go to York [to meet her there].

Monday 24 April

Dinner at 6–20, at which hour Mr Freeman [a Halifax attorney] came ... [I] asked him 'Why not appoint Mr Briggs steward?' Mr Freeman has nothing against him ... *but he was afraid he was poor. When he ought to have been saving he spent it all in fancies; gigs, horses, etc.* Tea & coffee at 8½. My aunt & I talked over the choice between Mr Parker & Mr Briggs for a steward. Inclined to the former. *The latter being poor sticks in my throat. Poverty makes people not always the safest.* Talked over our affairs *& the propriety of being away from here, out of my father's reach for borrowing money of us.*

Tuesday 25 April

Wrote 2pp to Mr Duffin to ask him to give me a bed on Thursday night & Friday night. Expected Mariana to bring me back on Saturday ... Mr Priestley wished me to see Mrs Lees [who was going to be Anne's tenant at Northgate House once Anne and her aunt had gone abroad and Anne's father and sister had moved into Shibden Hall as temporary residents until Anne's return]. She [Mrs Lees] wants several more alterations. Went & called on her about 2 ... [She] would shake hands with me & would have talked I know not how long but luckily she had her wants written down. I begged to have the paper – said we would be glad to do anything to make the thing comfortable to all parties. Thought there would be no difficulty between us. Agreed to meet her at one tomorrow & came away, thinking the time I had stayed long [enough], not caring to know the state of the bowels, etc., which made a water-closet (which I said at once we could not manage) necessary. She said she would come and call on my aunt. Had before intended it but had been so great an invalid. I bowed and as soon afterwards as seemed civil said I feared my aunt was too unwell to be able to see her. She took the hint. Poor soul! thought I to myself, she knows no better. Those whom we visit here must wait for <u>us</u> to visit <u>them</u>.

YORK

Friday 28 April

Got to the Henry Belcombes' [Steph's] at 12½. Mariana had gone into Micklegate for me ... Waited till 2½ then went towards Horner's to meet Mariana (she had 6 teeth stopped with gold) ... Had my hair cut at Parson's, Mariana with me all the while. We parted there just before 5 struck & I got back here to dine at 5–06 ... Tea here at 8 ... I went to spend the remainder of the evening in the Minster Yard [with Mariana at Steph Belcombe's home] ... Sad accounts of the riots in Lancashire.[1] Pulling down the power loom machinery. In coming [to York] yesterday, [I] met 2 troops of the 5th Dragoon Guards called off to quell the rioters. 'Tis said several of the mob have been killed.

HALIFAX

Sunday 30 April

Two last night & one this morning. Good, but never quite so much so the first night as afterwards. Mariana very sick & bilious & lay in bed all day, only getting up in time for dinner.

Thursday 4 May

Mariana got ready & we set off about 12¼ [to go to Halifax] ... The town rather disturbed. Riots expected. Messrs Edwards of Pye Nest, Kershaw, Ackroyd & Peter Bold have power looms & they expect them to be attacked. Some Dragoons came in this morning. Sad rioting at Bradford. Several people wounded. Marian [Lister] croaking, as usual, over the distresses of the people – gives much more in charity than she ought to do. More than my father can afford & I can't think that this is right. In returning, Mariana & I went down the fields ... *On returning up the new bank, a man said, 'Are them man & wife?' Mariana & I both coloured but she laughed & said she did not mind it, nor do I think she did. She says she is not worldly now. When we got home I took her into the stables. I thought not of James Sykes being at his dinner in the barn & believe he must have heard me say, 'I have brought you in here to give you a kiss.'*

Friday 5 May

In talking to Mrs Priestley & on her saying I should not come back to live here – should not make great alterations in the house, etc., 'Ah, I don't think so,' said Mariana, inadvertently, 'I think we might.' The we was tell-tale. Mrs Priestley had noticed it & looked as if it was not lost upon her. Mariana coloured deeply – talked of 'we' & 'we' as much as she could afterwards in such a manner as to turn it off, but probably only made bad worse. On Mariana's telling me this as we returned, we both laughed heartily. I told her Mrs Priestley would instantly guess all about it. I had told her I should one of these days have a friend with me, had long made up my mind, etc., – that she [Mrs Priestley] would like her exceedingly but on her asking if she had ever seen her, for fear of her guessing rightly & by way of a blind, I had said no. She would naturally be struck by what Mariana had so inadvertently let slip & would be au fait at the whole matter. Mariana said she did not care.

Sunday 7 May

We went to the old church. Got there just after the service had begun. Mr Hudson read the prayers. The curate preached 27½ minutes from Acts i. ii. I heard not much of it, rather dozing all the while. Mariana & I staid the sacrament – the 1st time we ever received it together in our lives. Returned very slowly up the old bank & got home at 2¼.

Monday 8 May

A very long, good kiss last night, after having talked above an hour. Said Dupuytren has examined me. [He] *evidently did not believe the story of my being married. Insinuated that he thought me singularly made. He had recommended that a seringue à manivelle which might be used by a man. He had so mercurialised me, etc., that it had brought on profuse bleedings. I used to sit on the pot & bleed like a stuck pig.*

Wednesday 10 May

Latter from Maria Barlow (Paris) – 1p. She has been dangerously ill. Only just out of danger. Had 7 leeches hanging on the nape of her neck at the time she received my last. Inflammatory fever ... *Poor soul! She likes, perhaps loves, me still & I feel for & pity her. I will write kindly but,* as Mariana says, *give no delusory hopes. The letter made me look & feel grave. Mariana is sorry for her & behaves very well.*

Friday 12 May

Mr Parker came & brought me the probate copy of my uncle's will . . . Told him I should appoint Mr James Briggs [as] steward, at which he was evidently much disappointed. He asked if speaking to my father would do any good, to which I of course said no! & begged he would not. Said my uncle had thought of appointing Mr James Briggs. Everyone startled at the thought of making an attorney steward.[2] He allowed this was natural enough.

Tuesday 16 May

Message to Mr James Briggs to say I wanted to speak to him. He came at 9¾. Dressed & went down to him at 10¼. Told him what I wished him to do as steward and told him he should have the appointment, with which he seemed well pleased. Mariana came into the breakfast room & thought him the very person to suit us. Then spoke to him in the drawing room. Could not get him to fix his terms. He said he should be easily paid – should be very happy to do his best for us. He had been long in the family (this meant so long accustomed to act as clerk to my uncle & father, as Commissioners of Taxes) that he felt quite an interest in the estate & for the family. Mr Washington came. Said they trespassed very much in Yew Trees wood. Had cock fights there. Gave him 20 papers [notices against trespassing] to put up.

Friday 19 May

Hunting up old silver, money chiefly, to take to the bank . . . Drove to Mr James Briggs' . . . Told him I would give him £20 a year for his trouble & that he must charge postage & any other extra that he thought he ought to be charged. He seemed well satisfied & said it was enough . . . Then drove to the bank.

They could not take the old silver coin. It had been called in by government & was not payable now ... Drove to Adams & Mitchell's shop. Took 40 crowns of Chas 2, William 3 and Anne; 14 half ditto [half-crowns] of these & later reigns; 70 shillings; 16 sixpences, & 4 shillings & 3 sixpences, worn quite plain (of every reign from Charles 2) which altogether weighed 61 oz., for which, at 4/6 per oz., I got £13.14.6. I also took & sold a light ½ guinea for 9/6 & a light sev. [seven?] shilling piece for 6/8, getting altogether £14.10.8.

Tuesday 23 May

Took Mariana to Southolm. She was beginning to be tired. Rested at Southolm an hour & had bread & butter & a glass of beer ... In returning from Southolm, persecuted by Miss Delia Walker. Turned into a cottage at Lower Norcliffe to avoid her & Mariana & I sat there 10 minutes till she went away. She said she meant to do herself the honour of calling here [at Shibden Hall]. I said we were going to leave the place immediately. From Lower Norcliffe by John Balmforth's to George Naylor's. Mariana rested there another hour. Sent for George Naylor & his wife out of the fields, which pleased them much. Promised to go see them again some time when we came back again. Mariana promised the lady a riband for a keepsake. George Naylor shewed his well-farmed land. Beautiful corn & greensward ... Sauntered to Beacon Hill.[3] Loitered there, looking at the town below & all the fine country around, admiring the prospect – speculating when we should next so regard it. Returned to our own fields opposite the house.

Thursday 25 May

At 12, Mariana & I set off to the Yew Trees ... In returning, caught by a shower. Took shelter at the Traveller's Inn at Hipperholme lane ends. A very civil young woman shewed us into the parlour where we sat about ¼ hour ... *We had talked of the management my temper required. Mariana knew it well. It had its peculiarities but she did not fear. Talked of the Blackstone Edge business*[4] *& that at Scarbro' & Miss Morritt & Goodrick*[5] *& my sensitiveness of anything that reminded me of my petticoats. Mariana behaved very well & I was satisfied. She will know & manage me better in future. I do not, cannot, doubt her affection. I think we shall get on well together in time to come. We both of us better know ourselves & what we are about.*

---

1. Riots in Lancashire – These were the most serious attacks launched against power looms in the South Pennine area: '... From April, 1826, 21 mills were attacked and more than 1,000 power looms destroyed in disturbances which began in Accrington and quickly spread across East Lancashire and later across the Pennines to Skipton and Bradford ...' J A Hargreaves, *Factory Kings and Slaves: South Pennine Social Movements 1780–1840* (p 8), Pennine Heritage Network, Hebden Bridge 1982.
2. 'Everyone startled ... an attorney steward ...' – See p 146, J V Beckett's *The Aristocracy in England:* '... agricultural experts were almost unanimous in condemning the employment of lawyers as stewards ... [because] lawyers were frequently accused of neglect; but the real complaint – which became more pertinent as the agricultural revolution proceeded – concerned their ignorance of farming practice ...'
3. Beacon Hill – Originally known as Gletcliffe or Gletclyffe, the first mention of this commanding hill which overlooks the town of Halifax is in the Southowram deeds of 1553. It derived the name which it holds today from the erection of a beacon pan, which formed part of the chain of beacons in Yorkshire and Lancashire used to pass on warnings of approaching danger, e.g. the approach of the Spanish Armada in 1588; of invading armies during the Glorious Revolution of 1688; and in 1745, when the Highlanders invaded England. In more peaceable times, the Halifax beacon is lit for occasions of national rejoicing.

4. *The Blackstone Edge business* – See note 7, p 171.
5. *Scarbro' & Miss Morritt & Goodrick* – See pp 316–322 of Volume One *The Secret Diaries of Miss Anne Lister.* Anne was socially snubbed at Scarborough by the Misses Morritt and Goodrick and was also hurt by Mariana's reluctance to be seen in public with her, because of her pronounced appearance of masculinity.

Ménage À Trois

Anne's life had taken on more definite contours as she settled into her new role as an independent woman of means. There was no-one to whom she had to defer, therefore her decision-making was untrammelled by having to consult the wishes of some over-riding figurehead. Her aims, at this time, were threefold. Firstly, she wished to return to Paris, using it as a base for a more extended tour of Europe. Secondly, she wished to ensure that her estate was run efficiently in order to maintain her lifestyle and pay for her travels, and to this end she had employed Mr Briggs as steward. Thirdly, having brought Charles Lawton into a state of conciliation, she wanted to establish her role firmly as that of family friend *par excellence*, to both the Lawtons and the world, so that the gossips could not speculate too freely about the intimacy between herself and Mariana. Charles' presence as the friendly husband, accepting the bond of friendship between his wife and her 'best friend', sanctioned the relationship and cloaked it with an air of respectability which silenced any would-be scandalmongers, while allowing the women to continue their affair.

With typical thoroughness, Anne began to put her plans into action. First of all, the social tie-in with Charles had to be displayed to the world. Anne planned a short tour of Wales and Ireland with Mariana and Charles, at the end of which they would all return to Lawton Hall, with Anne and her aunt as house-guests there. Having thus fulfilled the social requirements of husbandly approval and acceptance, the next step was to obtain Charles' agreement to Mariana's visiting Paris without him, in the company of Anne and her aunt.

The period between 16th June 1826, when Anne and her aunt left Shibden Hall to join Mariana and Charles in Cheshire, and the end of August 1826, when Anne and Mariana arrived in Paris, is a time of rather hectic travelling for the Listers and the Lawtons. Anne and her aunt, with George Playforth, their manservant, and MacDonald, their new Highland maidservant, met Mariana and Charles with their manservant, Christopher, at Parkgate, Cheshire, where they stayed for a few days at Mrs Briscoe's Hotel. Anne then had to visit York and return to Shibden Hall for business reasons and Charles returned to Lawton Hall. They left Mariana at Parkgate to look after Aunt Anne.

On Anne's return, she, Mariana and Charles, accompanied by the Lawtons' manservant, Christopher, set off for a short tour of Wales and then travelled over to Dublin. They again left Aunt Anne at Mrs Briscoe's Hotel in Parkgate, as so much travelling was exhausting for her. Once the party became reunited a second time with Aunt Anne, they all travelled on to Lawton Hall, Cheshire.

Friday 16 June

Breakfast at 12. Off at 1–05. All the house in tears – yet my aunt behaved better than I expected. She had said yesterday she could have cried all day but she thought it would be foolish & did not give way to it. I talk of our returning this summer 2 years to see them all. Alas! Will my aunt live to return? . . .

Stopt for a moment en passant at Northgate. Marian [Lister] gave me the receipt for her legacy of £50 [from her late Uncle James]. Poor girl! She hurried off after shaking hands & saying goodbye. Did she think she might not meet us all again? My father in better spirits than one might have fancied ... Off from Halifax at 1¾. Took our 4 horses to Rochdale town (under 17 miles from Shibden) yet did not get to the Roebuck [Inn] till 4½. The carriage, being new, ran heavily. A very good pair of horses from the Roebuck to the new Bridgewater Arms or Royal Hotel. Manchester ... My aunt better than expected. Lifted on a chair into the carriage on leaving Shibden but got out without one at Manchester & walked upstairs to our sitting-room ... Had a letter from Mariana (Lawton) to say she & Charles would meet us tomorrow at Chester. Stay and go with us to the cathedral & all go together to Parkgate in the afternoon of Sunday ... Charles says if she will give [up the idea of] going to Paris this year, he will go with her next year. She thinks nothing like time present. He is behaving beautifully.

CHESTER

Saturday 17 June

George had let Campbell, the coachmaker at Manchester, put common oil on the wheels. What ignorance. Common grease oil will not do with antiattrition. Obliged, therefore, to use kitchen fat at Northwich. By the way, told George last night, on settling with him, that as he was now out of livery he must behave very steady, etc. I should depend on him for all being right about the carriage & that he must now be called by his surname ... Alighted at the Royal Hotel, Chester [at 5–25] ... Charles out at the moment. Mariana looking out for us ...

delighted to see us ... Charles soon came in. Went up & shook hands with him & said I was glad to see him, as if nothing had passed disagreeably between us. All passed off remarkably well. Dinner at 6½. All quite at our ease ... excellent friends. *Mariana says he was very nervous all the morning. We both behaved uncommonly* [well]. *My manners soon set him at his ease. I had two glasses of Madeira at dinner & three of port afterwards but it was good & did not affect my head at all* ... Charles retired at 10. My room next to theirs & Mariana & I came in in 5 or ten minutes. *She undressed in my room. So did I, quite, & in half an hour we had been in bed, had two or three kisses & Mariana was gone to Charles. She says she cannot live without me. Charles is altered. I think he will not be another ten years in our way.* Mariana left me at 10–40 ... Mariana likes the look of MacDonald [Anne's new maid] very well. Sent her out this morning to buy a new bonnet, price 10/-, trimmed (straw, white) & gave it to her. *Told Mariana she had a pint of beer every afternoon about five-o-clock, which I did not like. Mariana did not seem to mind it – said she dared say Watson drank as much beer. If she did not get tipsy it did not signify. I must not be so fastidious.*

PARKGATE, CHESHIRE

Sunday 18 June

All off to Parkgate (Charles drove his own horse in the phaeton) at 2–25. Got out at Mrs Briscoe's Hotel in exactly 2 hours. A sick old lady, a Mrs Perrin, dying in the house. Her daughter in the house & had the room I was to have had. Obliged to take up with an indifferent one, but [it was] the room next to Mariana & Charles' and theirs so hot Charles glad to have it to himself & Mariana slept in mine.

Tuesday 20 June

Two very good kisses, last night, at once. We got into the other bed this morning that it might seem as if we had not slept together. Luckily, Charles could not get another room & it was too small & hot for him to care about having Mariana ... Mariana & I went out, walked a mile or more towards Hoylelake, along the shore. Sat down on a little grass-covered sand hillock for ½ hour. Had a pleasant chat & got back about 3. We had slunk off to avoid Charles ... *He is very attentive to my aunt & all goes on beautifully . . . Determined to part with George, he is such a lout. And probably MacDonald, too.* To get a professed lady's maid. A professed lady's maid would not take Mariana's place some time ago (when she feared losing Watson) because they were not in the habit of going to London. A professed servant wants to go every 2 years, to keep up what they have learnt.

Wednesday 21 June

Letter, 2pp., forwarded from Shibden, from Maria Barlow, Paris. Wondering she has not heard from me. She has been unwell. *Poor soul! In love with me as ever.* [She says that] *when she wrote me last – ' . . . I was not good. I was wicked. I set in array before me another beloved* [meaning Mariana] *& when that idea fills my mind I am half a maniac & it is then I detest myself. But I am better in every way. I shall be satisfied with my doom. There is no remedy & I hope resignation will again restore some peace to my wretched bosom. When the postman disappoints me of a letter, I am then made fully aware how precious your paper regard is to me. It is my only consolation, my best comfort . . . My real regard has never changed but to be more intense & it will ever remain so until I have breathed my last. How much I would have sacrificed for you I scarcely like to own to myself . . . Heaven bless you, dear Anne . . . You understand not, perhaps, the depths of woman's real regard – of such feelings as mine* *which, thanks to Providence, are not general in the sex. I am ever your sincere friend, C.M.B.' Poor soul! I pity &, were it not for Mariana, should love her. She would have me still . . . I must see her again. Let me try my regard for her – see how she looks & how she could please me now when Mariana is mistress of my thoughts & hopes.*

Saturday 24 June

At 5, Mariana & I went out. Strolled to the Ferry house . . . Looked at a pretty little cottage under the same roof as the Ferry house which the people (Bloor) let off in the summers. 1 parlour, 3 or 4 best beds & a servant's bed. 2 guineas a week. We must have a cook to cook for us. She would ask £10 for the six summer months. Mariana & I could economise there – could perhaps get the cottage for 30 guineas for 6 months [*sic*] & live for £70. Bring all to about £100.

On Monday 26th June, Anne travelled to York in order to have some dental treatment and to arrange for the drawing up of her will. She then went back to Shibden to attend to the half-yearly collection of rents and one or two other matters. Charles Lawton returned to Lawton Hall for a few days to attend to his own concerns, while Mariana and Aunt Anne remained at Parkgate, Cheshire.

As Mr Duffin was unable to offer Anne a bed at his house, she stayed with Miss Marsh during her short visit to York.

Thursday 29 June

At 11½, set off (by myself) over the bridge to shew him [Horner, the dentist in York] a tooth decaying at the far end of the upper left jaw. Waited about ½ hour. Then about ½ hour undergoing the operation of having the tooth filled with leaf tin (the material as pure tin as possible – always fills with this when the hole is very large). Suffered nothing from the tooth itself but a sympathetic affection of the nerves of the great tooth in the under jaw gave me excessive pain. Strong spasms of these nerves and a bad toothache in this tooth all the rest of the day. My jaws, too, were cramped from being held so long & wide open. The side of my face swelled a little & I could scarce eat anything at dinner that required chewing ... Dr H.S. Belcombe [Steph] came to call on me. Brought me a written list of things for our medicine chest. He was going to visit a patient in Spurriergate at 10. Walked there with him for the purpose of a little tête-à-tête. Said how well all had gone at Parkgate – *what Charles had said about the five hundred a year being secured to Mariana*[1] *– that Jonathan Gray was making my will, by which I* [left] *... Mariana a hundred a year ... At all events, she was sure of six hundred a year.*

HALIFAX

Friday 30 June

Took a hasty leave of Miss Marsh & off in the new mail at 7½. One nice-looking, civil gentleman inside (I could not go outside[2] – no room) ... Soon found my friend – a respectable Liverpool merchant – a Unitarian & for reform in Parliament & for having, like the Americans, no established religion. My friend argued mildly & certainly as well as such sentiments could permit & is evidently one of the Liverpool savans. He is an advocate for the more sound & liberal education of girls, for the better strength of their minds & bodies & enabling them to be more independent and fight their way, if necessary. Does not see why they should not be as clever as boys ... [On reaching Halifax] wished my friend good luck & got out a few minutes before 1 at this end [nearest Shibden] of the bridge. Joseph Smith, passing on horseback at this time, brought up my travelling bag, etc., & I followed. Got here in about twenty minutes. Musing, as I walked along, on the changes that death & time had wrought at Shibden. Found my father & Marian quite well. The roof off the drawing-room end of the house ... On coming upstairs, found a letter from Mariana ... It seems Miss Pattison [a good friend of Mariana's] was in Chester the Saturday we arrived there but her Blue politics kept her from the Orange precincts of the Royal Hotel. Of course we were there on account of the Lawtons. Mariana Blue, Charles Orange[3] but moderate.

Saturday 1 July

Wrote to Mr Gray *to entail the property on the oldest male or female issue of John Lister's eldest son or daughter.*[4] *If none from this stock becomes entailed to the estate,* [then] *to give it to Marian* [Lister] *for life & then in trust for her eldest son or daughter. If Marian leaves no issue, Mariana* [Lawton] *to have it for life & a power to leave it by will as she thinks proper, provided she leaves it to my right heir-at-law and, if she make no will at all, the right heir to have it unconditionally.* My *aunt to have it to do as she likes with* [should Anne predecease her aunt] *but if she does not revoke my will, it is to stand good. If my father survives her, he is to have the rents and profits for life. Marian's three hundred a year to commence from my aunt's death. The new trustees to have a hundred each.*

Monday 3 July

Washed & dressed & sat down at my desk, or rather at my table, at 8–20, to prepare the rent-roll, etc., for Mr Briggs at the rent-day ... All the day making out a proper rent-roll on account of the property income & outgoings.

Tuesday 4 July

On meeting my father, Mr Briggs *went & shook hands with him. I don't like this. I fancy him* [Mr Briggs] *not quite satisfied with twenty pounds a year tho' he says he is.* Came upstairs at 12. Making out for myself memoranda of what I have to receive this rent-day from one source or other & what, probably, to pay. *Perhaps there will be between seven & eight hundred left for us to live & travel upon.*

Wednesday 5 July

Waited a while for my father. We got to the Mytholm [Inn] at 11 ... & then to business. Settled with all the tenants before dinner except Mark Hepworth, who would not come ... Joseph Hall wanted me to pay the Lord's rent[5] for him – said my uncle would have done it. No. I could not, tenants always paid these charges. I really could not. 'It would be a bad precedent,' said Mr Briggs afterwards. I thought so decidedly yet felt annoyed to refuse. Hemingway behaved very well about having no allowance made him – said little or nothing about it. Why, if it must be so, it must be so. Balmforth would have it, not that my uncle had made him an allowance but that he had actually lowered his rent, & was for paying only 60 guineas – & was for paying only £31–10s instead of £36–15s [a half-year's rent] but I was decided so he paid the whole, making out with guineas which he said he had had a long time & was sorry enough to part with. I thought to myself, 'I am decided enough. They will think me "very hard" but I like it not, tho' this man is evidently wanting to take advantage & I shall remember this trick.' I thought of my uncle & wondered not he was so talked out of his money by such people. Thought I, gentlemen ought to have stewards. I am glad I have Mr Briggs. He shall do the business in future. I shall not trouble them much again. Dinner ready before 1. Kept them waiting a few minutes till I had done. Mr Briggs & I then went down. My father & the rest had eaten the pudding.[6] I on my father's right at the top & Mr Briggs on our left. The room full of people. The table full of smoking meat. My father turned sick & went out. Called Mr Briggs into his place. [I] staid a minute or 2 to drink a glass of water then wished all the tenants their health & goodbye, saying it was quite uncertain when I should see them again, & came away. Jackman followed, sent by the party to ask for our footing.[7] My father gave a pound, I ditto & 10/- for Mr Briggs & went back & gave it to Mr Briggs, for which all bowed & seemed much pleased ... About 8, Mark Hepworth came & paid all his rent & £5 towards his debt of £46.6.3. Told him I should divide his farm. He begged to be tried (said Mr Briggs) another year & he would farm well & pay rent & [debt] too. Hardcastle had told Mr Briggs Mark had borrowed £20 of him the last rent day & he had heard nothing more of it ever since. Told Mr Briggs to make the best of it & try Mark another year. Coffee at 9 ... My father will pay me Hampstead house rent[8] & the £9.16.2 James Smith owes me. I certainly did not expect this & all has turned out well. All the tenants have paid every farthing. This, too, is more than I counted upon.

Sunday 9 July

Mr Briggs came ... He explained the nature of account by a treble entry – day book, cash book, ledger. [I] came up & tried the cash-book system. I have too little time at present. Puzzled. Must go on my own way just now ... Oh! that I had 'retirement, books, domestic quiet' once again. I am all bustle.

LIVERPOOL

Monday 10 July

Packed my travelling bag & trunk, which is literally full of books for making out my accounts, etc., & Gifford's 'English Lawyer' which I have borrowed of my father, thinking it well to have some keys to the laws of my own country with me. Had Marian upstairs a little while. Explained how I wished things to be put away. Gave her all my keys but those [of] my letter drawer & journal book drawer ... Off from Shibden at 12–20 ... At the Waterloo Hotel [Liverpool] at a minute or 2 before 10 ... Charles here – arrived at 1 today ... His room next to mine. [He was] in high good humour – most attentive.

Tuesday 11 July

Very good bed. Very comfortable room ... Met Mariana [who had travelled from Parkgate, Cheshire]. Shopped a little then came home [to the Waterloo Hotel] ... Dinner at 6. Capital turtle, good soals [*sic*], etc. Good Madeira port & claret. Everything very good. Iced water – iced punch to the turtle ... Charles & I sauntered out together for a little air. Very fine, warm day. Sat with all the windows open. *Charles seemed inclined to let Mariana sleep with me. However, she went to him after she got into bed to me for a few minutes & given me a tolerable kiss. We heard him snoring all the while. Mariana dresses in my room, which gives us opportunity.*

Wednesday 12 July

Could not sleep last night. Had the toothache all the night & found the gent^y. [gentility? meaning bugs?] had been at both my eyes. Mariana came for a few minutes cuddle. Breakfast at 9–20. Charles' door open. Partly dressed in his room. We are all exceedingly sociable. Mariana & I set off for sightseeing ... We went to the Bluecoat School[9] in Church St. Mr William Forster, the teacher, house steward and manager, altogether most civil – a very clever young man, filling his situation admirably. 311 boys & 96 girls. Go to their chapel on a Sunday evening. The institution well worth seeing ... Paid off our coach. Had had it 3¾ hours, charge 12/- . . . In the evening we all went to the play, 'John Bull', 'Just Twelve at Night' & something else which we did not stop to see. The playhouse very hot tho' the boxes not near full. Got home at 10–50 . . . We are to be up at 5 tomorrow to pack & sail for Bangor at 8½.

MONA, WALES

Thursday 13 July

[At 9 am] on board the Prince Llewellyn steam packet . . . Not water enough for us in the Hoyle channel (spelt according to pronunciation) so obliged to go above 20 miles round about, by Formby. Soon sick – 4 times. Dozed between times. Could not bear to speak or move. Never so ill at sea before. All the rest of our party on deck, apparently well. The rain continued 2 or 3 hours. When the Lesser Orme's head came in view, roused myself to look at the fine lines of the Welsh coast. Felt better . . . [Got to] Mona at 11. A handsome looking house. Had to wait some time (all in bed) to see the rooms. Very good. Resolved to stay all night. Ordered mutton chops. I paid the drivers & did all. The wine hot but Charles called it good & liked the chops but hardly spoke & left Mariana & me & we sat up twenty minutes & then went to bed, Mariana sleeping with me.

HOLYHEAD

Friday 14 July

Off at 5¾ [pm] to Holyhead, 13 miles. Stopt at Spencer's, the Royal Hotel, at 6–30. Going in a hack, they were shewing us into an indifferent sitting-room but Mrs Spencer remembered Charles the moment she saw him (she & her husband used to keep the George Inn, now Mrs Briscoe's Hotel at Parkgate). This set all right. She lent us her little phaeton & pony to drive about to see the pier & the docks & we had everything the best the house could afford . . . Mrs Spencer's remembering him put Charles into good humour & so far it was worth much. Except along the Menai, not a tree to be seen in Anglesea [*sic*]. Dreary looking island . . . Holyhead a picturesque looking little town. The houses generally whitewashed.

DUBLIN

Saturday 15 July

On board the Cinderella mail packet . . . landed at Howth at 1½ . . . off in a chaise that was waiting, about 2 . . . Dublin bay on our left. Could see but little of it. Quite low water. Could not have seen it to advantage . . . All of us much struck with the magnificent appearance of the public buildings & the width of the streets, Lower Sackville St. etc., & Dawson Street, where we are [at Tuthill's Hotel] . . . Dinner at 5–40. Very good madeira port & claret. The soup & fish very good. Besides these, beef steaks & veal steaks, red currant tart & green apricot ditto. Charles delighted with the town & with our accommodation. Owns himself repaid for coming. At 7, went to the theatre. Shakespeare's 'Comedy of Errors'.

Sunday 16 July

Mariana & I set off at 11–35 to the Roman Catholic chapel in Marlborough St. Took a boy from the house as guide & walked. While we went into the chapel, sent him for a coach to take us to Christ church. The Roman Catholic service having begun at 11, the high mass was over . . . Got to Christ church in our wretched vehicle at 12½ . . . Many of the congregation seemed to have come on purpose to hear the singing. Very good – but give me York ... Got home about 2¾. Mariana had biscuits & I a glass of warm lemonade. *Charles never heard of such a thing. Nobody would, or ever did, take it but myself. Then he began about Mariana's shawl & mine being for winter, not summer. Nobody wore such here, etc. Tiresome. I am sick of travelling with him. Heaven defend* [me] *from such another tour. I wish this was over.* I *came off to my own room for a while* ... At 7½, had a job coach (shabby – all the hired vehicles seem so – the hackney coaches are quite terrible) & drove round Phenix [*sic*] park & the principal streets. The park pretty but wants wood. Abundance of large old thorns which constitute almost all the wood there is in the park, 4 or 5 miles around. Got home at 9¼. Had tea ... Mrs Lloyd said the Marchioness of Wellesley[10] was very proper. Very attentive to everybody & made the Marquis[11] so, too. Made him, in this respect, more proper than he was before.

Anne and the Lawtons spent a few more days sightseeing in and around Dublin and then decided it was time to return to Aunt Anne in Parkgate, Cheshire.

LIVERPOOL

Thursday 20 July

All of us on board the Lord Barney steam packet [at 8–25 am] ... Sheep & cattle in the hold & in large sheds on deck alongside the engine wheels, & hampers full of geese on deck & geese loose in the hold. One of the sheds full of narrow stalls, just large enough to hold one horse each, filled with Irish harvest men[12] squatted close together on the floor. More of them on deck. A motley scene, aided by sellers of oranges, etc., & people not going to sail with us . . . I fell asleep. Soon awakened by Mariana's being very sick. Could sleep no more – nor speak to her – so sick myself. The sea rough. The vessel tossed about, the excessive trembling, lateral motion, added to the up & down, made Mariana & me suffer much. She crawled on deck about 10½ & I about 11 am. The night had been very rough.

PARKGATE, CHESHIRE

Saturday 22 July

Mariana low at the thought of my leaving her . . . but did not say much. In tears at, and after, dinner. She came up into my room for 2 or 3 minutes. Charles hurried her off [back home to Lawton Hall] at 7 &, he & I having before parted very good friends, I saw them no more . . . At 7–05 off from the Waterloo Hotel (Liverpool) . . . in a postchaise. The man drove me here [Mrs Briscoe's Hotel, Parkgate, Cheshire] in 1¼ hours & I alighted at 9¼ by these clocks – forwarder than Liverpool's. Found Miss Fletcher sitting with my aunt – a tall, large, plain, dark, elderly or middle-aged person . . . Miss Fletcher's attention to my aunt has been most kind & useful. She seems an excellent sort of person. She say she is 'stay-at-home'. This, one might guess.

Wednesday 26 July

At 7¾ Miss Wilbraham, Mrs & Miss Cottingham called & sat till 8–20 . . . Miss Cottingham a lively Irish girl. Miss Wilbraham said our motive, my aunt's & mine (for living reasonably in Paris, should we get there) was not economy – it was not necessary. *They all think us people of fortune & gentility, & probably of talent.*

Thursday 27 July

Mrs Buchanan came up to me & sat with me till now – 4½. Great deal of conversation about the Lawtons. *She, & everybody, wonders why Mariana married* [Charles]. *Says it must always be an enigma to her. Mr Buchanan does not like Charles. Won't visit them. Met him at Westhouse some time ago. His conversation shockingly gross* . . . [I said] *Charles' manners gauche but I pitied him. His caprices so sometimes unaccountable, I thought him not always responsible for himself. This, it seems, has also entered the heads of others. They say he was quite silly when at school . . . Several gents said, after the ball at Lawton, what a pity Mariana had not a different husband.*

Thursday 3 August

Packing my boot-trunk & seat-box, etc. Looking over, trying on, & writing my name in my 13 prs of new gloves put into my boot-trunk – besides having 3 prs new ditto elsewhere & 4 pairs in wear. Looking a little at the contents of my writing-box . . . Had tea. Settled & paid everything, that I shall have nothing of this sort to do in the morning.

---

1. '. . . *five hundred a year being secured to Mariana* [by Charles] . . .' – The terms of Charles Lawton's will, proven in March 1860, some twenty years after Anne Lister's own death, show that he left Mariana an annuity of £50, in addition to all his household effects, monies from insurance policies, his horses and carriages, some cottages, an inn and the lands attached to them. Whilst not inheriting the Lawton estate, she was, by the standards of the day, reasonably well provided for, for the last eight years of her life. She died in 1868, at the age of eighty, according to her death certificate, although her date of birth was given as 1790.
2. '. . . I could not go outside . . .' – Anne preferred the unladylike way of

travelling on the outside of the coach. When possible she would take the reins although at that time it was against the law for coachmen to allow passengers to do so. The rule was regularly broken.

3. '... Mariana Blue, Charles Orange ...' – Blue was then, as now, the political colour of the Conservative or Tory party. Orange was a variation of the Whig yellow. An article in the *Halifax Guardian Almanack* (1903–1905) entitled 'A Halifax Election Riot', which took place in 1832, states that: '... blues and yellows were busy in preparation for the contest. Flags were hung out of the windows of the Committee Rooms. Those of the Conservatives were blue ... The yellow flags [of the Whigs] were of one genus as to colour, but of varying shades of complexion, from the deep orange glow of the large banner to the modest tints of gamboge [a yellow-producing pigment] that appeared on the more humble streamers ...'
4. Anne Lister's will – See ref SH:1/SH/1836/2, Calderdale Archives Dept. Anne's last will and testament bequeaths all the income from her property to her then (in 1840) companion, Ann Walker, for life provided she remained unmarried. On Ann Walker's death, the estate was to pass to John Lister Esq, the only son of John Lister of Swansea. There is no mention of any annuity, or anything else, for Mariana Lawton.
5. '... The Lord's rent ...' – i.e. monies paid to the lord of the manor. In the case of the Listers and their tenants on the Shibden estate, this rent was paid to the Lord of the Manor of Southowram. It was also called 'free rent'. James Lister paid the sum of three shillings and eightpence in 1811, that sum being two years' rent which he owed, to the Lord of the Manor. (See ref SH: 1/SH/1809/1–5, Calderdale Archives Dept.)
6. '... eaten the pudding ...' – Anne probably refers here to the savoury Yorkshire pudding, a batter pudding which is served with gravy before the main course, in Yorkshire.
7. '... footing ...' – A gift of money to the workmen, usually given when the foundation of a building or wall was laid down. On this occasion it seems to have been customary to treat the tenants with money for drinks on rent-days, once business had been concluded.
8. '... Hampstead house rent ...' – Captain Jeremy Lister had inherited some houses in Hampstead, London, from his aunt, Mary Rose *née* Lister, who had married George Rose of Hampstead. It appears he

must have owed Anne some money and was repaying her with the 'Hampstead house rent'.

9. '... The Bluecoat School ...' – so called because the pupils of the original early eighteenth century educational establishments were clothed in the rough, blue material worn by servants or charity pupils. The Bluecoat schools were financed from private donations and usually run by religious bodies. Their aim was to eradicate poverty through education. They became the foundation of English elementary education in the nineteenth century.
10. Marchioness of Wellesley – *née* Marianne Patterson (nd), whom the marquis married in 1825, much to the anger of his brother, the Duke of Wellington, who had entertained a *grande passion* for Marianne. She was an American Roman Catholic, the widow of Robert Patterson and daughter of Richard Caton of Baltimore. Her grandfather, Charles Caroll of Carollstown, who died in 1832, was the last surviving signatory of the Declaration of American Independence.
11. Marquis – Richard Colley (1760–1842), First Marquis of Wellesley and Second Earl of Mornington. Elder brother to the Duke of Wellington, he held many government posts, including the Lord-Lieutenancy of Ireland in 1821–1828 and again in 1833–1834.
12. '... Irish harvest men ...' – i.e. Irish labourers who regularly came over to England to earn money harvesting crops in England. 'Successive failures of the potato-crop [in Ireland], notably the famine of 1821–2, drove forward the migration ... [of] the harvest workers, whose "spirit of laborious industry" was commended as against the "greedy" Lancashire labourer ... [They were] the cheapest labour in Western Europe.' Pp 471–472, *The Making of the English Working Class* by E P Thompson.

An Idyll in Paris

The Lawton family had lived in the village of Lawton for many generations. Lawton Hall,[1] their family seat, is near the Cheshire/Staffordshire border and is described as a mid-eighteenth century house built of 'red Flemish bond brick with ashlar dressings'. From the accounts in Anne's journals it seems that Mariana was not happy there. How much this was due to Anne's wishful thinking or to Mariana's desire to keep Anne's interest alive by denigrating her life with Charles, is hard to determine. Certainly the place has an isolated feel about it, even today. The little village church is the next building to it, set in the same wooded surroundings. The Lawton Arms, a small village alehouse, is a mile or so down the road from it, where carriages and coaches would stop for refreshments or the ordering of fresh horses. Coming, as she did, from the lively bustle of York city centre and the company of her large gregarious family, Mariana would, no doubt, have felt her isolation keenly. She depended heavily upon protracted visits from her sisters until she had established her position in Cheshire society as a wealthy landowner's wife. Life became more bearable once she made her own friends, and became engaged in charitable pursuits and the social life of the local gentry. Charles' life at Lawton was already well-established. He regularly had a few of his male cronies staying at Lawton Hall, but their totally masculine pursuits of shooting, drinking, gambling and womanising (the latter usually carried on away from home) brought nothing of interest into Mariana's life. Charles was often away from home, carousing in London or wherever else his interests took him.

Understandably, it gave Anne some satisfaction to accentuate the negative aspects of Mariana's marriage and Mariana happily contributed to this view. Thus neither Charles nor Lawton Hall received a good press at Anne's hands. The York gossip and that of the servants at Lawton never failed to reach Anne's ears or the pages of her journal. In the absence of anything more positive, we are perhaps left with a distorted image of a man who may have been no better or worse than many of his contemporaries. What is certain is that he never replaced Anne in Mariana's affections, never showed the slightest inclination to change his way of life in order to make Mariana a happier woman, and thereby contributed to the destabilisation of the marriage.

Now that the long ban on Anne's visit to Lawton Hall was lifted, she hurried there to consolidate her victory and to establish her presence as Mariana's oldest and most valued friend in the eyes of Cheshire society. She and her aunt left Parkgate and travelled via Chester and Middlewich, reaching Lawton around 4.15 pm, on Friday 4th August 1826.

Friday 4 August

Miss Pattison [Mariana's closest Cheshire friend] here. Saw her for ¼ hour. Her voice very disagreeable. *Shews no blood. Not taken with her at first sight. Mariana had been fancying we should not come tonight. Delighted to see us. Charles meaning to be very civil but desperately gauche. Said how he had been disappointed not to be able to go to Buxton today & stay till* Monday, *as he had fixed.*

I would not be much in his house on any consideration. I cannot endure his manners.

Saturday 5 August

Had Watson [Mariana's personal maid] *up. She staid talking, I think an hour. I cannot think her otherwise than an honest, virtuous woman & servant.* [She said] *Charles as bad as ever out of doors. Perhaps there is more foolishness than wickedness in it but he has such a trick of calling after women & talking to them. Uses very gross language. Said to have been, the other day, in the plantation with a low, bad woman. Will walk with any sort of trull. The Irishman who assaulted the dairymaid the other day declared all the servants were bad & he was no worse than his master. Shameful . . . Grantham* [the lodgekeeper at Lawton Hall] *says he is sure Mariana will never end her days there. Her leaving Charles would not surprise any of them . . .* Dinner about 6–20. Afterwards, went into the saloon. Played the hand organ. Had Watson in to turn for us while Mariana & I danced in remembrance of former times to the tune of Smith's Hornpipe & then I sang 'Early Days, How Fair & Fleeting'; 'In Thee I Take So Dear a Part'; 'I Dreampt My Heart Was Laid One Day', etc.

Monday 7 August

Mariana & I strolled along the walk by the water-side, into her flower garden. Had only time to wash our hands for dinner at 6¼. *At dinner Charles said, speaking of ale ten years old, it was to be kept till his son was of age, adding, 'I have a son & you shall see him by & by.' He said he would bet me a wager he had a son. I had better see him now or I should have no opportunity. Mariana called him gently to order. As we got up from the table he took me into the saloon & told me it was* Mrs *Grantham's* [the lodgekeeper's wife's] *second son, Joseph, & who was very like him, Charles. Mariana was deceived in her but was sure he had not been near her these two years. He could not bear deceit. Wished me to break it to her. He had thought of it for some days & had once thought of telling Miss Pattison. I told him I was very glad he had not. 'Well, no,' he said, 'perhaps it is better. She might have told.' Again I advised him saying nothing about it. Mariana would be annoyed if she knew it. Oh, no. She would care nothing about it. 'Ah,' said I. 'I know her better,' and went to get my things on to walk . . .* with Charles & Mariana to the Lodge. Somehow missed them both. Went by myself. Spoke to Mrs Grantham. Her son, Joseph, a stupid-looking, white-headed boy. In returning, met Mariana. *Told her what had passed. We both laughed tho' Mariana really seemed vexed at his having talked so before the servants. Wicked thus to injure so good a servant as Grantham. Would not have a mistress of Charles' at the Lodge.* It was 9½ when Mariana & I got home to tea. All went off to bed a little after 10. *Presently came Mariana into my room. She had dignifiedly told Charles all this, & that if she found the thing out, she would tell Grantham, to which he said not one single word &, being frightened, she had left the room. Then sat talking to me. Would have me see & tell him in the morning this thing & that, or leave a note for him not to tell Miss Pattison, etc.; that no wife would bear these things, etc. Mariana sat with me till after one.*

Tuesday 8 August

Mariana came about 8¼, for ½ hour . . . *Charles had been very low. He had entreated her to take care of herself for his sake. Given her fifty pounds. Could not* [give] *more because he had not it. Almost crying. Mariana thinks he must be cracky but all this, of course, disarmed the shew of* [Mariana's] *displeasure.* Breakfast at 10¼ . . . *Charles held out his face for me to kiss & I did so & we parted very good friends.*

After Charles' confessional outburst, whether true or not, he was hardly in a position to object any further to his wife's trip to Paris without him. Leaving him in a suitably humble and contrite frame of mind, the two women gleefully set off on their long-planned Parisian idyll, taking Aunt Anne with them, of course. Before leaving England they took in a few places of interest, travelling first to Birmingham, then to Stratford-upon-Avon, Oxford, Henley-on-Thames, London, Reigate and, finally, Brighton, where they embarked for the Continent on the 26th August. Landing at Dieppe on Sunday 27th August, they travelled to Versailles. They took time to visit the Palace of Versailles then travelled on to Paris, where Anne contacted Maria Barlow, rather cruelly not warning her that Mariana was to be with her in Paris. Mariana, for her part, knew that Anne would be seeing Maria Barlow but, secure in her reaffirmed position in Anne's affections, she felt she could face her rival with equanimity and even afford the luxury of feeling compassion for her.

Saturday 2 September

Off for Paris at 5. Changed horses at Sèvres at 5–35. All of us interested on seeing Paris. A thousand reflections crowded, perhaps on us all – not less on Mariana than myself. We had got into the Rue de Rivoli when Mariana saw a little figure in white dart out of the Hôtel de Terrasse (No. 50) & call out to the postboys to stop. Said Mariana, 'Mrs Barlow.' There was Jane, too. Mrs Barlow as pale as death. I felt a little less so. Jumped out of the carriage. Met her. No room at Meurice's.[2] She had taken us a rez de chaussée for my aunt & lodging rooms à la entresol du premier for us at Hôtel de Terrasse. Her attention to my aunt unbounded. Evidently [she was] rather constrained to me & I to her. Mariana had come upstairs to our room & did not come down till Mrs Barlow was gone, who staid surely about ½ hour. I walked home with her & went upstairs into her salon for a few minutes. In crossing the Tuileries gardens, mentioned Mariana's being with us. Mrs Barlow agitated. Said I had behaved dishonestly not to tell her before. Should have written on purpose from London & she would have got out of the way – gone into the country. 'And I have seen her,' said she. 'I took her for your lady's maid & wondered to see another ugly woman stuck up behind'!!! I took no apparent notice of this splenetic, ill-judged speech but turned it over in my mind & repeated it on getting home, observing that surely Mariana was prettier than MacDonald. We all felt annoyed at this. [I] *said* [to Mrs Barlow] *it was not my fault Mariana was with us, etc. She would stay perhaps a few days. On mentioning lodgings, 'Why,' said she peevishly, 'should I settle Mrs Lawton?' This struck me much. 'She is, indeed, then,' said I to myself, 'ill-tempered.'*

Monday 4 September

Did not get out till 1¼. Direct along the Rue St Honoré to the Palais Royal (to Joseph's, the money-changer). Mariana exchanged £30 at 25.45. Sent the money home by George, then along the Rue Vivienne, staring in at the shop windows for a bonnet for Mariana. Ordered Galignani's paper – for 3 months. No letters there for me . . . Thence to the Palais Royal to buy Mariana a sac & thence to the Mesdames Romatier & Huchet (29 & 14, Rue St Anne) to order stays & gowns for Mariana. Thence to Madame Cor, No. 4, Rue de Marche St Honoré, & Mariana bought a bonnet. Thence to La Belle Anglaise, Rue de la Paix, where Mariana bought a tippet. Then set about looking for lodgings & did not get home till 7. Dinner immediately. Found my aunt <u>very</u> poorly – spasms – thinks she got cold with sitting with all the windows & doors open at Nantes & her room here is damp. Came up to bed at 9½. Sat up talking about my aunt – *what to do if she died soon. I had suddenly said, when dinner was half over (my aunt too unwell to be with us & was gone to bed), 'Perhaps I might go to Mrs Barlow,' & this had spoiled poor Mariana's appetite – but she would have me do whatever seemed best. I said I had said it suddenly, without thought, & it would not do. Should think of it no more.*

Tuesday 5 September

Mariana & I out at 12, seeking lodgings till after 3. Then went into the [Tuileries] gardens (at the far end) & round the bottom of them & along the Terrace d'Eau to Quai Voltaire. Mariana waited at the porter's till I went upstairs. Mrs Barlow in bed. Had been there all yesterday, very ill. Had me into her room. Sat by her bedside. Said not a word of Mariana. Mrs Barlow 'sorry she had not met her with becoming dignity'. Would have no objection, it seems, to see her. Strange! Inconsistent! Talked of lodgings. *She told me of the Droz's* [former acquaintances of Anne's in Paris]. *They do not like to walk with me. He would not like to be obliged to offer me his arm, etc. She* [Mrs Barlow] *seemed composed. It was a nervous complaint in her bowels of which she was ill. I made no attempt to salute, or made any advance at all.* Mariana waited for us patiently 55 minutes tho' I had promised to stay only ¼ hour. *She had been overwhelmed with miserable reflections but behaved beautifully* ... Dinner at 5. Afterwards, went out – along the Rue St Honoré to the Palais Royal. Walked leisurely all round it that Mariana might see it by candlelight. She, much pleased, thought it well worth seeing.

Wednesday 6 September

Leave Mariana writing out her journals & at 3¾ go to consult with Mrs Barlow (about apartment-hunting). As usual on such occasions, not much the better for my consulting! All I learnt was that my allowance for £50 for wood would be enough for the year but we should burn more than £25 the next 6 months. The conversation turned to other matters. Jane had left the room both yesterday & today as I entered it. *I said I had done Mariana injustice – been mistaken about her – en revient toujours à ses premier amours* [one always goes back to one's first love]. *'Then,' said Mrs Barlow, 'you love her. You love another & you tell me so yourself. I did not think you could have so soon forgotten me & met me thus,' etc., & we had a scene. At last I said I durst not presume to talk of love without her (Mrs Barlow's) express permission under my present circumstances, which could not be changed, etc.* [She said] *she could permit it – it was different now after the manner* [in which] *we had lived together. 'Well, then,' said I, 'I love you as well as ever,' & prest her hand. (Alas! I felt something like disgust.) She smiled as if she had gained a victory & I hurried off, for she had called me back two or three times – & once, when I said I would call no more – 'What! Have you then returned to desert – & that, after all you said when I would not see you?' I felt shocked as I returned, musing on what had passed. She will take me on any terms. Poor Mariana! I looked, she & my aunt said to each other, very ill. I daresay I was as white as a sheet. I know not what to make of her. Mariana has a bad opinion of her, I see, & she would not judge harshly, even in this case* . . . Mariana & I sat talking of Mrs Barlow. *Told as gently as I could the main of what had passed & we agreed that I should try whether she would really take me on any terms or not. If she would, I would be shocked & be off. If she would not, of course I should stand excused from lovemaking scenes.*

Having made their plans to manoeuvre Maria Barlow firmly into a catch-22 situation, the two women set about enjoying their few weeks together in Paris. Mariana was very much the tourist, seeing Paris in a carefree way. For Anne and her aunt it was a more serious matter. They intended to settle in Paris for some time and needed to set up a private, domestic household in order to live as cheaply as possible, while not sacrificing their comfort too much. The responsibility for this, of course, fell on Anne. On Friday 8th September, six days after their arrival in Paris, the party was installed in an apartment at 6 Rue de Mondovi (just off the Rue de Rivoli) thanks to Anne's energetic efforts. She had looked at quite a few others but rejected them. The Rue de Mondovi apartment was airy and conveniently placed for shopping and sightseeing. It had rooms enough to give herself and her aunt their own private quarters, and also to house George and MacDonald. There was a stand nearby on which they could pay six francs a month to station their carriage. Mariana shared Anne's rooms until she left Paris.

Meals were a problem. For a few days after the move, Anne and Mariana dined out at nearby restaurants, sending meals up to the apartment for Aunt Anne and the servants. This obviously could not continue indefinitely and, initially, a cook was engaged at a salary of 400 francs a year plus 50 francs for doing the laundry. Mrs Barlow sent her butterwoman along, from whom Anne could buy butter, poultry and vegetables each week. Anne ordered milk to be delivered daily to the apartment. After a few days Anne decided the expense of the cook was rather extravagant and she fired her. MacDonald would have to learn to cook for them, an experiment which was not very successful.

This ordering of a domestic household was a tedious business for Anne, keeping her from her social and intellectual pursuits as it did. Her servants, George and MacDonald, were hampered by language difficulties and Anne had to shop for food herself. She was convinced that the Parisian shopkeepers were out to cheat the well-off English customer and this meant that every shopping expedition was turned into an argumentative, bargaining session between Anne and the shopkeepers, with Anne returning home tired and aggrieved.

Despite these drawbacks, Anne and Mariana enjoyed their Parisian interlude together. Mariana took lessons in embroidery while Anne contacted Mme Galvani again with a view to resuming her lessons in French and Italian. Strolls in the Champs Élysées, the Tuileries gardens and up and down the boulevards were enjoyed daily. Shopping expeditions, in which Mariana indulged her taste for French fashions, were frequent.

Anne spent her money, as usual, on books, buying a complete set of Byron's works in seven large volumes. Visits to the theatre in the evenings were frequent, as were excursions in and around Paris to places of historical and educational interest. They took great delight in eating pastries at the many small pâtisseries in the city, and also in drinking delicious, fresh lemonade. Fresh fruit was high on their menu, particularly grapes and pears, and they bought all sorts of 'sweetmeats and bonbons', which they no doubt ate with their evening tea or coffee, around nine o'clock at night, sitting before a wood fire in their apartment, Mariana practising her newly-learnt embroidery stitches, while Anne read aloud to her or wrote up her journal. For, running through the entries during the days of this month of September, is a joyous sense of togetherness – of closeness and intimacy – an elation at being together in Paris without the irritation of Charles' presence. Given the choice, these halcyon weeks would have become protracted into a lifetime's enjoyment of each other's company, with few outside distractions to disturb them.

Apart from Anne's fretting over domestic details, two things spoiled their Parisian idyll. The first was the knowledge that it would inevitably end when Charles Lawton crossed the Channel to reclaim his wife early in October. The second was the presence of Maria Barlow in Paris, jealous and alert to every opportunity which might bring Anne to her side. Mariana's certain departure from Paris filled Maria Barlow with hope. She counted on Anne's inability to resist sexual activity with her once Mariana was out of the way. Meanwhile, she played a not-so-patient waiting game, becoming ill and fretful, causing scenes with Anne, making half-hearted overtures to Mariana and attempting to ingratiate herself with Aunt Anne. There was no doubt in Mariana's fearful mind that Mrs Barlow was all set to mount a sexual offensive once Anne was alone in Paris, far away from Mariana's restraining presence.

Friday 8 September

Mariana & I went shopping, buying bread, butter, groceries – tiresome but necessary. What folly to have English servants. They can do nothing of this sort for you & ten times worse to provide for them yourselves!

Sunday 10 September

Left Mariana sitting at the porter's while I went up to Mrs Barlow. In bed. Very poorly. Much pain. Inflammatory symptoms in her bowels. Says she must be bled. Pain & weight at the back of her head. Had near sent for me. *Wanted one word of kindness from me. Better now she had seen me. Her eye caught the ring on my right third finger. She burst into tears. Luckily Jane came. She had said before she was very ill on Friday night. Had burnt many papers & had now all my letters under her pillow, ready to give me. I turned the subject, not wishing to agitate her. Poor soul, I pity her.*

Monday 11 September

Thro' the Tuileries gardens to Quai Voltaire, No. 15. Left Mariana at the porter's for ¼ hour while I sat with Mrs Barlow. Then brought Mariana upstairs & Jane played to her & amused her for 1 hour, 10 minutes, while I sat by Mrs Barlow's bedside. *She behaved very well.*

Thursday 14 September

Spoke seriously to MacDonald about her not suiting us. No fault to find with her moral character – thought her very good & worthy – but disappointed in not finding her a more complete servant & must really send her home if she did not suit us better. She could get nothing out of her hands [i.e. she had no skills].

Was not at all angry but thought it right to tell her all this. She was very sorry – hoped she would do better. Perhaps she will. Mariana & I went out at 2 & took George to the Feydeau theatre to find out the bureau for taking places at night. Thence to the new Bourse.[3] They have made considerable progress in finishing it since I last saw it 18 months ago. English workmen employed for the steam apparatus to heat the building. 5 hundred English (workmen, women & children) living at Charenton where the iron foundry is, under Mr Manby. All employed by the kg. Have from 5 to 10 francs a day. Have a church & clergyman – 'very fine preacher' – at Charenton. Quite an English village. Gave them (3 of them) 1/- to drink. ¾ hour at the Bourse. Magnificent building. Mariana delighted . . . Went out at 6½ along the Champs Élysées to the Barrière de l'Étoile. In returning, sat in the grande avenue listening to the singing & music of some Italians. This reminded me of this time 2 years [ago]. The evening delightful. Mariana much pleased . . . Lovely moonlight evening.

Sunday 17 September

Off to the Ambassador's chapel in our remise, taking MacDonald & George, at 10¾. Service began at 11. *Mariana nervous at seeing Mrs Barlow. Jane introduced them on coming away. Both of them nervous. Asked Mrs Barlow to come back with us but she declined* . . . Got out of church at one. Came home for a minute or 2 & then drove to the Louvre. Walked thro' the statuary halls & thro' the gallery. 50 minutes there. Mariana delighted. Thence thro' the Bois & the village of Boulogne to the fête at St Cloud. No carriages allowed to pass the bridge, that we had to walk a considerable distance. Just got into the park at 3¼. Fixed up a spot where to find George at 6 & then sent him off & sauntered about by ourselves. Left the crowd and sat down under a tree & ate our grapes & bread that we had brought with us. Just got back to the great fountain in time to see it play. Soon after it began, probably at 5, 4 of the royal carriages passed & repassed us 3 times. The king,[4] duke & duchess d'Angoulême,[5] the two children[6] & their governess in the 1st carriage. All the party looked well – very smiling & gracious. Then [we] mingled completely with the crowd & at 6, found George & took him with us. Booths & shews as usual. Gave 5 sols each to enter the circle railed off for the dancers. Then visited the inferior dancing parties . . . Had seen a man (in the open air) walk up a rope to the top of a tree. Afterwards went to one of the shews where a little girl of 7 or 9 walked up a rope to a great height & a man balanced a great cart-wheel, fixed to a ladder, on the point of the ladder on his chin. Then to a Fantocini performance[7] of the Brigands de Pologne* & to a similar sort of representation of the Deluge, both which were laughable enough. Very low, of course, but nothing disagreeable save the strong smell of humanity. Mariana much amused with novelty of the thing. Certainly well worth a stranger's seeing. Came away at 9–10.

Monday 18 September

[Mariana] & my aunt talked of Mrs Barlow. Mariana against our having her here to keep house for us. Says she will never consent to it. My aunt thinks Mrs Barlow is trying to make up to her.

Tuesday 19 September

Mariana & I peeped into the morgue.[8] 3 men exposed there. Thence to the Notre Dame. Very clean & neat – newly painted instead of washed. Very nice & neat.

Sunday 24 September

Off at 6½ [in the evening, to the grand fête at Tivoli]. ½ hour going. Quite in the style of Vauxhall[9] but not so brilliant.

---

*I have been unable to trace the origins of this particular drama/opera.

Dullish evening. The clouds dark. The torrents of rain that fell about 5 o'clock this morning had made me sensible of damp in the gardens. The fireworks very good. Better than those at Vauxhall – but not ½ over when the rain fell in such torrents (it had lightened very much ½ hour or more before) the gardens were immediately cleared. [We] had taken our umbrella. Tiresome to have waited even a minute. Of course, no fiacres to be had. No shelter. The cafés locked lest we should all rush in. Away we came in the rain. Rained heavily all the way home but we had 2 showers tremendously heavy. It was quite wading thro' the streets. Crossing the Rue St Honoré from the Place Vendôme, Mariana was literally above her knees. It was quite a river that ran down the middle of the street. The umbrella kept our shoulders dry. Came in at 10–10 – sad objects. George sadly wet, having no umbrella. Undressed. Got into bed as fast as we could & had some warm wine & water. MacDonald having not been well for several days, gave her 15gr. julep & 5 gr. calomel.

Monday 25 September

Drove to Quai Voltaire, No. 15. Left Mariana to amuse herself & went up to Mrs Barlow. *She kept me one & a quarter hour. Sent Jane out of the room. Quite a scene. Said I behaved ill to her – did not care for her – treated her with no respect – was a slave to 'that creature'. I found fault with this manner of expression. Said my circumstances were fixed & I had promised to live with Mariana & Charles if anything happened to my aunt & if we staid here* [in Paris] *they might come next winter. All this seemed to upset her. She cried. Sent me away then called me back. I was weary of her & really cared very little, except to be pothered & annoyed. Poor Mariana waiting. Mrs Barlow said she* [Mrs Barlow] *was a Corinne.*[10] *I see I shall be quite sick of her. She generally ends by asking me for one kind word. What must Jane think of it all?* Mariana had waited at a shop near, during the heavy rain, very good-humouredly.

Tuesday 26 September

Mariana & I took George & went shopping. Bought various little things. Saw a nice little stove at 24/. Think to buy it for our kitchen. It will soon save itself in charcoal ... Mariana bought a beautiful 'satin chaconné rose' i.e. pink figured satin, at 10/50, 8½ aunes for the dress. Then chose her a bonnet in the Galerie Vivienne, lilac silk, 25/. Then ate pâtisserie in the Palais Royal & sauntered about there. The Russian coral Mrs Henry Belcombe wants is nothing but a large red berry – 'fruit de Sibérie' – not coral. Quite out. Not to be had. When it was la mode it was dear but now people knew what it was & would not wear it, it was nothing. Nobody had it.

Friday 29 September

Drove off to the Conservatoire des Arts & Métiers,[11] Rue St Martin. 1 hour, 10 mins there. Mariana much interested with the models (scale – 1 inch to a foot) made at the suggestion of Mme de Genlis[12] for the instruction of the children of the Duke of Orléans.[13] Very expensive on account of the diminutativeness of the size. An Englishman wanted a facsimile of one of the trades & the artist said he could not do it for under £320 ... The concierge at the Conservatoire said the Duke de Bordeaux[14] had not been there. The Duchess[15] had but would not bring him for if he saw the models he would want them & he was a little gentleman that, if they did not give them to him, he would break them. 'What will he do, then,' said I, 'when he is king of France?'[16] 'Ah,' said the man, 'il brisera tout.' [He will break all] ... Not having an express permission, we could not see the chambres particulières but the man (in king's livery) said they were not interesting to ladies – full of mathematical instruments, chronometers, etc. ... At 7½, went to Mrs Barlow. Found her alone. *She behaved very well at first. At last, got on to the old subject.* [She] *thinks she is mine by right. Nobody – no married woman – can have so good a right to me as hers.* [I] *told her Mariana would not let me have her keep house for us* [in Paris, after Mariana's departure]. *Thought it would be bad for all parties. Mrs Barlow owns she would only have attached herself to me more – but said she would not have come to us. I think she probably had a thought or hope of this. Jane came from downstairs & I got away.*

Sunday 1 October

Mariana & I read aloud the whole of the morning service & I afterwards read aloud sermon 15, on the right principle of moral conduct ... The porter's wife gave me a note (per post) from Mme Galvani, Rue des Marqis, No. 65, Fb. St Germain, to say she had got us 6 cases of eau de Cologne for Mariana ... Mariana & I had talked of going to the Louvre but it shut at 4. We sauntered round the Tuileries gardens, lastly along the Terrasse d'Eau, then sat down under one of the statues near the summer house on this side. *Talked earnestly about Mariana's leaving Charles. She has a sad dislike or misgiving about going back to Lawton. Thinks she cannot get over this business about Mrs Grantham* [Charles' supposed mistress] – *cannot stay.* [I] *bade her tell Willoughby Crewe*[17] *& Steph & let the latter arrange the matter. Not to consult me by letter but tell Steph to write to me about it. Let the thing be done leisurely & properly. Mariana very low.* [We had some] *talk of her bringing him to Paris, for she would do all she could to stay with him. Her leaving him will never surprise me but I wish to have nothing to do with it.* At 5, went to Mme Galvani. Mariana likes her. She was very agreeable – *said Mrs Barlow was ugly. Could believe Mariana pretty in her youth. Seems to like & admire her. Gave a good imitation of me, saying both she & Mariana were 'plus femme que moi'* [more womanly than me]. *I have the figure & nature of a man. Have not beauty but agreeable features tho' not those of a woman. I joked, pretended to be shocked.*

Mme Galvani so agreeable we staid far too long, above an hour. Hurried & heated ourselves in returning & did not get home till 6–50. My aunt had ½ dined. Afterwards, wrote all the above of today. Very fine day. Settled my accounts. Went to bed at 10½. Sat up, eating grapes & talking, as we generally do.

Tuesday 3 October

At 1–50, went to the top of the column in the Place Vendôme – 176 deepish steps. Mariana almost sick at the top from the height. 5 minutes in ascending, as long in descending & ¼ hour at the top. The day not very clear but tolerably favourable. Beautiful view of Paris. Mariana thought it worth the trouble. In returning from the column to the Rue St Honoré, met Mrs Barlow & Jane. Stopt to speak & shake hands. *Mrs Barlow's lips trembled. Mariana set wrong & nervous by the meeting but all behaved very well.* Mariana bought tin molds [*sic*] & ordered a black velvet cap ... thence to the Galerie Vivienne where Mariana bought 5 prs of shoes ... Got home at 6¼.

Wednesday 4 October

Dinner at 6½. Not enough. Hardly enough for the servants. MacDonald had told my aunt, & my aunt told me, there was <u>quite</u> enough. I must look after <u>everything</u> myself. Sent the meat away & we had none at all. Dined on carrot soup (do not like it) & potatoes. Mariana ate a small bit of artichoke & fromage de Gruyère & grapes. A couple of petit pâtes each & some baba, which Mariana did not like – too much saffron for her. My aunt has complained of cold ever since we came here. Quite shivering this morning. Cold at dinner. At 8, Mariana & I lighted a fire in the salon. An hour's work before we could get it to burn well ... *Mariana very low for several days past – particularly so today. In tears all dinnertime & afterwards, till amused by lighting the fire &, afterwards, fell asleep for a little while. Poor Mariana. She is very low at the thought of leaving me with such a friend* [as Maria Barlow] . . . *Going with* Mariana to Boulogne on Saturday. Charles to meet us.

Thursday 5 October

A letter from Charles to tell Mariana it would be quite soon enough if we were at Boulogne on the 10th. He had staid for a little shooting at home. In doubt whether to go on Saturday or not.

In the event, Anne and Mariana did decide to leave Paris on Saturday 7th October, and spend a couple of days together in Boulogne, waiting quietly for the arrival of Charles. Mariana took a tearful leave of Aunt Anne and departed from Paris at 7 am on Saturday morning, to the huge relief of Maria Barlow. Anne paid extra to have the coupé to themselves in view of Mariana's possible distress along the way. However, she coped very well and they reached Boulogne the following day, Sunday 8th October, in time to have an evening meal and fall exhausted into their beds. Monday found them rested and refreshed, bracing themselves to meet Charles and the inevitable parting which would follow.

Monday 9 October

We both observed how much colder it was here than in Paris. *Cleaned her* [Mariana's] *head. She frets at her hair coming off so very much. It is indeed reduced to almost nothing.* Tidying the room. Dawdling over 1 thing or other. I must have a servant that can do everything of this sort & leave me time to myself. Mariana in better spirits this morning. *The comfort of not* [yet] *meeting Charles here, but of having a little time to ourselves seems to have quite comforted us. It is indeed a godsend.*

Tuesday 10 October

Had our room done & then sat down to breakfast at 12–05. Afterwards, Mariana took her work & I sat by, talking on one subject or other till nearly 4. *Talked quietly on what we had to gain by Mariana's staying with Charles. If possible, she had best get the upper hand & stay it out* [until his hoped-for early death]. *I would make myself happy & comfortable. It might make a difference of five hundred a year to us* [the annuity which Charles had finally agreed to leave to Mariana after his death] *besides the additional respectability – & we should find the money useful. But I left her at liberty to do which way she chose. She owned my talking had done her a great deal of good* ... A little before 4, we went out to the ... Darvall's ... Sat with them near 2 hours. They very civilly asked us to stay to dinner. Saw 3 girls & a boy – very ugly children. Shewn into a great long salon furnished with English furniture – rez de chaussée. A little garden at the back, a court in front, close to a dirty, half-built street with a great ditch, like a common sewer, down the middle of it. A row of shabby trees on each side. Mariana & I both exclaimed we could not live there. Damp & disagreeable & close. 'Il n'ya que Paris' [There is only Paris]. Who would live at Boulogne? The Darvalls give a hundred a year for their house, unfurnished. Had a permit to lend [use in the house?] their English furniture. May bring out anything that is not new. Going to Paris for 2 or 3 weeks in the spring, to shew Miss Pringle the lions [i.e. the sights]. Will call upon me ... [I] fought rather shy. Will have no hand in helping to shew lions.

Wednesday 11 October

Got to ... the Sturts'. Not admitted. The servant came running after us to call us back. Returned. Sat an hour with Mr & Mrs & Miss Jane Sturt & his niece, Miss Emily Denvers. 2 pretty girls. The latter not straight – the former squalled so loud in speaking I could scarce endure it. Mrs Sturt looking insignificant & cowed. He, a bashaw – seeming to talk & act for his wife & manage all . . . Thence direct to the port & sands. The latter excellent, hard & dry. Several people riding & walking there. In returning, Mrs Darvall passed us in their carriage & took us up, at 4 . . . to her house to dinner. Went up into Mrs Darvall's room. Mariana curled my hair, I perfectly at ease. Mrs Darvall played a little on the piano before dinner – played & sang prettily. Dinner at 5½. Roast fillet of veal & goose-sides, pigeons & harico'd mutton, mashed potatoes & kidney beans, baked bread pudding, apple pie, custard and fritters. Cheese, then apples, pears, grapes & common biscuits. Too much a made meal for us. Boulogne porter (Mariana said very good), beer, vin de pays ordinaire & 2 bottles white wine Frontignac, & strong, hot wine, bordering on Spain & Champagne.

Thursday 12 October

Went out at 2. Walked to the great news-room close upon the sea, a handsome-looking, 1 story [*sic*], pillared building with a nice sort of little garden in front towards the town & a broad walk or plot of ground, gravelled, towards the sea. The people have a largeish monkey chained at the North end. Mariana & I stood a considerable time, watching it balance itself on the slack rope suspended between 2 poles close to its kennel. Then [we] contemplated the sea, then sauntered homewards . . . On passing our hôtel at 4, saw Charles & Mr Darvall standing at the door. It was well to have met in this way. *The suddenness left Mariana no time for reflection. We were taken by surprise. It was best . . .* Dinner at 6 . . . All passed off well. Mariana left us, to pack. *I took the opportunity, as preconcerted, to tell Charles Mariana had been very miserable.* [She] *could not forget what he had said – alluding to Mrs Grantham – & that if she could find out that he had so abused both herself and Grantham, she would not stay another minute in the house. I had begun the subject by charging him, that whatever he did, never to let Mariana find out about Mrs Grantham. He said no sensible woman would think of such a thing a moment. He had been very unhappy but never would be so again. I said Mariana had told me of the anonymous letters she had had. He said it was impossible she could have any, yet when I said she had shewn him one, he owned it but said many men did worse than he, etc. I answered that might be true but I thought people ought to make their own house respectable & at all rates, I was sure Mariana would not allow it to be otherwise while she was in it &, if she could not make it respectable, I did not believe her friends would let her stay.* [I] *said that if he saw Mariana low he had best take no notice. He seemed to wish the subject turned & I let him have his wish & we talked of indifferent things. I went up to Mariana for some money. Told her all that had passed & hurried down for fear he should think I was telling her . . .* Mariana has really behaved very well this afternoon – *very stoutly. I believe she thinks she shall soon be back to me.*

Friday 13 October

Mariana & Charles breakfasted on board the Medusa (a very small packet but said to be a very good one) at 8. Weighed anchor & off at 8½. *Mariana had not shed a single tear this morning & behaved very well saying, when I told her I expected her back within the year, she thought so too. Bade her care nothing for our fine schemes of saving, & managing Charles, etc., but come to me at once if she could not be comfortable with Charles.* I walked along the pier-side as far as I could, as they passed, & Mariana waved her handkerchief as we took our last look. I went to the news-room & sat under the colonnade on one of the benches, watching the vessel. My head & eyes ached & the speck was gone beyond my sight. The sea was very rough & as I watched the vessel heave among the breakers my heart heaved with it and I hoped Mariana & I would never meet to part again.

1. Lawton Hall – The house still stands although it is now a gated luxury residence, having been in use as a private school in years past. It is classified as a grade II listed building.
2. *Meurice's* – 228 Rue de Rivoli, the Hôtel Meurice was the most famous hotel in Paris in Anne's day. It was particularly patronised by the British abroad. Both Thackeray and Dickens stayed there in the 1840s. On 2nd November 1826, Sir Walter Scott mentioned, in his journal, that: '. . . Monsieur Meurice writes to me that he is ready to hang himself that we did not find accommodation at his hotel . . .' (p 229, *The Journal of Sir Walter Scott*, ed W E K Anderson, Oxford University Press 1972.) During the Second World War, the hotel became the headquarters of the German army of occupation.
3. The new Bourse – See note 18, p 131.
4. The king – Charles X. See note 16, p 38.
5. Duke & Duchess d'Angoulême – See note 17, p 38.
6. '. . . the two children . . .' – A rather puzzling reference. The Duc and Duchess d'Angoulême, to their great distress, did not have any children. The children referred to here could perhaps have been their niece and nephew, children of the assassinated Duc de Berri.
7. A Fantocini performance – i.e. a puppet or marionette show, so-called from the Italian *fantoccino*, meaning puppet.
8. The morgue – A visit to the Paris Morgue, on the Quai du Marché-Neuf, was apparently a customary item on the itinerary of English visitors to Paris. Charles Dickens, in particular, felt a morbid attraction towards the spectacle of near-naked corpses laid out behind a glass partition for public exhibition, probably to enable people to identify a missing relative, particularly in the turbulent days of the Revolution.
9. Vauxhall – Situated on the south bank of the Thames, in the borough of Lambeth, near Vauxhall Bridge, public gardens were laid out c1661. They became fashionable as a pleasure resort from the time of Samuel Pepys and feature in the novels of such writers as Fanny Burney and W M Thackeray. Due to the spread of urbanisation, the site was closed in 1859 and buildings were erected there.
10. Corinne – *Corinne or Italy* (1807), a romantic novel by Madame de Staël (1766–1817), woman of letters and an important figure in French political and literary circles during her lifetime. Her novel

Corinne portrays a woman who dies of grief because her lover marries another woman.

11. Conservatoire des Arts et Métiers – An institution founded in 1794 by the Revolutionary Convention for the purpose of technical instruction. It is now an industrial museum, lecture centre and laboratory.
12. Mme de Genlis – See note 20, p 158.
13. The children of the Duc of Orléans – The Duc d'Orléans (later Louis-Philippe, king of the French, 1830–1848) had a large family of six sons and three daughters.
14. Duc de Bordeaux – see note 19, pp 38–9.
15. The Duchess . . . – This would be the Duchesse de Berri, widow of the assassinated Duc de Berri and mother to the Duc de Bordeaux, who would be around six years old at this time.
16. '. . . king of France?' – In fact, he never became king of France. See note 19, pp 38–9.
17. Willoughby Crewe – A sympathetic friend to Mariana Lawton in her marital troubles. See Ormerod's *History of Cheshire* vol 3, p 314 (1819/1882) for the pedigree of the Crewe family of Crewe Hall, Cheshire.

Epilogue

The year 1826 ended despondently for Anne. Paris, without Mariana, no longer sparkled. Maria Barlow, although at first gleefully triumphant at being rid of her rival, soon fell back on jealous scenes. For although the relationship between herself and Anne was re-established, it was very much on terms of Anne's choosing. Her emotional commitment to Mariana had been brought out into the open. Mrs Barlow had seen for herself the strength of the tie which bound the two women. She had witnessed the primacy of Mariana's place in Anne's life and had no alternative but to concede defeat. This did not stop her from continuing her emotional demands on Anne. Nor did it prevent Anne from resuming sexual relations with her, albeit in a half-hearted fashion and mainly at the latter's instigation. Anne was careful, however, to conceal the fact of the renewed affair in her letters to Mariana.

In 1827, Anne, Mrs Barlow and Jane made an extended tour of Switzerland and Northern Italy, leaving Aunt Anne in Paris, well cared for by friends and medical advisers. The tour, with its enforced intimacy of shared carriages and accommodation, finally convinced Anne that she and Maria Barlow were not, and never could be, compatible. When they arrived back in Paris she was relieved to part company with the Barlows.

Anne spent the winter of 1827–8 cultivating a new acquaintance, a pretty, young, Parisian widow called Madame de Rosny. Eventually, to the astonishment of her aunt and the Barlows, she moved into Madame de Rosny's house as a lodger. Anne's reason, ostensibly, was to perfect her French. In reality she had become attracted to Madame de Rosny, not least because of the fact that she had access to the circle of aristocrats which surrounded the French royal family and was able to gain entry into the king's social gatherings and *levées*. Anne's ambitions were rising and, although it was not possible for her to be presented at the French court unless she had first been presented at the English court, Anne felt that it could only be advantageous to have one or two influential friends in high circles in Paris when she returned there.

A light-hearted affair took place between Anne and Madame de Rosny, with the jealous Maria Barlow hovering in the background and doing all she could to blacken the name of Madame de Rosny. She warned Anne that Madame de Rosny moved in dangerous circles. It is true that Anne did become marginally involved in Madame de Rosny's underground life of smuggling activities, in which travellers were bribed or enticed into fetching and carrying contraband goods between England and France. Anne found herself involved in this business, even though she had previously disapproved of such things:

'... [I] *said she might arrange as she chose for the contraband. If she chose to land at three different ports, I would meet her at each – Dover, Brighton, London ...*'

(Sunday 20 January 1828. Paris)

Luckily, nothing seems to have come of these arrangements and Anne's heart was never really in such an adventure. She stayed with Madame de Rosny for a few weeks longer, then returned to her own apartment at 6 Rue de Mondovi in order to settle her affairs and return to England. Business affairs at Shibden were becoming pressing. She also longed to see Mariana again. So, leaving her aunt in the charge of Mrs Barlow, Anne left Paris in March 1828 and, on reaching England, she hastened to Lawton Hall to visit Mariana.

Following the sad parting of the lovers at Boulogne, Anne's mind had dwelt with happy anticipation on their meeting again in England. It had been the one sustaining thought which had carried her through the bleak Parisian winter and the unsatisfactory companionship of Mrs Barlow on her European tour. It was a shock to Anne, therefore, when she found herself looking at Mariana Lawton through disillusioned eyes. For, to her dismay, she found that Mariana now seemed dull and provincial after the sophistication of Parisian women, particularly those in Madame de Rosny's set. Anne tried to muster up a warm, enthusiastic manner with which to greet Mariana but, as she recorded in her journal:

> '*. . . the real fact was, I had come on her account yet her manner was warmer than mine.* [I] *said I was harrassed tho' in fact I felt more as if I had been so long absent from Mariana I did not know what to do with her. She looked tall and big. She seemed to have grown taller. I felt awkward & said to myself, "Why, what have I to do with having such a woman?" . . .*'
>
> (Sunday 23 March 1828. Lawton Hall, Cheshire)

This objective appraisal of Mariana acted as a catalyst for Anne, releasing her from the enchantment of her youthful passion for Mariana with a finality which Anne had never before been able to accept. But now, her increased sophistication and financial independence had served to foster ambitions in Anne which were strong enough to overcome youthful idealism. These ambitions held no place for Mariana, who would be a financial liability to Anne. Anne now wanted a woman who could bring money, social status and, preferably, the *éclat* of a title to the partnership. Mariana had none of these things to offer and, at thirty-eight, was no longer a young woman by nineteenth century standards. Although Anne stayed on at Lawton Hall for a few days and acted the part of lover, her obsession with Mariana Lawton was over for good. She was now no longer hostage to the binding force of an unattainable dream. The future lay before her and Anne was prepared, financially and emotionally, to face the realism of that future.

For the next four years, from 1828 to 1832, Anne made some attempts to find a new lover. Through the family connections of an old friend Sibbella MacLean, Anne was introduced to people who belonged to the English and Scottish aristocracy. Through these connections, she began to move in socially elevated circles and, when she next visited Paris, was made a welcome visitor at the British Embassy in Paris, a privilege which delighted Anne's aspiring heart. However, after the death of her friend, Anne's connections with her new aristocratic friends weakened. Once more, the Shibden estate began to absorb all her time and energy. For, if she wished to pursue her career of travel and socialising, Shibden must be made to produce the sort of income which would finance her schemes.

One hard fact of life which had struck Anne as she moved amongst her newly-acquired friends in Paris and England was that she would never be rich enough to sustain the lifestyle enjoyed by the aristocracy. It became imperative that she should join her fortune to that of another woman of means. Realising also that the aristocratic women she had met were not prepared to move beyond their own kind when choosing a life-partner, Anne began to look nearer home and nearer her own rank in life. In 1832, she began fostering an acquaintance with a twenty-nine-year-old woman called Ann Walker, who was heiress to an estate near to Shibden, on the outskirts of Halifax. Anne began wooing her assiduously, but with many misgivings from the start about whether or not they would be able to live happily together. In September 1834, Ann Walker came to live at Shibden Hall, combining her fortune with Anne Lister's. It was not a happy relationship.

The death of her parents had left Ann Walker a rich woman. However, she already had a past history of neurotic illness when she and Anne Lister began their affair. Soon Anne Lister began to find that her early misgivings were all too well founded. Tears, moody silences, days spent on the sofa in a state of extreme languor or depression, dominated their relationship. Nothing could have been in greater contrast to Anne Lister's outgoing and energetic character than Ann Walker's cultivated illnesses and neuroses. Anne made great efforts to bring the younger woman round to a more amenable form of companionship. She took her to see various doctors, one of whom dismissed Ann Walker impatiently, saying, in effect, that 'if Miss Walker were not rich, she would not be ill'. Anne Lister took her on trips in and around England and for one or two brief jaunts in Europe, but the determined invalid responded poorly to these efforts.

Finally, after great preparations and much resistance from Ann Walker, the two women set off for what was to be Anne Lister's final escapade. All her adult life she had wanted to travel to the more exotic parts of the world. Russia, Persia and Turkey in particular drew her irresistibly. On 20th June 1839, she and Ann Walker left Shibden Hall for just such destinations. By September 1840, after a year of hard travelling and many memorable encounters and adventures, they reached the foothills of the Caucasus Mountains in Georgia, the most southern province of the then Imperial Russia. Alas, Anne was never to reach the more exotic parts of the Orient. She caught a plague-like fever, there in the mountains, and died on 22nd September.

To date there is no record of how the embalmed body of Anne Lister, in its lead coffin, travelled from the wilds of the Caucasian region back to her home town of Halifax. From the reports given in the local paper, the *Halifax Guardian*, the journey took seven months. On 31st October 1840, the press carried a notice of Anne Lister's untimely death, likening her to other famous women travellers:

'... In mental energy and courage she resembled Lady Mary Wortley Montagu[1] and Lady Hester Stanhope;[2] and like these celebrated women, after exploring Europe, she extended her researches to those Oriental regions, where her career has been so prematurely terminated. We are informed that the remains of this distinguished lady have been embalmed and that her friend and companion, Miss Walker, is bringing them home by way of Constantinople for internment in the family vault ...'

(*Halifax Guardian*, 31 October 1840)

Six months later, the *Guardian* carried the following notice:

'The late Mrs Lister. The remains of this lady (who, our readers will remember, died at Koutais, in Imerethi, on 22 September last), arrived at Shibden Hall late on Saturday night and were interred in the parish church on Thursday morning.'

(*Halifax Guardian*, 1 May 1841)

One can only too well imagine the gloomy scene at Shibden Hall on that dark April night when the body of Anne Lister was returned to the home from which she had set out with such high expectations on her last adventurous journey. Now she was returned to:

'… the little spot where my ancestors had lived for centuries …'

(Friday 29 October, 1824. Paris)

There was still much history to be lived through at Shibden Hall, but never again would it house so colourful a character or one so prepared to record, in such honest and faithful detail, the workings of an all too human heart and mind, as Anne Lister, diarist extraordinaire.

---

1. Lady Mary Wortley Montagu – (1689–1762). English poetess and letter-writer. Daughter of Evelyn Pierrepoint, first Duke of Kingston. In 1712, she married Edward Wortley Montagu, travelling with him to Constantinople (1716–18). From there originated her *Letters from the East*. She was instrumental in introducing inoculation for smallpox into England on her return from the East. She separated from her husband and settled in Italy (1739–61). From there, she wrote letters to her daughter, the Countess of Bute. Her friendships with Pope and Swift ended in quarrels in 1722.
2. Lady Hester Stanhope – Hester Lucy (1776–1839), eccentric eldest daughter of the third Earl of Stanhope and Hester, sister of William Pitt. She left England in 1810 for the Levant and, in 1814, settled down amongst tribespeople on the slopes of Mt Lebanon. After becoming increasingly eccentric, she eventually died, a recluse, in 1839.

English Glossary

Antiattrition	Any compound applied to machinery to resist the effects of friction such as black lead mixed with grease, etc.
Aperient (Draught)	A laxative drink.
Baba	A rum-flavoured currant or plum cake.
Bashaw	A haughty, imperious man.
Bombazine (Bombasine)	A twilled dress material composed of silk and worsted, cotton and worsted, or worsted alone. In black, much used in mourning because of its dull texture.
Calomel	Mercurous chloride or proto-chloride of mercury (Hg_2Cl_2), much used as a purgative; also found native as 'horn-quick silver'.
Compeer	One of equal rank or standing.
Contemn	To treat with scorn or disdain.
Crape (Crepe)	A thin, transparent, gauze-like fabric, plain woven, of highly-twisted raw silk, with a crisped surface.
Ell	A measure of length, varying in different countries. The English ell equals 45 inches.

Gig	A light, two-wheeled, one-horse carriage.
Habit-Shirt	A kind of chemisette (or bodice) with linen collar, worn by women under the outer bodice.
Hack-Chaise	A pleasure or travelling carriage; a light, open carriage for one or two persons, with a top or folding hood, originally drawn by one horse. (A hack.)
Hackney Coach	A four-wheeled coach, drawn by two horses, with seating for six persons, kept for hire.
Harico'd (Mutton)	Stewed with vegetables and highly flavoured seasoning.
Jointure	The holding of a property to the joint use of husband and wife for life, or in tail as a provision for the latter during widowhood. Also, a sole estate limited to the wife, to take effect upon the death of her husband for her own life, at least.
Kerseymere	A twilled, fine woollen cloth of a particular texture.
Kiss	A euphemism for sexual intercourse.
Leghorn (Bonnet)	Name of a straw plaiting, used for hats and bonnets, made from a particular kind of wheat, cut green and bleached and imported from Leghorn in Tuscany.
Levantine	A very rich, stout, twilled black silk.
Merinos	A soft, woollen material, like fine French cashmere, originally of wool obtained from a variety of sheep originally bred in Spain and prized for its fine wool.
Packet (Steam-Packet)	A boat which travelled regularly between two ports, conveying mail and also goods and passengers; a mail boat. (Often shortened to packet.)

Pathetics	A way of producing an effect upon the emotions: moving, stirring, affecting.
Pelerine	A name for various kinds of mantles or capes worn by women: in recent use, a long narrow cape or tippet, with ends coming down to a point in front.
Pelisse	An outdoor garment similar to a cloak or mantle, worn by women, reaching to the ankle.
Phaeton	A light, four-wheeled, open carriage usually drawn by a pair of horses and with one or two seats facing forward.
Pilaster	A square or rectangular column or pillar, engaged in a wall, from which it projects a third, fourth or other portion of its breadth.
Postchaise	A travelling carriage, hired from stage to stage on the journey.
Post-Horse	A horse kept at a post-house or inn for the use of post-riders or for hire by travellers.
Posting-House	An inn, or other house, where horses are kept for the use of travellers.
Pothered (Bothered)	Put into a fuss; flustered; worried.
Puff	A boaster, a braggart.
Purse-Slider	A kind of tongueless buckle or ring used as a fastener, clasp or brooch.
Quiz	A piece of banter or ridicule; to make fun of a person or thing.
Redingote	A corruption of English 'riding-coat'. In France, a double-breasted, outer coat with long plain skirts, cut away in front when worn by women, but not when worn by men.

Rood — Used here as a linear measure; a rod, pole or perch. Now only local and varying from 6 to 8 yards.

Rumble — The back part of a carriage which can be arranged to provide extra seating or to carry luggage.

Spar Shop — Souvenir shop. Spars were crystalline fragments often fashioned into ornaments.

Spencer — A short, close-fitting jacket cut like a bodice, usually with long sleeves and a high neck, commonly worn by women and children in the early nineteenth century.

Taber (Tabor) — A small kind of drum used chiefly as an accompaniment to the pipe or trumpet – a taborine or tabret.

French Glossary

Amant	Lover.
Amarantha	A purple colour.
Amoureuse	Being in love.
Au fait	To be thoroughly conversant with.
Aune	Ancient measure of length – 1.88m in Paris.
Bain d'odeur	Scented bath.
Baiser	To kiss; could also be used as a euphemism for sexual intercourse, as was the word 'kiss' in England at the time.
Beaucoup	A lot; very much.
Bien bon	Quite good.
Billets	Official passes or tickets of entry.
Bon marché	Cheaply.
Bourse	Stock Exchange.
Brodeuse	Embroideress.
Cabinets d'aisances	Water closets.
Cabinet d'eau	A wash-room.

Cabriolet	Two-wheeled, one-horse, large hooded carriage, designed to seat two to three people.
Cents, Centimes	French coins equal to one hundredth of a franc each.
Chambres à coucher	Bedrooms.
Chambre du domestique en haut	A servant's bedroom in the attic.
Chambres particulières	Specialised rooms.
Chargé d'affaires	One in charge of affairs; a minister who transacts business during the temporary absence of the ambassador.
Chinois	Chinese.
Chrysofraes (Chrysophraes)	The ancient name of a golden-green precious stone, perhaps a variety of the beryl or aquamarine.
Coiffée	Have one's hair dressed.
Comme il faut	Properly, in a proper manner.
Compote des pruneaux	Stewed prunes.
Concierge	Caretaker/porter of a large building.
Cor-beille (de mariage)	Present a man offers to his bride-to-be.
Cortège	Procession.
Cotillons	The name of several dances, chiefly of French origin, consisting of a variety of steps and figures.
Coup d'oeil	A view as it strikes the eye at a first glance.
Coupé	A short, four-wheeled, close carriage with an inside seat for two and an outside seat for the driver; also the front or after compartment of a Continental *diligence*.

Cuisine	Kitchen.
Cuisinière	The cook.
Députés	Deputies; Members of Parliament.
Deshabillé	Undress.
Diligence	A public stagecoach.
Distraite	Listless, absent-minded.
Du temps	Of the time.
Écarte	To discard. Also a game of cards for two persons, played with a pack from which the cards 2–6 are excluded. The players may discard any or all of the cards dealt and replace them from the pack, hence the name of the game.
Éclat	Social brilliance; lustre of reputation.
Écritoire	Writing desk (portable).
Emballeur	Packer.
Émigré	An expatriate (in this case a Royalist who fled France at the time of the French Revolution).
En amie	In friendship.
En critique	Critical.
En face	Facing, opposite to.
En passant	In passing by.
En sortant	Going out.
Ennuyée	Bored or wearied from want of occupation or lack of interest.
Entresol du premier	A mezzanine floor – a low storey between two higher ones – usually between the ground floor and the storey above.
Étage	Floor, storey (of a building).
Étrennes	New Year's gifts.

Femmes galantes	Prostitutes.
Fiacre	A small, four-wheeled, hackney carriage, named after the *auberge* (inn or hotel) of St Fiacre, where the first carriages for rent were housed.
Filles publiques	Prostitutes.
Franc	Unit of French currency, a silver coin, first struck in 1575. Valued in the eighteenth century at 9d or 10d.
Fromage de Gruyère	A Swiss cheese.
Frontignac	A muscat wine made at Frontignon.
Garde du corps	Bodyguard.
Garde Nationale	National Guard.
Garde Royale	Royal bodyguards.
Gâteau de pommes	Applecake/tart.
Gaucherie	Awkwardness; clumsy behaviour.
Gens d'armes	Men at arms; soldiers who were employed on police duties.
Gros de Naples	Coarse material of Naples.
Haut ton	High tone; fashion.
Hôtel garni	Furnished apartments.
La mode	The fashion.
Livre	An old French unit of currency, divided into 20 sols (or sous) and about equal to the present franc.
Napoléon	A gold coin issued by Napoleon I, of the value of 20 francs.
Omelette aux fines herbes	Chopped herbs (chives, chervil) omelette.

Parure	A set of jewels or other ornaments intended to be worn together.
Passé	Past the prime; past the period of greatest beauty.
Pâtisserie	Cake-shop, confectioners.
Pendule	Clock.
Petit paquet	Small parcel.
Petit pâtes	Meat patties; small pork pies.
Plafond	Ceiling, roof.
Potage	Soup.
Potage à la julienne	Vegetable soup.
Potage au vermicelli	Fine noodle soup.
Propriétaire	Proprietor.
Pucelle	Virgin.
Quadrille	A card game played by four people with forty cards, the eights, nines and tens of the ordinary pack being discarded.
Quadrilles	A square dance of French origin, usually performed by four couples and containing five sections or figures, each of which is a complete dance in itself. Also called 'a set of quadrilles'.
Quincaillier	Hardware dealer, ironmonger.
Reaumur	A temperature scale established in 1730 by the French naturalist Rene-Antoine Ferchault de Reaumur, with its zero set at the freezing point of water and its 80° mark at the boiling point of water at normal atmospheric pressure. Use of the Reaumur scale was once widespread but by the late twentieth century it had practically disappeared.

Remise	A carriage hired from a livery stable, of a better class than the ordinary hackney carriages.
Rez de chaussée	Ground floor.
Rouleaux	Rolls (of wallpaper, etc.).
Sac	Bag.
Salle à manger	Dining room.
Salon	Lounge, sitting room.
Salon du trône	Throne room.
Savant	A man of learning or science, especially one engaged professionally in learning or scientific research.
Séance	A sitting of a deliberative or other body or society or of a number of persons assembled for discussion, instruction, etc.
Seringue à manivelle	A syringe with a small wheel or handle.
Soirée	Evening party, gathering or social meeting.
Sol (or sou)	A former coin in France, etc., usually equal to the twentieth part of a livre, but of varying actual value. Now used to designate the five centime piece.
Spirituelle	Of a highly refined character or nature, especially in conjunction with liveliness or quickness of mind. Clever, smart, witty.
Triste	Sad, unhappy.
Vin de pays	Regional wine.
Vingt-cinq-sols	1.25 francs.
Volage	Fickle, inconstant.

Bibliography

Archival Sources

The documents listed below are held at Calderdale Archives Dept, Halifax, West Yorkshire, under the references shown:

The journals of Anne Lister, 1806–1840. SH:7/ML/E.
The letters of Anne Lister, 1800–1840. SH:7/ML.
Captain Jeremy Lister, 1771–1828. SH:7/JL.
Legal deeds, etc., concerning Shibden properties. SH:1/SH.
College of Arms (re Lister pedigree). SH:7/ML/B.
Lister accounts, 1815–1840. SH:7/ML/AC.
Lister wills, inventories, etc. SH:2–6.
Pedigree of the Lister family of Ovenden and Shibden Hall. SH:3/LF/27.
Genealogy of the Lister family, drawn up by John Lister MA. SH:3/LF/28.
Schedule A Militia Act. SH:4/T.HX/1803.
Shibden Estate Ledger, 1808–1826. SH:2/SHE.
Ramsden, Dr Phyllis: *Anne Lister (1791–1840) A Chronology*. RAM:52.
Three Journeys from the Journal of *Anne Lister of Shibden Hall*. RAM:43.

Anne Lister in France. RAM:26,27,28.
Luddism, Halifax. 1811–1813. MIC:5.
Luddism, Halifax. 1814. HAS:1383.
Parliamentary boroughs of Halifax, *c*1832. HP:95.
Protestant declaration of loyalty to the Crown. (Halifax, nineteenth century.) HAS/B:20/240.
West Riding election; 1809. HAS/B:9/2.
Yorkshire election; 1807. HAS/B:9/1.
Yorkshire election; nineteenth century. HAS/B:9/10.
Yorkshire election; 1831. HAS:430/240.

Unpublished Theses

Green, Muriel M (ed) 'A Spirited Yorkshirewoman: The Letters of Anne Lister of Shibden Hall, Halifax'. A thesis for the honours diploma of the Library Association. Ref L359236. Calderdale Reference Library.
Ferguson, M J 'York Parliamentary Elections, 1807–1835'. A thesis for the University of Hull. Ref 7324–42. York Reference Library.

Articles and Newspaper Cuttings

The unpublished articles and newspaper cuttings listed below are held in the Horsfall Turner Collection (ref HTQ.070) at Calderdale Reference Library, Halifax:

Bretton, R 'Banking, 1922–23 and 1933–34'.
'Beacons and Bonfires, 1935'.
'Beacon Hill'.
'Beacon Pan'.
'Diary Extracts'.
Hanson 'Story of Spen Valley'.
Hartley, R J Newspaper Cuttings, 1868–1898. (3 vols.)
Lister, J 'Diary Extracts'.

Porritt, Arthur 'Election of 1807'.
Turner, T 'Beacons and Bonfires'.
'Captain Jeremy Lister's Army Career'.
'Extracts from Anne Lister's Diaries'.
'Halifax and the 19th Century'.
'Lister, Anne: Social and Political Life in the 19th century'.
'Politics in Halifax'.
'The town of Halifax in 1797'.
'Political Life in Halifax in the 19th century'.

The item below is held at Calderdale Reference Library, under ref L9762/3:

Innes, R A 'Jeremy Lister, 10th Regiment, 1770–1783' from 'Army Historical Research'.

Reference Books Consulted

British Journal of Venereal Diseases (1971).
British Library General Catalogue of Printed Books to 1975 (vol 260).
Burke's Peerage and Baronetage.
The Complete Peerage.
Concise Oxford Dictionary of Opera.
Dictionary of National Biography.
Encyclopaedia Britannica (1988 ed).
European Authors, 1000–1900.
Handbook of World Opera.
London Encyclopaedia (ed Weinreb, B, and Hibbert, C. London. Macmillan. 1983)
Oxford Companion to Medicine (vols I, II).
Reader's Encyclopaedia (ed Benet, W R. London. 1974).
Webster's Biographical Dictionary.

British History

Aspinall, A A and Smith, A E (ed) *English Historical Documents. Vol XI: 1789–1832*. London. Eyre and Spottiswoode. 1959.

Beckett, J V *The Aristocracy in England, 1660–1914*. Oxford. Basil Blackwell. 1986.

Butterfield, Herbert *George III and the Historians*. London. Cassell. 1988.

Davidoff, L and Hall, C *Family Fortunes: Men and Women of the English Middle Class, 1780–1850*. London. Hutchinson. 1987.

Defoe, Daniel *A Tour thro' the Whole Island of Great Britain*. London. 1725.

Mathias, Peter *The First Industrial Nation: An Economic History of Britain, 1700–1914*. London. Methuen & Co Ltd. 1969.

Mitchell, Leslie *Holland House*. Duckworth. 1980.

Thompson, E P *The Making of the English Working Class*. London. Pelican Books. 1976.

Wood, Anthony *Nineteenth Century Britain, 1815–1914*. Longman. 1989.

French History

Cobban, Alfred *A History of Modern France. Vol 2. 1799–1871*. Penguin Books. 1976.

Collingham, H A C *The July Monarchy: A Political History of France*. London and New York. Longman. 1988.

Goodwin, A *The French Revolution*. London. Hutchinson University Library. 1966.

Hampson, Norman *A Social History of the French Revolution*. London. Routledge and Kegan Paul. 1976.

Hemmings, F W J *Culture and Society in France, 1789–1848*. Leicester University Press. 1987.

Jardin, Andre and Tudesq, Andre-Jean *Restoration and Reaction, 1815–1848*. Cambridge University Press. 1983.
Mansel, Philip *Louis XVIII*. Blond Briggs. 1981.
Mansel, Philip *The Court of France, 1789–1830*. Cambridge University Press. 1988.
Mercier, Louis Sebastien *The Picture of Paris Before and After the Revolution*. London. Routledge & Sons Ltd. 1929.
Porch, Douglas *Army and Revolution: France, 1815–1848*. Routledge and Kegan Paul. 1974.
Resnick, D P *The White Terror and the Political Reaction after Waterloo*. Harvard University Press. 1966.
Schama, Simon *Citizens: A Chronicle of the French Revolution*. London. Penguin Books. 1989.

English Regional History

Bradford, West Yorkshire:

Turner, J W 'The Bradford Piece Halls'. *Bradford Antiquary*. Vol 1. 1884.

Buxton, Derbyshire:

Bower, Alan *The Water Cure*. Derby. J H Hall and Sons Ltd. 1985.
Hall, Ivan *Georgian Buxton*. The Derbyshire Museum Service. 1984.
Langham, M, and Wells, C *Buxton Waters: A History of Buxton, the Spa*. Derby. J Hall & Sons Ltd. 1986.
Milton, W Allan *The Historic Places Around Buxton*. Derbyshire Printing Co. 1926.
Montell, Keith H *Haddon Hall*. Derby. English Life Publications Ltd. 1987.

Halifax (and environs), West Yorkshire:

The Halifax Antiquarian Society Tracts, which are published annually, have been an invaluable source of information on the history of Halifax. References to the Lister family are scattered throughout the publications, as are articles on many other Halifax families and topics of local interest. In addition, the following publications have been useful and interesting:

Halifax Guardian Almanack 1903–1905 'A Halifax Election Riot. Political Amenities Seventy Years Ago'.

Hargreaves, J A *Factory Kings and Slaves: South Pennines Social Movements, 1780–1840*. Hebden Bridge. The Pennine Heritage Network. 1982.

Hartley, W C E *Banking in Yorkshire*. Dalesman Books. 1975.

Marsh, John 'A Victorian Woman's Wanderlust'. *Country Life*. 8th March 1973.

Roth, H Ling *The Genesis of Banking in Halifax*. Halifax. H F King. 1914.

Watson, Rev John *The History and Antiquities of the Parish of Halifax in Yorkshire*. T Lowndes. 1775.

York/Yorkshire:

Page, William *The Victoria History of the County of York* (vol III). Constable and Co Ltd. 1913.

Thompson, Hamilton A (ed) *York Minster Historical Tracts, 627–1927*. London. 1927.

Wood, G Bernard *Historic Homes of Yorkshire*. Oliver and Boyd. 1957.

Medical/Sexual History

Ackernecht, E H *Medicine at the Paris Hospital, 1794–1848*. Baltimore. Johns Hopkins University Press. 1967.

Cooper, Sir Astley 'Surgical Lectures. Lecture 54. Venereal Disease'. *The Lancet*. Vol III, no 7. London. 15th May 1821.

Laqueur, Thomas 'La Difference: Bodies, Gender and History'. *The Threepenny Review*. Spring 1988.

Lesbian History and Culture

Faderman, Lilian *Surpassing the Love of Men: Romantic Friendship and Love Between Women from the Renaissance to the Present*. London. The Women's Press. 1989.

Lesbian History Group *Not a Passing Phase: Reclaiming Lesbians in History, 1840–1985*. London. The Women's Press. 1989.

Sappho (Translated by Josephine Balmer) *Sappho: Poems and Fragments*. London. Brilliance Books. 1984.

Biographies

Baily, F E *Lady Beaconsfield and Her Times*. London. Hutchinson and Co. 1935.

Cecil, David *Melbourne*. London. Constable. 1986.

Clive, John *Macaulay: The Shaping of the Historian*. New York. Vintage Books. 1975.

Collins, Herbert F *Talma: A Biography of an Actor*. London. Faber and Faber. 1964.

Cooper, Duff *Talleyrand*. London. Cassell. 1987.

Gittings, Robert and Manton, Jo (ed) *Dorothy Wordsworth*. Oxford University Press. 1988.

Herold, J Christopher *Mistress to an Age: A Life of Madame de Staël*. London. Hamish Hamilton. 1959.

Hibbert, Christopher *George IV*. Penguin Books. 1988.

Jones, R Ben *Napoleon, Man and Myth*. Hodder and Stoughton. 1972.

Lloyd, Alan *The Wickedest Age: The Life and Times of George III*. David and Charles. London. 1971.

Longford, Elizabeth *Wellington: Pillar of State*. London. Panther Books. 1985.
Mansel, Philip *Louis XVIII*. Blond Briggs. 1981.
Thompson, J M *Leaders of the French Revolution*. Oxford. Basil Blackwell. 1988.
Tomalin, Claire *The Life and Death of Mary Wollstonecraft*. Penguin Books. 1985.
Ziegler, Philip *King William IV*. Newton Abbot. Readers Union. 1973.

Letters and Journals

Adeane, J H and Grenfell, M (ed) *Before and After Waterloo: Letters from Edward Stanley, Sometime Bishop of Northwich. (1802:1814:1816)*. London. T Fisher Unwin. 1907.
Anderson, W E K (ed) *The Journal of Sir Walter Scott*. Oxford. Clarendon Press. 1972.
Bernier, O, and Bourhis, K le *At the Court of Napoleon. Memoirs of the Duchesse d'Abrantes*. New York. Doubleday. 1989.
Blanch, Lesley (ed) *Harriette Wilson's Memoirs*. London. Century Publishing. 1985.
Bury, J P T and Barry, J C (ed) *An Englishman in Paris: 1803. The Journals of Bertie Greatheed*. London. Geoffrey Bles. 1953.
Colvin, Christina (ed) *Maria Edgeworth in France and Switzerland: Selections from the Edgeworth Family Letters*. Oxford. Clarendon Press. 1979.
Schrank, Barbara G and Supino, David J (ed) *The Famous Miss Burney: The Diaries and Letters of Fanny Burney*. New York. The John Day Company. 1976.
Suddaby, Elizabeth and Yarrow, P J (ed) *Lady Morgan in France*. Newcastle upon Tyne. Oriel Press. 1971.
Surtees, Virginia (ed) *A Second Self. The Letters of Harriet Granville, 1810–1845*. Norwich. Michael Russell. 1990.
Whitbread, Helena (ed) *I Know My Own Heart: The Diaries of Anne Lister*. London. Virago Press. 1988.

Index